SETTING GLOBAL STANDARDS

GUIDELINES FOR CREATING
CODES OF CONDUCT
IN MULTINATIONAL CORPORATIONS

S. PRAKASH SETHI

John Wiley & Sons, Inc.

Published by John Wiley & Sons, Inc., Hoboken, New Jersey.
Published simultaneously in Canada.

For general information on our other products and services please contact our Customer Care Department within the U.S. at (800) 762-2974, outside the United States at (317) 572-3993 or fax (317) 572-4002.

Wiley also publishes its books in a variety of electronic formats. Some content that appears in print may not be available in electronic books. For more information about Wiley products, visit our web site at www.Wiley.com.

Library of Congress Cataloging-in-Publication Data:

Sethi, S. Prakash.
  Setting global standards : guidelines for creating codes of conduct in
multinational corporations / S. Prakash Sethi.
      p.   cm.
  Includes bibliographical references.
    ISBN 0-471-41455-7 (cloth)
    1. International business enterprises—Management.   2. Business
etiquette.   3. Corporate culture.   I. Title.
  HD62.4 .S48   2003
  658.3'14—dc21   2002153264

Printed in the United States of America.

10 9 8 7 6 5 4 3 2 1

Acknowledgments

No scholar works in a vacuum. In the process of writing this book over the past three plus years, I have constantly benefited from discourse with my academic colleagues, members of civil society, and corporate executives. It would be well-nigh impossible for me to recognize everyone and acknowledge my debt of learning. Nevertheless, my gratitude to them remains undiminished.

There are, however, a number of people who have been more intimately involved and their assistance is specifically recognized. This book contains a number of case studies pertaining to individual corporations as well as codes created by industry-based or other types of organized groups. These studies were enriched from the support of many corporate executives and representatives of other organizations who provided me with data and internal documents, and also shared details of their organizations' efforts in code development and implementation.

The most important contributors to this effort have been the executives of Mattel, Inc. It was Mattel's commitment to creating and implementing an independent external monitoring system that gave concrete shape to the ideas I had been advocating for a long time. The code initiative at Mattel started in 1997 when its then top management team took the lead against skepticism as to the advisability of this course of action. Mattel's code, called the Global Manufacturing Principles (GMP), had the full support of Mattel's then CEO, Jill Brad; Ned Mansour, President of Corporate Operations; Joseph Gondolfo, President of Worldwide Operations; and Sean Fitzgerald, Vice President of Corporate Communications and Corporate Social Compliance. GMP also enjoyed total support at the board level, which was led by one of the senior outside board members, Ronald M.

Loeb, who also serves as the general counsel of Williams-Sonoma, Inc. The success of the code and its implementation was further assured by many professional staff members both in the head office and in the field. Notable among these were Frank Canko (chief internal auditor), as well as Fermin Cuza and Ken Meashey, who as Sean Fitzgerald's successors strengthened the compliance effort with even greater vigor.

The importance of institutional values and leadership in the case of Mattel has been reaffirmed by the fact that the company's current leadership remains united in its unwavering commitment to the code, independent external monitoring, and full public disclosure. As chairman of Mattel Independent Monitoring Council (MIMCO), I, together with my colleagues, have received total support from Robert A. Eckert, Mattel's Chairman of the Board and CEO; Bryan Stockton, Executive Vice President, Strategic Planning and Business Affairs; Tom Debrowski, Executive Vice President, Worldwide Operations; James Walter, Vice President, Quality Assurance and Social Compliance; and Lisa Marie Bongiovani, Vice President, Corporate Communications and Government Affairs.

Further thanks are due to Caitlin Morris, Jeff Denchfield, and Katrice McCorkle, who have worked in the trenches to ensure protection of all the soldiers in this common endeavor from those who continue to have misgivings about the code's value to the corporation and the community. I have also benefited from the practical wisdom of Mattel's many plant managers, notably Arun Kochar (Malaysia), Tracy Rogers (Indonesia), and Rug Burad (China).

I am grateful for the support and encouragement provided by executives from other companies, nongovernmental organizations (NGOs), and members of the press. Special thanks are due to Mark Spears and Lisa Kantor (both of Disney). Among other notable mentions are Dan Chally (McDonald's); Dusty Kidd (Nike); Shawn MacDonald (Fair Labor Association); Georg Kell (United Nations Global Compact); Alex Kaufman (Kenan Asia Institute, Thailand); Heather White (Verité); Steve Koppich and Donna Isralsky (both of Williams-Sonoma); Meg Voorhes (Investor Responsibility Research Center); Tion Kwa (Far Eastern Economic Review, Hong Kong); Aaron Bernstein (*Business Week*); and Charles Riley (Baruch College).

The onerous task of reading multiple versions of different chapters of the manuscript and offering frank, often harsh but always supportive and thoughtful advice was patiently and happily shared by a multitude of friends and colleagues of long standing. There is not enough that I can say to express my gratitude to them. They are (in alphabetical order), James Armstrong (Rollins College); Pauline Baker (Fund for Peace); Christian Barry (Carnegie Council on Ethics and International Affairs); Thomas Bausch

(Marquette University); Robert Dilenschneider (The Dilenschneider Group, Inc.); Thomas Donaldson (University of Pennsylvania); William Frederick (University of Pittsburgh); Richard Howitt (British Member of European Parliament); David Lowry (Freeport-McMoRan); Paul McCleary (ForChildren Inc., and MIMCO board member); Lee Preston (University of Maryland); Timothy Smith (former Executive Director of Interfaith Center on Corporate Responsibility, and currently Vice President of Walden Asset Management); Jeffery Sonnenfeld (Yale School of Management);· Murray Weidenbaum (Washington University, St. Louis, and MIMCO member); and Oliver F. Williams (University of Notre Dame).

The research effort for the data collection, tracking source citations for accuracy, and finding materials from archives with only the vaguest direction from an absent-minded professor was brilliantly carried out with utter dedication by Olga Emelianova, Pinar Imer, and Sandeep Hajare, all graduate students at the Zicklin School of Business.

The task of managing the logistics of communications through different stages of manuscript preparation was carried out by my administrative assistant, Olinda Anderson, who is one of the best when it comes to creating order from chaos. In this effort, she was assisted by Dawn Evans, Tricilia Jacob, and Sulma Villatoro and blessed by Chris Koutsoutis.

I am grateful to Lawrence Alexander (Publisher of Wiley Business Books), Jo-Ann Wasserman (Associate Publisher of Wiley Journals), and Paula Sinnott (Assistant Editor) for their faith in this book despite numerous and frustrating delays on my part. The copyediting chores were efficiently and competently handled by Jay Boggis.

Notwithstanding all the good advice and support that I have received from my friends and colleagues, I alone must bear total responsibility for any and all sins of omission and commission that readers might find in this book. I beg their indulgence and forgiveness and earnestly hope that in their reading they will find some kernels of truth and interesting ideas that would justify their patience and forbearance.

And finally, on a personal note, I enjoy my good fortune in having a loving wife in Hillary, and two wonderful sons in Amit and Ravi (and Ravi's bride Josephine), who make me very happy just by thinking about them.

S. Prakash Sethi

New York, New York

More Accolades for *Setting Global Standards*

"This book transcends the emotional name-calling between the advocates and opponents of globalization. Sethi offers a brilliant and courageous statement of the responsibilities of global citizenship with fresh, wide-ranging perspectives, hard evidence, compelling examples, and constructive options. This timely piece will help corporate leaders, social activists, policy makers, and management students discover the ample common ground in their collective efforts to forge a better world."

> —Jeff Sonnenfeld, Associate Dean of Executive Programs,
> Yale School of Management
> President of the Chief Executive Leadership Institute

Contents

Preface

In a market economy, business institutions are an integral part of the social system, and their actions, despite assertions to the contrary, have a profound influence on other societal institutions. The relationship, however, is not all in one direction. No matter how much business may yearn for the unfettered marketplace, the aspirations and behavior of every businessperson and institution are governed by the internal gyroscope of society's values and cultures.

The nature and scope of international business, along with the role of multinational corporations (MNCs), have witnessed strong growth during the past two decades. The increasing trend toward globalization has contributed enormously to the production of wealth. Intertwined with an increase in international trade and movement of capital, this growth has also brought about significant changes in the way business is conducted in different parts of the world. Unfortunately, the benefits of accelerated economic growth and rising levels of income have not been equitably shared by all segments of society. International trade and investment have distributed gains in favor of those who control the capital and against those who contribute human labor, especially in developing countries.

The changing political and economic environment has introduced further uncertainty and risk in the global business and economic environment, where a variety of current and new groups are jockeying to fill power vacuums and shape the course of future events. Public concern against MNCs has been heightened by many nongovernmental organizations (NGOs) and other international bodies that have played a critical role in putting these issues on the public agenda. As the primary engine of globalization and economic growth, MNCs have become the focus of public scrutiny as to the role they might play to ameliorate the negative side effects of globalization. MNCs have responded by creating codes of business conduct, indicating their commitment to good corporate citizenship in countries where they operate. These codes also address many problems that have become endemic to MNCs' overseas operations, such as treatment of workers, protection of the environment, and dealing with local governments. Unfortunately, this approach to date has failed to achieve its goal of reducing public criticism and decreasing demand for greater national and international regulation of MNCs.

We submit that the issues of labor, human rights, and the environment will continue to escalate in importance, both in business operations at the micro level and in international trade and investments at the macro level. The next decade of globalization will be quite different from the previous two. To date, policy discussions among academics, governments, and corporations have focused on economic issues such as the free flow of capital and the relatively unhindered movement of goods and services. The focus of debate in the coming decade will be on political issues, such as the impact of international trade and investment on institutions—economic and political—in the host countries, especially the developing countries of Asia, Latin America, Eastern Europe, and Africa. All around us, we can see how international trade issues have become politicized. And the political character of globalization cannot be denied because, in the final analysis, distributive justice—that is, equitable and fair distribution of the gains from globalization—is as important as the aggregate increase in wealth created by globalization.

Even a cursory review of events during the past 20 years suggests that MNC leaders have not sufficiently grasped the importance of this time frame and of the sociopolitical events that have brought them to the forefront of the new economic era. The decline of the nation-state, accompanied by the rise of economic institutions that support unhindered movement of capital and goods, has allowed the large multinational corporations to exert enormous influence on the lives of people around the world without creating any countervailing power exercised by the nation-states.

If history is any guide, MNCs are unlikely to sustain this gain in economic power and affluence unless they take voluntary steps to ensure that the terms of international trade and investment are not rigged unfairly to their advantage. We need to ensure that the poor are not deprived of a fair share of the gains from international trade and productivity through lack of bargaining power. We need to protect the working and living environments of the poor in developing countries, which are being polluted and degraded, inflicting heavy damage to the health and well-being of current and future generations.

MNCs are at a turning point and must decide the direction of their future. They own and control the present, and they can certainly act as if the future will be no different. But this would be dangerous. The current phase of globalization is fairly new in a historical context. Its gains are all too apparent; but its negative impacts are still buried among the dusty roads and mud villages of the poor in developing countries. The public awareness of these issues, both here and abroad, is increasing, however, and will reach ominous levels if no action is taken.

MNCs cannot ignore this persistent criticism because it reflects a growing gap between societal expectations and corporate performance. Such a widening gap should be a cause for concern for MNCs because it invites further government regulation of their activities. It may also damage their reputations and undermine public confidence and trust, eroding their sociopolitical legitimacy and weakening their economic and political franchise.

The notion of enhanced responsibility on the part of multinational corporations, in its most basic form, must meet three conditions:

1. MNCs must deal with all of their stakeholders, and not merely stockholders, in a fair and equitable manner. This is especially so in the case of developing countries and among poor people, who lack the necessary economic and political power to bargain with MNCs on more equitable terms.

2. MNCs must act as positive and proactive agents of change through the use of their enormous economic power, and, where necessary, even against the express wishes or prevailing customs of host countries, so as to protect and foster basic human rights and democratic values that are the foundation of the MNCs' own economic strength and prosperity in their home countries.

3. MNCs must not consider these actions either as discretionary matters or as necessary inconveniences, such as a cost of doing business. Instead, these actions must be treated as minimum standards of behavior, compliance with which must be mandatory, transparent, and subject to external validation.

This book is divided into six parts. The first part begins by focusing on the expanding role of multinational corporations in developing countries within the context of globalization and free trade. Chapter 1 examines the impact of increased globalization in aggregate terms and also as it affects countries and people in industrially advanced as well as in developing countries. Chapter 2 looks at the nature of sweatshop-like working conditions and human rights abuses in different parts of the world and how they relate to various industries and companies. This analysis is based on the information generated through the creation of a database of news reports published in English-language newspapers and magazines and indexed in the Dow Jones Interactive Electronic Network.

Part Two examines MNCs' current response patterns to external pressures for change. Chapter 3 evaluates MNCs' communications strategies in responding to external criticism and examines reasons for the failure of these strategies. Chapter 4 develops a framework to analyze the links between MNCs' external environment and the ways it impacts corporate strategies. Chapter 5 focuses attention on some of the more proactive responses undertaken by multinational corporations in the form of voluntary codes of conduct and their relative effectiveness.

Part Three is devoted to an analysis of group-based approaches that are being tried by some corporations and industry groups as their collective response to public criticism of their conduct in developing countries. Three such efforts are studied: the Sullivan Principles in South Africa, the United Nations Global Compact, and the Fair Labor Association. The analysis suggests that any industry-wide approach to creating initial codes and standards—where none existed before—is doomed to failure because of the free rider problem and adverse selection. The need to bring a large group of companies yields greater leverage to the recalcitrant companies, which use this leverage to delay the process and weaken it through endless negotiations and other tactics. At the same time, the good companies are reluctant to take the initiative because the recalcitrant companies would benefit at their expense and may also harm them by not complying with the group's standards.

Part Four is devoted to case studies of two companies: Nike, Inc. and The Walt Disney Company (Chapters 9 and 10). These companies have followed the go-it-alone approach. The chapters demonstrate the strengths and weaknesses of this approach when it is used under severe boundary constraints imposed by the companies.

Part Five offers a new approach to creating economically efficient and socially viable codes of conduct. Chapter 11 offers detailed guidelines for the creation of a model code of conduct. A corporate code of conduct is in the nature of a "private law" or a "promise voluntarily made" whereby an institution makes a public commitment to certain standards of conduct.

The nature of voluntariness and, by implication, the flexibility afforded to a corporation make it imperative that the codes pertain to issues that are important both to the MNC and to the individuals and groups that are affected by their operations. Chapter 12 addresses one of the most critical issues with regard to international codes of conduct—independent external monitoring and compliance verification. These codes must also be credible and believable, both in what they proclaim and in what they actually achieve. These voluntary efforts will be fatally flawed if they are not transparent and independently verifiable. Chapter 13 discusses the case of Mattel, Inc., whose code of conduct comes close to meeting the conditions of an ideal code as described in Chapter 11. Equally important, Mattel is the only company in the world that has fully embraced and implemented an independent external monitoring system.

The final section (Part Six) is devoted to the lessons that can be learned from current initiatives in creating and implementing voluntary corporate codes of conduct. We conclude by observing that the failure to undertake meaningful reform in this area will hurt the path of globalization and its potential attendant benefits to all concerned. Even more ominously, such a failure will seriously undermine democratic values and thus erode the very foundations of political and economic freedom in large parts of the world that sustain private enterprise, property rights, respect of individual freedom, and protection of human rights.

PART ONE

The Role of Multinational Corporations in the Context of Increasing Globalization and Free Trade

CHAPTER 1

The Blessings and Perils of Globalization: A Tale of Two Peoples

A strong argument can be made that globalization and the unrestricted flow of capital, goods, and services lead to creation of wealth and prosperity among all participating nations. Comparative advantage allows both industrially advanced nations and developing countries to maximize their gains from trade. Industrially advanced countries make better use of their technology and capital by exporting it to less developed or poorer countries, which in turn make better use of their cheap and abundant labor by exporting their low-tech, labor-intensive products to the richer countries.[1] Globalization also leads to economic integration and convergence in economic policies around the world. Economic integration leads to economic growth through reform and harmonization in the countries' fiscal and monetary policies, tax systems, ownership patterns, and other regulatory arrangements.[2]

In the current context of globalization, with its concomitant free trade and global integration of national economies, the role of large multinational corporations (MNCs) is becoming increasingly critical to the growth and development of emerging nations. MNCs have become an engine of change through their injection of capital, technology, organizational skills, and a competitive environment. Foreign corporations not only bring with them new technologies and management systems, they also bring a different kind of corporate culture and new assumptions about the relations between a national government and a country's economic and sociopolitical institutions. At the same time, national control over a country's economic and sociopolitical arena is constantly being challenged, if not already considerably eroded.

Advocates of globalization point to increases in wealth creation in all parts of the world following moves toward open markets since the 1970s. They point to the increase in merchandise exports from developing countries, both in absolute terms and in percentage terms of their gross domestic product (GDP). Developing countries have witnessed large inflows of capital and technology, and have recorded high rates of GDP growth. Trade liberalization (read globalization) has been inextricably linked with a country's economic reforms and growth in GDP.[3] This has been evident in the economic growth of the Asian Tigers like South Korea, Taiwan, and Hong Kong since the 1970s, and more recently in the cases of China and India.[4]

There is evidence of strong linkage between participation in international trade and domestic economic growth. In "The Promise and Pains of Globalization," Dennis Rondinelli and Jack Behrman state that between 1960 and the early 1990s, the economies of countries that exported only a small proportion of their output grew less than 3 percent a year, compared with growth rates of 5 to 7 percent a year for countries exporting a large proportion of their output.[5] Economist Murray Weidenbaum asserts that globalization has been singularly successful in reducing poverty in the world.[6] The number of people in abject poverty in East Asia, living on less than $1 a day, has been reduced from 450 million to 280 million between 1990 and 1998. "Wars, natural disasters, totalitarian governments, pervasive corruption, mismanagement and anarchy must share the blame for the remaining abysmal poverty."[7]

Globalization has also contributed to substantial economic progress in the United States. For example, between 1993 and 1998, the real income of the poorest 20 percent of families increased at an average of 2.7 percent a year, while the top 20 percent averaged gains of 2.4 percent annually.[8] We are also told that evidence all around the world shows that economic freedom equates with higher living standards. In 1997, for example, the per capita income of the most economically free nations averaged over $18,000 against $1,700 for the least free.[9]

It should be pointed out that the current wave of globalization is neither the first nor the largest. The world has witnessed at least five prior waves of globalization: in the United States (1870–1890), Western Europe (1890–1913), Japan (1913–1938), the United States (1970), and

Western Europe (1950–1992).[10] Most of these waves eventually petered out because of their adverse impact on the social infrastructure of the countries involved. Most notably, these adverse impacts were related to increasing income disparities and unequal sharing of gains from globalization between countries and among different groups within individual countries. Another adverse impact was felt by the poorest segments due to the dismantling and dislocation of the "social safety net," which resulted from changes in income distribution and government reallocation of social expenditures.

The proponents of globalization cite data on economic growth to support their case for even greater globalization. Unfortunately, these numbers do not tell the entire story. The benefits of globalization are greatly exaggerated by its proponents, who tend to ignore or understate many, if not all, of its adverse consequences. As Jeffrey Sachs and Andrew Warner point out:

> Long-held judgments about the development process, as well as the workhorse formal models of economic growth suggest that the poorer countries should tend to grow more rapidly than richer countries and therefore should close the proportionate income gap over time. The main reason for expecting economic convergence is that the poorer countries can import capital and modern technologies from the wealthier countries, and thereby reap the "advantage of backwardness." Yet in recent decades, there has been no overall tendency for the poorer countries to catch up or converge with the richer countries.[11]

Globalization and economic growth have had adverse side effects. Distribution of gains from international trade and investment has been highly skewed in favor of those who control the capital and against those who contribute human labor, especially in the developing countries. According to the World Bank, the disparity between rich and poor countries has grown 10 times wider during the past 30 years.

The number of people living on less than $1 a day may have been reduced by over 60 percent in an eight-year period, but it should be clear that the 1998 $1 is grossly decimated by inflation. Moreover, the current prevailing rate of $1.50 to $2 per day for 10-hour days, worked by most low-skilled and unskilled workers in Asian and Latin American countries, can hardly be called progress when one realizes the abysmally unsafe working conditions under which these workers toil to earn what we euphemistically call "a living."

The poorest 20 percent in the United States may be increasing their earnings at a rate of 2.7 percent compared with the 2.4 percent rate of increase earned by the wealthiest. This is not progress but a statistical artifact. Income growth from $1 to $2 a day would be a 100 percent increase while income growth of $200,000 when income was already $1 million would be 20 percent or just a fifth as much. It is disingenuous to claim progress by showing a percentage increase over a small base, while the actual disparity in income between the poor and rich has actually widened. Similarly, although the average "economically free" person may be earning $18,000 per year, this figure does not say anything about the political freedom of people in economically free nations. Nor does it say anything about how the income is distributed among the richer and poorer segments of the population in these countries.[12]

In their overseas operations, MNCs have ensured that products made for them in developing countries meet quality standards acceptable to consumers in the industrially advanced countries. However, when it comes to workers and working conditions, MNCs have been indifferent, if not downright negligent, about ensuring the health and welfare of the workers who make those products. Consequently, we are finding widespread worker exploitation and abuse, and harm to the environment.[13]

As globalization has progressed, political boundaries have blurred, and the control of national governments in the domestic arena has diminished. Both the governments of industrially advanced countries and multinational corporations have sought to exploit this weakness to promote their own goals. The governments of the industrially advanced countries have essentially used their influence to protect the interests of MNCs based in their home countries as these companies expand their business activities abroad.[14] MNCs and the governments of industrially advanced countries have asserted, albeit gratuitously, that the greater expansion of international trade and economic growth will lead to a fostering of democratic institutions and improvement in the human rights records of developing countries where authoritarian and totalitarian regimes currently hold sway.

Such assertions are made almost as truisms. Yet they are actually untenable. America's trade with China has risen sixfold in the past 10 years and now stands at $85 billion. In the same period, U.S. investments there grew to $56 billion from $32 billion. Yet one would be hard-pressed to find commensurate gains in democratic institutions or human rights in China.[15]

The irony is that in their home countries, multinationals depend on democratic systems of governance, the rule of law, and open societies to protect their interests and enable them to thrive. At the same time, they make enormous gains in countries where authoritarian and nondemocratic regimes deliver on the promise of disciplined labor, low wages, and lax controls on environmental protection and human rights. Thus, they seek to protect the gains of their exploitation in developing countries under the umbrella of their home country's democratic institutions.

The advocates of limitless globalization emphasize its role in economic growth and development around the world. The drive toward globalization is also linked with the rise of the private sector as if government per se was a prime detriment to a nation's economic growth and the prosperity of its people. That any constraints on the markets were per se constraints on economic growth and individual freedoms is, however, a very narrow construction of the social role of capitalism in general and corporations in particular. The market system is not a perfect mechanism. It requires a certain degree of state supervision to enforce the rules of the game. Moreover, as Irving Kristol observes, historically the virtue of capitalism was measured (1) in terms of its ability to maximize production of goods and services and provide people with maximum freedom to pursue their self-interest, and (2) to create a distributive system of social rewards and benefits that people considered just, fair, and equitable. Kristol suggests that modern defenders of capitalism have been emphasizing the former, while the survival of the system depends on the public's perception of capitalism's ability to deliver the latter. Devoid of its moral and aesthetic core, capitalism would be likely to lose its ethical mooring and social legitimacy.[16]

Multinational Corporations and Globalization— A Case of Neomercantilism

For the benefits of free trade to be distributed equitably, it is important that both capital and labor have maximum mobility, thereby allowing each party to maximize the reward from its efforts. However, in the new scheme of things, MNCs have all the advantages of moving capital between different sectors and nations in order to maximize their return on investment. Workers, on other hand, are disadvantaged because they lack such mobility. Workers in a country cannot easily migrate, if at all, to another country with labor shortages and thus bring about a better balance of supply and demand.

This situation is more akin to neomercantilism than to free trade. Multinationals use the threat of capital mobility to extract the maximum share of productivity gains from cheap and abundant labor. Unable to reduce supply through emigration, local workers compete with each other for available jobs, reducing their wages to subsistence level. At this level, wages may prevent starvation, but they do not allow for savings to be invested in the human capital of the current workers or future generations. Otherwise, how could one explain the fact that the minimum hourly wage rates are $5.15 per hour in the United States while they are less than U.S. $0.30 per hour in most developing countries, with essentially similar—and often higher— productivity levels in developing countries.[17] Given the large wage gap and similar or higher productivity rates, workers in Asian countries—other things being equal—should be able to extract somewhat higher wages and reduce the disparity between wage rates. However, their lack of bargaining power condemns these workers to work for subsistence wage rates and "be grateful for it."

This neomercantilism creates a monopoly-like condition in favor of MNCs and enables them to hire workers at subsistence-level wages. MNCs maintain their control on wage rates in several ways: (1) the MNCs minutely scrutinize the cost structure of local manufacturers, to enforce cost controls; (2) local manufacturers cooperate among themselves by not competing for workers on the basis of higher wages—a situation that is easily maintained because of abundant labor; (3) most workers come from rural areas to seek employment and are unaware of their rights under local laws; (4) labor authorities—induced by corruption and the need to protect their tax base—often collude with local manufacturers to violate even the rudimentary labor laws pertaining to minimum wages and working hours; and, finally, (5) the MNCs' power over local wages and working conditions becomes almost absolute because these MNCs control access to foreign markets through ownership of brand names, technical know-how, and supply chains.

An abundance of cheap labor leaves little incentive for MNCs to improve technology and thereby labor productivity. MNCs further exacerbate this situation through outsourcing most, if not all, of their production needs to local entrepreneurs. It is the predominant mode of operation by most MNCs in the poorer and developing countries of Asia, Latin America, and now Eastern Europe. This process places the entire burden of providing capital on local entrepreneurs. Available empirical data suggest that local entrepreneurs in developing countries have a short-term perspective on investment, enterprise growth, and profitability. Lacking capital and technology, these entrepreneurs resort to further exploitation of labor through long working hours, often without payment of overtime, and under dangerous and unhealthy working conditions.

The developing country is faced with a Hobson's choice of exporting at any cost or dying because of lack of foreign exchange and foreign capital. This dilemma "conveniently leaves out why a country exports in the first place: to favor the development of the internal market, which is another way of saying the collective well-being of society."[18]

The manifestation of the current forces of globalization creates fewer opportunities for a multiplier effect and backward transformation of physical, social, and economic infrastructure that would provide the developing country with the wherewithal for economic takeoff and sustained growth. "It benefits some people and modernizes some things, while excluding the bulk of the population, offering them only the fantasy that owning a cellular telephone will make them part of the new world order."[19]

The mobility of capital means that an important segment of the local governments' tax base can simply get up and leave, giving governments the unappetizing option of imposing disproportionately high taxes on income from labor,[20] agricultural products from even poorer rural areas, and household consumption, and higher taxes on local property. Short of resources, host country governments have been unwilling or unable to exercise regulatory oversight to enforce the already rudimentary infrastructure of labor and environmental protection laws.

Globalization and the dominant role of MNCs do not provide any mechanisms to enhance a country's economic infrastructure and instead push lower its already meager fiscal resources through tax abatement, tax holidays, and other esoteric techniques. Lest we forget, the growth of the industrialized nations was not achieved by private enterprise alone. Even in the United States, it was the government that created the vast state-supported educational infrastructure and the highly subsidized railroads that helped educate the populace and improved transportation systems.

Control of final product and distribution channels by MNCs leads to greater standardization in manufacturing processes, which emphasize use of labor over capital. This in turn leads to commoditization of labor and allows MNCs to shift production among suppliers in different countries in a seamless manner. It puts an added burden on manufacturers in one country to harmonize their production costs—in dollar terms regardless of different local conditions—to compete with manufacturers in other countries. An inevitable consequence of this process is that workers in one poor country must now compete with workers in other poor countries. This situation works to the advantage of MNCs by further depressing marginal wage rates because of the vastly expanded labor pool. Finally, subsistence-level wage rates propel rural families to produce more children to work in the factories, in order to sustain the family, which creates a self-perpetuating cycle of poverty.[21]

This situation is further compounded by the fact that most manufacturing operations primarily hire young workers between the ages of 16 and 18—except in high-skill areas—and do not keep them beyond the ages of 20 or 21, only to replace them with another wave of 16- to 18-year-old workers. The older workers, with few additional skills, are then thrown out to join the armies of the destitute and unemployed.

One must also add to this developing situation the impact of public interest groups, or nongovernmental organizations (NGOs) in the United Nations parlance, in the United States and other industrially advanced countries. These NGOs come from a variety of sources and include religious institutions, environmental groups, human rights organizations, organized labor, groups dealing in issues of public health, and groups concerned with global poverty, to name a few. NGOs have sought to hold multinational corporations accountable for the negative impact of their activities in developing countries. They have used mass media, direct action, governmental lobbying, and other forms of public and private pressure to force corporations to become more accountable. Avenues of protest have been the exposure and denunciation of corporations in the media, consumer boycotts, and other forms of pressure campaigns to embarrass the offending corporations. In the process, NGOs have brought these issues into the public forum and raised people's awareness of the need to seek greater accountability from MNCs in their overseas operations. There is every reason to believe that NGO activism is here to stay and will have an important role in most future deliberations on global economic, environmental, and human rights issues. Conflicts between market economies and democratic societies are not generally about aggregate economic growth or the activities of private sector institutions. Instead, the debate on business-society conflicts must be formed in broader terms, that is, the nature of public-collective goods and private goods. The former are viewed as society's endowments to be shared by all of its members without regard to one's ability to pay for them. The distributive criteria are those of need, social relevance, and collective enjoyment. Private goods are for the exclusive enjoyment of their owners and, within broad limits, to be bought, sold, and exchanged at their owners' discretion. Expansion of market activities, by its very nature, creates more private goods, often contracting the supply of public goods. While business institutions are applauded for their production of private goods and services, they also take the major blame for depleting the stock of public goods.

In one sense, society's moral and ethical values, concern for the less fortunate, and preservation of the natural environment are public or collective goods. All members of a society stand to benefit from an enhancement of these values regardless of their individual contributions to such enhancement. Here the nature of corporate mission and goals and those of private voluntary organizations stand in sharp contrast. This may partially explain the inherent discrepancy in public trust and goodwill enjoyed by public interest groups compared to the business community.[22]

The collective stock of a society's moral and ethical values will increase if more and more individuals and groups behave with a greater degree of altruism. In the case of public interest groups or NGOs, there is a presumption of altruism, which is further strengthened by their espoused missions and goals. Even when individual NGOs act in a manner that could be construed as antisocial in some quarters, they are still viewed as only hurting private greed for larger social good. The problem of a free rider—that is, one who takes a greater share of public-collective goods without adequately contributing to the enhancement of their stock or being concerned about depriving others of similar enjoyment—is not considered serious. NGOs are expected to behave in the public interest. It is their raison d'être. Ergo, there is no free rider.

MNCs, as private sector institutions, face the exactly opposite problem. They must always try to maximize gain by internalizing all possible profits and externalizing all possible costs. Given competitive markets, firms have a great deal to lose from contributing to general public trust and moral and ethical values and everything to gain from being a free rider. Since a firm cannot control the behavior of other firms, it must assume that other firms would behave equally aggressively as free riders. The exception to this rule would take place under conditions of imperfect markets, that is, where a firm is anxious to protect its strong market position and resultant nonmarket rent or above-normal profits by courting the goodwill of its customers, government regulators, or public at large.[23] The incentive to do so, however, is not altruism but a desire to preserve the firm's extra profits. Thus public goodwill is measured by its direct costs in terms of loss of potential profits. Both these conditions tend to undermine the value of business contributions to enhancing a society's ethical and moral values because companies are viewed to be primarily acting in self-interest, thereby discounting their claims of being good public citizens.

It is not now, and unlikely to be in the foreseeable future, that the traditional role of competitive markets, and corporations as their primary institutions, will be supplanted by other institutions in most democratic and industrially advanced societies. If anything, this role is gaining wider acceptance in other societies that had previously denigrated it or chosen to follow the path of a centrally managed, government-controlled system of economic growth.

The areas of conflict rest almost entirely on the means that business institutions allegedly use to circumvent the discipline of markets or to appropriate for their use gains from the marketplace arising out of their superior bargaining leverage, insufficient consumer information, and a host of other factors classified under the economic concept of "market failures" or "market imperfections." And yet MNCs rarely if ever address issues of social conflict or their adversaries along those dimensions until such time that an issue has reached crisis proportions with pressure from people and other institutions of society for companies to curb their behavior and provide greater accountability and justification for the harm that they have caused to noneconomic institutions of society.

The future challenge to globalization and the role of MNCs will not come from the opponents of free trade and economic growth. It will arise from the inability and unwillingness of multinational corporations to voluntarily act in a socially responsible manner, and their unwillingness to be accountable, and transparent, for the second-order negative consequences of their wealth-creating activities. The primary issue here is twofold: one, to ensure that economic growth is accompanied by a sense of fair distribution of gains from productivity between those who provide capital and those who provide labor; two, for MNCs to internalize more of the costs of appropriating public goods by using them more efficiently, and also by contributing to the increase in the stock of public goods.

Notes

1. Jagdish Bhagwati, *A Stream of Windows—Unsettling Reflections on Trade, Immigration, and Democracy* (Cambridge: MIT Press, 1998); Robert Baterson and Murray Weidenbaum, *The Pros and Cons of Globalization* (St. Louis: Center for the Study of American Business, Washington University, 2001), 22; "Globalization and Its Critics," *The Economist* (September 29, 2001), 30.
2. Jeffrey Sachs and Andrew Warner, "Economic Reform and Process of Global Integration," *Brookings Papers on Economic Activity* No. 1 (1995), 1–118.
3. Ibid.
4. S. P. Sethi and B. B. Bhalla, "Free Market Orientation and Economic Growth: Some Lessons for Developing Countries," *Business and the Contemporary World* 3:2 (Winter 1991), 86–101; S. P. Sethi, "Human Rights and Corporate Sense," *Far Eastern Economic Review* (October 19, 2000), 37; S. P. Sethi and B. B. Bhalla, "The Peril to the Global Environment: The Role of Globalism," *Business and the Contemporary World* (Autumn 1991), 114–125.
5. Dennis Rondinelli and Jack Behrman, "The Promise and Pains of Globalization," *Global Focus* 12:1 (2000), 6 (cited in Murray Weidenbaum, *Looking for Common Ground on U.S. Trade Policy* (Washington, D.C.: CSIS Report, August 2001), 6).
6. Weidenbaum, *Common Ground*, 6.
7. "World Development Indicators 2000" (Washington, D.C.: World Bank, 2000), Tables 4.10 and 4.11 (cited in Weidenbaum, *Common Ground*, 6).
8. John M. Berry, "This Time, Boom Benefits the Poor," *Washington Post* (February 14, 2000), C5 (cited in Weidenbaum, *Common Ground*, 6).
9. James Gwartney and Robert Lawson, *Economic Freedom of the World: 2000 Annual Report* (Vancouver: Fraser Institute, 2000), 15 (cited in Weidenbaum, *Common Ground*, 6).
10. Dani Rodrik, *Has Globalization Gone Too Far?* (Washington, D.C.: Institute for International Economics, 1997), 7. The current phase of globalization benefits mostly industrialized nations and a small set of developing countries in Asia. It excludes most of Africa and large parts of Latin America. These and other countries in Eastern Europe and other parts of the world have been left to their own devices to find a way to become part of the new world. The choice of which countries shall benefit from globalization is a function of the needs of MNCs in industrially advanced countries, and has little to do with the needs or the potential of developing countries. Thus we are faced with the phenomenon of an expanding disparity between the richer and the poorer countries, and also between the richer and poorer people in individual countries.
11. Sachs and Warner, "Economic Reform," 1–118.

12. S. P. Sethi, Joel Kurtzman, and B. B. Bhalla, "The Paradox of Economic Globalism: The Myth and Reality of the 'Global Village'—The Changing Role of Multinational Corporations," *Business and the Contemporary World* 6:4 (1994), 131–142.

13. "Global Capitalism: Can It Be Made Better?" *Business Week* (November 6, 2000), 72–90; "Take a Break, Trade Bullies," *Business Week* (November 6, 2000), 100–101; S. P. Sethi, "Human Rights and Corporate Sense," *Far Eastern Economic Review* (October 19, 2000), 37.

14. Fareed Zakaria, "Globalization Grows Up and Gets Political," *New York Times* (December 31, 2000), 24.

15. Sethi, "Human Rights and Corporate Sense," 37, note 13.

16. Irving Kristol, "When Virtue Loses All Her Loveliness: Some Reflections on Capitalism and the Free Society," *Public Interest* (Fall 1970), 3–16.

17. After more than 18 years of observing manufacturing operations in many developing countries, I have seen the truth in the notion that worker productivity in low-skilled and comparatively less capital-intensive manufacturing operations is considerably higher in developing countries. A large part of this productivity comes from long working hours and high production speeds. This also accounts for the fact that relatively young workers, 16 to 18 years old, perform most of these operations. The fact that such long hours and high manufacturing speeds lead to exhaustion, worker injury, and long-term health damage rarely enters into employers' considerations.

18. Oscar Ugarteche, *The False Dilemma: Globalization, Opportunity or Threat* (New York: Zed Books, 1997), xiii–xiv.

19. Ibid. xiv.

20. Rodrik, *Has Globalization Gone Too Far?*, 6.

21. Daniel Cohen has made a similar argument with respect to the use of women as beasts of burden in Africa. See Daniel Cohen, *The Wealth of the World and the Poverty of Nations* (Cambridge: MIT Press, 1998), 7.

22. In developing these ideas, I have greatly benefited from the writing of Fred Hirsch, *Social Limits to Growth* (Cambridge: Harvard University Press, 1976). See in particular Section II, "The Commercialization Bias," pp. 72–114, and Section III, "The Depleting Moral Legacy," pp. 117–158.

23. William Baumol, *Perfect Markets and Easy Virtue* (Cambridge, Mass.: Blackwell, 1991); Thomas Schelling, *Micromotives and Macrobehavior* (New York: W. W. Norton & Co., 1978), 9–45. See also Amartya Sen, "Behavior and the Concept of Preference," *Economica* (August 1973), cited in Hirsch, *Social Limits*, 139; and Robert H. Scott, "Avarice, Altruism, and Second Party Preferences," *Quarterly Journal of Economics* (February 1972), cited in Hirsch, *Social Limits*, 78.

CHAPTER
2

Sweatshops and Human Rights Abuses: Evidence from the Field

To date, there have been no systematic studies to assess the extent of sweatshop-like working conditions and human rights abuses among workers in different countries around the world. Nor is there any data showing linkages of these conditions with different types of industries and multinational corporations. To the best of my knowledge, no country has released such data. Although it stands to reason that most MNCs would track news stories concerning their overseas operations, no company has made such information publicly available.

This is an attempt to fill this void. In the absence of direct information, we have used the number of news reports pertaining to these issues as proxy for the prevalence of sweatshops and human rights abuses.

My primary source of data is from the Dow Jones Interactive (DJI)—an index of 6,000 full-text news wires, newspapers, magazines, and trade journals published in the English language. This is by far the most comprehensive database available. We have supplemented this database with other sources, such as individual national and international newspapers—*The New York Times*, *The Wall Street Journal*, *The Financial Times*, *Business Week*, and *The Economist*, for example. (See Appendix 2.1). In addition, web sites from various human rights groups, MNCs, and countries are important sources of information (see Appendix 2.2).

My sole reliance on English-language sources creates a certain bias in the

15

database. Most factories are located in the developing countries where English is not the primary language. English-language publications are likely to report only those stories that are newsworthy (i.e., that are out of the ordinary) and also relate to the MNCs from the home countries of the respective publications. This approach is likely to miss news reports of everyday sweatshop-related incidents that are more relevant to the local communities where these incidents have occurred. Therefore, our database doubtless underrepresents the magnitude of adverse conditions present in these countries. Similarly, English-language publications are likely to underreport news stories connected with MNCs whose home bases are in non-English-speaking countries (e.g., Japan, Germany, France, and South Korea), which are more likely to be covered by the news media of those countries.

Our unit of analysis is the number of news reports and, in particular, the number of mentions (e.g., name of a country or company, or the type of sweatshop condition, worker abuse, or human rights violation). No attempt has been made to undertake extensive analysis of individual news stories—except where they report an incidence of such severity that it deserves special attention. This approach runs the risk of underreporting the severity of the problem where frequency of news reports may not be an accurate reflection of their overall severity.

There are two additional issues with regard to counting that should be kept in mind. In a number of cases, a news report will mention multiple companies and types of abuses (e.g., nature of abuses, types of industries, and names of different companies involved). Therefore, the total number of mentions in various categories would exceed the total number of news reports in any time period.

This database covers 30 countries and identifies 55 multinational corporations. To facilitate our analysis, these companies have been classified into eight industry groups. These are: athletic footwear, apparel, automobiles, carpets, electronics, food and beverages, retail, and toys. Similarly, sweatshops and human rights abuses have been classified into six categories. These are: working conditions, wages, working hours, human rights violations, child labor, and other types of worker abuse.

The Persistent Character of Sweatshops and Human Rights Abuses

The data analysis contained in this chapter, and reinforced through the case studies and analysis contained in other chapters in this book, tells a distressingly sad and maddeningly simple story. The data demonstrates convincingly that a very large majority of sweatshops and human rights abuses are concentrated in such mundane issues as wages, working hours, and unhealthy working conditions. They are not the highly complicated and politically charged issues of human rights violations such as torture, coercion, and denial of due process, where companies are often at the mercy of host country governments and their despotic rulers. Even the widely talked about issue of child labor is not mentioned as often as the issues of wages, working hours, and working conditions.

The data for various types of sweatshop-like working conditions and human rights abuses is presented in Table 2.1 and Figure 2.1. It shows that the two top abuses, namely working conditions and wages, accounted for more than 50 percent of all mentions during the period 1994 to March 2002. This was followed by working hours as the third most prevalent element. Together, these three conditions accounted for 72 percent of all negative news mentions during this period. The remaining three conditions, namely human rights violations, child labor, and other worker abuse, represented 13 percent, 12 percent, and 4 percent respectively.

Table 2.1 Distribution of Negative News Mentions According to Different Types of Sweatshop Conditions and Human Rights Abuses, 1994 to March 2002

Type of Abuse	1994–1996	1997–1999	2000–2002 (March)	Total 1994–2002 (March)
Working conditions	20%	30%	33%	29%
Wages	33%	28%	26%	28%
Working hours	16%	14%	14%	15%
Human rights violations	12%	13%	13%	13%
Child labor	13%	11%	11%	11%
Other worker abuse	6%	4%	3%	4%
Total number of mentions	693	1,477	913	3,083

Source: Appendix 2.1.

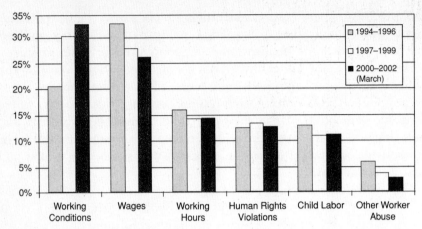

Figure 2.1   Distribution of Negative News Mentions According to Different Types of Sweatshop Conditions and Human Rights Abuses, 1994 to March 2002
Source: Appendix 2.1.
Note: The bar referring to the period 2000–2002 (March) covers only 27 months as against 36 months for the other two time periods. Therefore, the three time periods are not strictly comparable.

Country Concentration of Sweatshops and Human Rights Abuses

News reports of sweatshops and human rights abuses follow a predictable pattern; that is, their growth rates and country dispersion parallel the expansion and growth of MNCs' business in those countries. Our database of 1,682 news reports from the early 1980s through March 2002 contains 1,904 country mentions (Table 2.2). The number of country mentions is greater than the number of news reports since many news stories mention more than one country. There were only a handful of news stories on the subject prior to 1991; these accounted for 6.7 percent of all news reports during the period. However, starting in 1991 the number of news reports almost exploded and more or less doubled every three years. It has continued to expand as of March 2002, which is the closing date for the database covered in this analysis.

Among the countries, China has continued to top the list, and accounts for approximately one-fourth of all negative mentions in the news reports. Other countries with heavy concentration of negative news reports and mentions are: Indonesia, Vietnam, Mexico, Saipan and Northern Mariana

Table 2.2   Country Distribution of Negative News Reports and Mentions Pertaining to Sweatshops/Human Rights Abuses, Pre-1985 to March 2002

Country	1985 and Earlier	1986– 1990	1991– 1993	1994– 1996	1997– 1999	2000– 2002 (March)	Total
Bangladesh		1		5	3	11	20
Brazil					2	1	3
Cambodia					6	6	12
China		16	26	59	127	76	304
Colombia						1	1
Costa Rica					1		1
Dominican Republic						1	1
El Salvador	1			7	36	14	58
Guatemala				1	9	1	11
Haiti				24	20	1	45
Honduras				10	14	3	27
Hong Kong	3	1					4
India		1				5	6
Indonesia		7	17	45	66	44	179
Italy					1		1
Ivory Coast						3	3
Kazakstan						4	4
Malaysia		2		1	9		12
Mexico			2	11	30	48	91
Myanmar					1	1	2
Nicaragua					1	14	15
Pakistan		1		11	9	10	31
Philippines	1	3	1		4	2	11
Saipan and Northern Marianas			3		37	27	67
South Korea		17	16	18	15	6	72
Sri Lanka					2		2
Taiwan	2	11	11	2	2	1	29
Thailand	1	14	17	19	30	15	96
Turkey					1	1	2
Vietnam				24	49	23	96
General*	35	9	22	117	296	219	698
Total number of mentions	43	83	115	354	771	538	1,904
Total number of news reports	37	77	109	257	698	504	1,682

*Refers to news stories that discuss one or more topics pertaining to sweatshops and human rights abuses but do not mention specific countries. Instead they deal with issues in global terms or refer to one or more regions.
Source: Appendix 2.1.

Islands, Thailand, and El Salvador (Table 2.3, Figure 2.2). Excluding the general news reports, namely, the reports that do not identify individual countries but instead refer to particular regions or geographical areas, the top five countries that were the subject of news reports concerning sweatshops and human rights abuses accounted for 93.5 percent of total news reports from 1991 to 1993, 69.6 percent from 1994 to 1996, 66.3 percent from 1997 to 1999, and 68.3 percent from January 2000 to March 2002 (Table 2.4).

A reduction in the proportion of news reports accounted for by the top five countries does not mean a reduction in the incidence of sweatshops

Table 2.3   Country Ranks According to Distribution of Negative News Mentions on Sweatshops/Human Rights Abuses, 1994 to March 2002

Country	1994– 1996	1997– 1999	2000– 2002 (March)	Total 1994–2002 (March)
China	24.89%	26.74%	23.82%	25.41%
Indonesia	18.99%	13.89%	13.79%	15.03%
Mexico	4.64%	6.32%	15.05%	8.63%
Vietnam	10.13%	10.32%	7.21%	9.31%
Haiti	10.13%	4.21%	0.31%	4.36%
Thailand	8.02%	6.32%	4.70%	6.21%
Saipan and Northern Marianas	0.00%	7.79%	8.46%	6.21%
El Salvador	2.95%	7.58%	4.39%	5.53%
South Korea	7.59%	3.16%	1.88%	3.78%
Pakistan	4.64%	1.89%	3.13%	2.91%
Nicaragua	0.00%	0.21%	4.39%	1.45%
Honduras	4.22%	2.95%	0.94%	2.62%
Bangladesh	2.11%	0.63%	3.45%	1.84%
Guatemala	0.42%	1.89%	0.31%	1.07%
Malaysia	0.42%	1.89%	0.00%	0.97%
Cambodia	0.00%	1.26%	1.88%	1.16%
India	0.00%	0.00%	1.57%	0.48%
Philippines	0.00%	0.84%	0.63%	0.68%
Taiwan	0.84%	0.42%	0.31%	0.48%
Others*	0.00%	1.68%	3.76%	1.84%
Total number of mentions	237	475	319	1,031

*Brazil, Colombia, Costa Rica, Dominican Republic, Italy, Ivory Coast, Kazakstan, Myanmar, Sri Lanka, Turkey.
Source: Appendix 2.1.

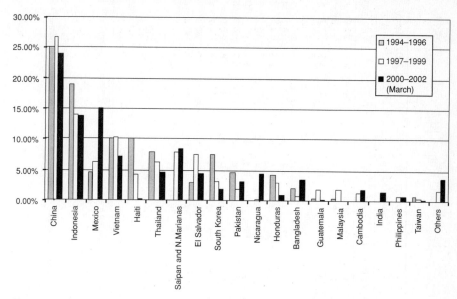

Figure 2.2 Country Ranks According to Distribution of Negative News Mentions on Sweatshops/Human Rights Abuses, 1994 to March 2002
Source: Appendix 2.1.
Note: The bar referring to the period 2000–2002 (March) covers only 27 months as against 36 months for the other two time periods. Therefore, the three time periods are not strictly comparable.

and human rights abuses in these countries since the total number of news reports containing these issues has increased more than fivefold in a little over 11 years from January 1991 through March 2002. Instead, it suggests that additional countries have joined the ranks of nations with sweatshops and human abuses as MNCs have expanded and diversified their foreign sources of supply in order to seek continuously cheaper workers and reduce their labor costs. This is confirmed by the increase in news reports in the "general" category from 10.8 percent in 1986–1990 to 40.7 percent in the period from January 2000 to March 2002 (Table 2.4). It also reveals that these issues are becoming more endemic and characteristic of conditions associated with "manufacturing for export" in countries around the world. Figure 2.2 offers another perspective by comparing the persistence of news reports concerning sweatshops and human rights abuses within and between major countries.

Table 2.4 Top Country Distribution of Negative News Mentions Pertaining to Sweatshops and Human Rights Abuses, 1986 to March 2002

Country	1986–1990 News Reports				1991–1993 News Reports				1994–1996 News Reports				1997–1999 News Reports				2000–2002 (March) News Reports			
	No.	% (A)	% (B)	Rank	No.	% (A)	% (B)	Rank	No.	% (A)	% (B)	Rank	No.	% (A)	% (B)	Rank	No.	% (A)	% (B)	Rank
China	16	19.3	21.62	2	26	22.6	28.0	1	59	16.7	24.9	1	127	16.5	26.7	1	76	14.1	23.8	1
Indonesia	7	8.4	9.459	5	17	14.8	18.3	2	45	12.7	19.0	2	66	8.6	13.9	2	44	8.2	13.8	3
Vietnam									24	6.8	10.1	3	49	6.4	10.3	3	23	4.3	7.2	5
Saipan and Northern Marianas					3	2.6	3.2	5					37	4.8	7.8	4	27	5.0	8.5	4
El Salvador									7	2.0	3.0	8	36	4.7	7.6	5	14	2.6	4.4	7
Mexico					2	1.7	2.2	6	11	3.1	4.6	6	30	3.9	6.3	6	48	8.9	15.0	2
South Korea	17	20.5	22.97	1	16	13.9	17.2	3	18	5.1	7.6	5	15	1.9	3.2	8	6	1.1	1.9	10
Taiwan	11	13.3	14.86	4	11	9.6	11.8	4	2	0.6	0.8	10	2	0.3	0.4	14	1	0.2	0.3	15
Honduras									10	2.8	4.2	7	14	1.8	2.9	9	3	0.6	0.9	13
Thailand	14	16.9	18.92	3	17	14.8	18.3	2	19	5.4	8.0	4	30	3.9	6.3	6	15	2.8	4.7	6
Subtotal	65	78.3	87.84		92	80.0	98.9		195	55.1	82.3		406	52.7	85.5		257	47.8	80.6	
Others	9	10.8	12.16		1	0.9	1.1		42	11.9	17.7		69	8.9	14.5		62	11.5	19.4	
General*	9	10.8			22	19.1			117	33.1			296	38.4			219	40.7		
Total number of mentions	83	100	100		115	100	100		354	100	100		771	100	100		538	100	100	
Total number of reports	77				109				257				698				506			

*Refers to news stories that discuss one or more topics pertaining to sweatshops and human rights abuses but do not mention specific countries. Instead they deal with issues in global terms or refer to one or more regions.

% (A) refers to percentage based on total number of mentions including general category.

% (B) refers to percentage based on total number of mentions excluding general category.

Note: Quite often news stories report on multiple countries, companies, or issues (e.g., child labor, wages, worker abuse). Therefore, the number of issues mentioned will be greater than the total number of news reports surveyed.

Source: Appendix 2.1.

Figure 2.2 suggests that during the period 1994 to March 2002 in China, there has been no noticeable reduction in the negative news reports of sweatshops and human rights abuses. In China's case, a somewhat shorter bar for the period January 2000 through March 2002 is a statistical artifact since this period covers only 27 months while the other two periods consist of 36 months each. A similar observation is relevant in the case of other countries like Indonesia, Mexico, Vietnam, Thailand, and Saipan and Northern Mariana Islands. These news reports tell a disappointing story about the progress made by MNCs in ensuring better compliance with their codes of conduct in countries like China. This is an important observation given the large concentration of manufacturing facilities and also the presence of a large number of MNCs in that country. One would like to think that this magnitude of concentration would facilitate cooperative and collective action on the part of the MNCs to curtail the incidence of sweatshops and human rights abuses. Further, such a concentration of manufacturing facilities would yield economies of scale toward more effective monitoring of local plants and their compliance with MNC codes of conduct. Instead the message seems to be that a repressive work environment and a regulatory regime that is indifferent to human rights abuses create a more inviting business environment for the MNCs. The sharp decline in the case of Haiti in the latest period, 2000 to March 2002, does not reflect any improvement in the working conditions in that country. This decline is the result of one or more major foreign multinationals leaving that country for greener pastures elsewhere.

Table 2.5 and the bar chart in Figure 2.3 further reaffirm the concentration of sweatshops and human rights abuses in different regions of the world. It is a mirror image of the concentration of factories manufacturing goods for the MNCs. The highest concentration is in the Pacific region: 62.7 percent during the latest period, 2000 to March 2002. This is followed by the Central America and Mexico region (25.7 percent), and the South Asia region (8.5 percent). In the case of the South Asia region, the sharp increase in the latest period is indicative of the increased activity in exports-related production from this region.

Another interesting feature of the country mentions is the sharp decline in the case of South Korea, similar to the situation in Taiwan. This reflects a migration of MNCs to other cheap labor countries once Taiwan and South Korea had developed their economies and were able to create higher-paying jobs for their better-trained workers. Distribution of sweatshop-like conditions and human rights abuses among countries within each region are presented in Tables 2.6 to 2.8 and Figures 2.4 to 2.6.

Table 2.5   Within Region and Between Region Comparison of Negative News Mentions Pertaining to Sweatshops/Human Rights Abuses, 1994 to March 2002

Regions	1994– 1996	1997– 1999	2000– 2002 (March)	Total 1994– 2002 (March)
Pacific region	70.89%	72.63%	62.70%	69.16%
Central America and Mexico	22.36%	23.37%	25.71%	23.86%
South Asia region	6.75%	3.16%	8.467%	5.63%
Latin America region	0.00%	0.42%	0.63%	0.39%
Rest of world	0.00%	0.42%	2.51%	0.97%
Total number of mentions	237	475	319	1,031

Note: Pacific Region: China, Indonesia, Malaysia, Philippines, South Korea, Taiwan, Thailand, Vietnam, Cambodia, Saipan, Northern Marianas.
Central America and Mexico: Costa Rica, Dominican Republic, El Salvador, Guatemala, Haiti, Honduras, Mexico, Nicaragua.
South Asia: Bangladesh, Myanmar, India, Pakistan, Sri Lanka.
Latin America Region: Brazil, Columbia.
Source: Appendix 2.1.

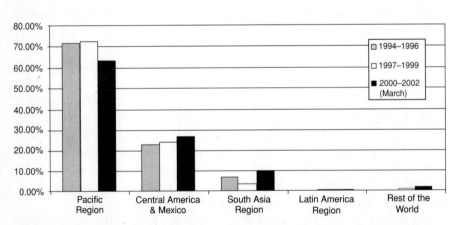

Figure 2.3   Within Region and Between Region Comparison of Negative News Mentions Pertaining to Sweatshops/Human Rights Abuses, 1994 to March 2002
Source: Appendix 2.1.
Note: The bar referring to the period 2000–2002 (March) covers only 27 months as against 36 months for the other two time periods. Therefore, the three time periods are not strictly comparable.

Table 2.6   Pacific Region: Distribution of Negative News Mentions Pertaining to Sweatshops/Human Rights Abuses, 1994 to March 2002

Country	1994–1996	1997–1999	2000–2002 (March)
China	35.12%	36.92%	38.00%
Indonesia	26.79%	19.19%	22.00%
Vietnam	14.29%	14.24%	11.50%
Saipan and Northern Marianas	0.00%	10.47%	13.50%
Thailand	11.31%	8.72%	7.50%
South Korea	10.71%	4.36%	3.00%
Cambodia	0.00%	1.74%	3.00%
Malaysia	0.60%	2.62%	0.00%
Taiwan	1.19%	0.58%	0.50%
Philippines	0.00%	1.16%	1.00%
Total number of mentions	168	344	200

Source: Appendix 2.I.

Table 2.7   Central America, Mexico, and Caribbean: Distribution of Negative News Mentions Pertaining to Sweatshops/Human Rights Abuses, 1994 to March 2002

Country	1994–1996	1997–1999	2000–2002 (March)
Mexico	20.75%	27.03%	58.54%
Haiti	45.28%	18.02%	1.22%
El Salvador	13.21%	32.43%	17.07%
Honduras	18.87%	12.61%	3.66%
Nicaragua	0.00%	0.90%	17.07%
Guatemala	1.89%	8.11%	1.22%
Dominican Republic	0.00%	0.00%	1.22%
Costa Rica	0.00%	0.90%	0.00%
Total number of mentions	53	111	82

Source: Appendix 2.1.

Table 2.8   South Asia Region: Distribution of Negative News Mentions Pertaining to Sweatshops/Human Rights Abuses, 1994 to March 2002

Country	1994–1996	1997–1999	2000–2002 (March)
Pakistan	68.75%	60.00%	37.04%
Bangladesh	31.25%	20.00%	40.74%
India	0.00%	0.00%	18.52%
Sri Lanka	0.00%	13.33%	0.00%
Myanmar	0.00%	6.67%	3.70%
Total number of mentions	16	15	27

Source: Appendix 2.I.

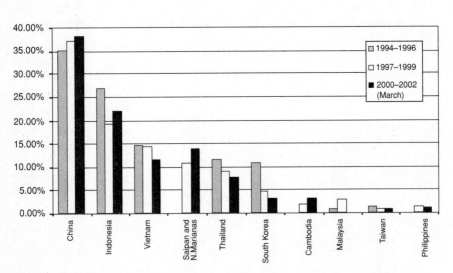

Figure 2.4   Pacific Region: Distribution of Negative News Mentions Pertaining to Sweatshops/Human Rights Abuses, 1994 to March 2002

Source: Appendix 2.1.

Note: The bar referring to the period 2000–2002 (March) covers only 27 months as against 36 months for the other two time periods. Therefore, the three time periods are not strictly comparable.

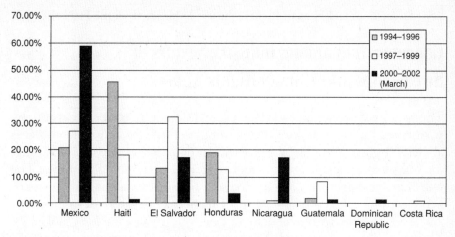

Figure 2.5   Central America: Distribution of Negative News Mentions
Pertaining to Sweatshops/Human Rights Abuses, 1994 to March 2002
Source: Appendix 2.1.
Note: The bar referring to the period 2000–2002 (March) covers only 27 months as against
36 months for the other two time periods. Therefore, the three time periods are not strictly
comparable.

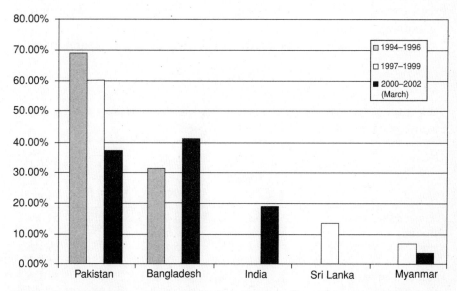

Figure 2.6   South Asia Region: Distribution of Negative News Mentions
Pertaining to Sweatshops/Human Rights Abuses, 1994 to March 2002
Source: Appendix 2.1.
Note: The bar referring to the period 2000–2002 (March) covers only 27 months as against
36 months for the other two time periods. Therefore, the three time periods are not strictly
comparable.

Concentration among Industry Sectors of Sweatshops and Human Rights Abuses

The next phase of our analysis focuses on different industry sectors and the persistence of news reports concerning sweatshops and human rights abuses. Of the eight industry sectors in our database, we report our findings on four sectors, namely athletic footwear, apparel, retailing, and toys. The four remaining sectors, namely food and beverages, automobiles, carpets, and electronics, had a relatively small number of negative news mentions and accounted for 1.97 percent of all mentions in our database (Table 2.9). Therefore, they were excluded from our analysis. Our data shows that athletic footwear industry has the worst record among all industries in terms of sweatshops and human rights abuses over the entire period covered in this study. The four industry groups also varied in terms of growth patterns (Figure 2.7). The athletic footwear industry, having reached saturation point, stayed at the 50 percent plus level across the entire period. The apparel industry, however, showed a sharp upward spike in the number of mentions. This growth rate may be explained by the expansion of outsourcing in the apparel industry. Another contributing factor may have been the lack of success on the part of MNCs in the apparel industry

Table 2.9 Industry-Based Distribution of Negative News Mentions Pertaining to Sweatshops/Human Rights Abuses, 1994 to March 2002

Industry	1994–1996	1997–1999	2000–2002 (March)	Total 1994–2002 (March)
Athletic footware	53.20%	47.34%	55.26%	51.22%
Apparel	9.46%	23.26%	26.53%	21.51%
Retail	24.55%	24.54%	9.42%	19.45%
Toys	11.51%	3.70%	4.87%	5.71%
Food and beverages	0.26%	0.58%	2.20%	1.06%
Automobiles	0.51%	0.58%	0.16%	0.42%
Carpets	0.00%	0.00%	1.26%	0.42%
Electronics	0.51%	0.00%	0.31%	0.21%
Total number of mentions	391	864	637	1,892

Source: Appendix 2.1.

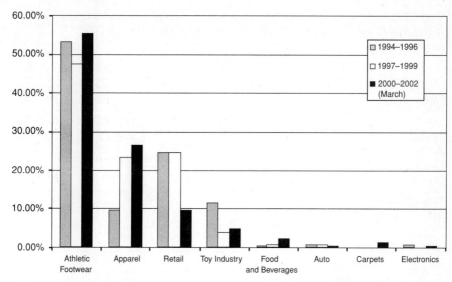

Figure 2.7 Industry-Based Distribution of Negative News Mentions Pertaining to Sweatshops/Human Rights Abuses, 1994 to March 2002

Source: Appendix 2.1.

Note: The bar referring to the period 2000–2002 (March) covers only 27 months as against 36 months for the other two time periods. Therefore, the three time periods are not strictly comparable.

to control sweatshop-like conditions and human rights abuses in the factories manufacturing apparel. Of the remaining two industry groups in our analysis, retail recorded a decline in negative news mentions during the latest period, and toys rose slightly.

ATHLETIC FOOTWEAR INDUSTRY

The athletic footwear industry comprises three major multinational corporations: Nike, Reebok, and Adidas. In addition, it includes some minor players such as Puma and Timberland. This industry accounted for over 50 percent of all mentions. These negative news mentions were more than twice the number for apparel, the next worst industry (Table 2.9). In the footwear industry Nike accounted for over 82 percent of all negative mentions for sweatshops and human rights abuses (Table 2.10, Figure 2.8). However, Nike's position remained relatively unchanged during the entire period of 1994 to March 2002.

Table 2.10   Athletic Footwear: Distribution of Negative News Mentions Pertaining to Sweatshops/Human Rights Abuses, 1994 to March 2002

Company	1994– 1996	1997– 1999	2000– 2002 (March)	Total 1994– 2002 (March)
Nike	93.27%	71.75%	92.35%	82.91%
Reebok	5.77%	7.32%	4.25%	5.98%
Adidas	0.96%	2.85%	2.55%	2.37%
Others*	0.00%	1.22%	0.57%	0.76%
Total number of mentions	208	492	353	1,053

*New Balance, Puma, Timberland
Source: Appendix 2.I.

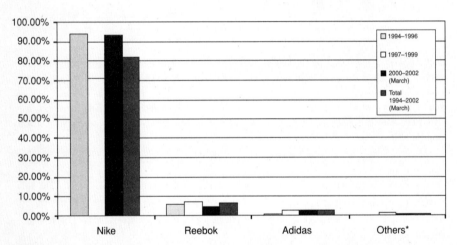

Figure 2.8   Athletic Footwear: Distribution of Negative News Mentions Pertaining to Sweatshops/Human Rights Abuses, 1994 to March 2002
Source: Appendix 2.1.
Note: The bar referring to the period 2000–2002 (March) covers only 27 months as against 36 months for the first two time periods. Therefore, the time periods are not strictly comparable.

APPAREL INDUSTRY

The situation in the apparel industry is more fragmented than in the footwear industry. It is also quite revealing to the extent that we can draw certain inferences about corporate conduct from the data with regard to number of mentions about sweatshops and human rights abuses

(Table 2.11, Figure 2.9). During the period 1994–1996, Disney accounted for 81 percent of all mentions, while Nike accounted for only 8 percent of such mentions. However, in the next period (1997–1999) Nike's negative news mentions increased more than fourfold, from 8 percent to 36 percent, while Disney's decreased fourfold from 81 percent to less than 21 percent and further declined to 17 percent in the subsequent period. A somewhat similar, but smaller, decline was noticed in the case of Gap. Relative declines between two time periods were recorded for J. Crew, Tommy Hilfiger, and Liz Claiborne. The remaining companies recorded substantial relative increases although most started from a smaller base.

RETAIL STORES

Wal-Mart was the principal culprit in the retail store segment and accounted for over 50 percent of all negative mentions. Wal-Mart's negative mentions also remained at a high level through the entire eight years

Table 2.11 Apparel Industry: Distribution of Negative News Mentions Pertaining to Sweatshops/Human Rights Abuses, 1994 to March 2002

Company	1994– 1996	1997– 1999	2000– 2002 (March)	Total 1994– 2002 (March)
Nike	8.11%	35.82%	36.09%	33.58%
Disney	81.08%	20.79%	17.16%	24.75%
Gap	10.81%	8.42%	3.55%	6.62%
Tommy Hilfiger	0.00%	5.45%	5.33%	4.90%
J. Crew	0.00%	5.94%	3.55%	4.41%
Polo Ralph Lauren	0.00%	3.47%	5.33%	3.92%
Warnaco	0.00%	3.96%	4.14%	3.68%
Calvin Klein	0.00%	1.98%	5.92%	3.43%
Levi Strauss	0.00%	1.98%	5.33%	3.19%
Liz Claiborne	0.00%	3.47%	2.96%	2.94%
Jones Apparel	0.00%	1.98%	4.14%	2.70%
Others*	0.00%	6.44%	6.51%	5.88%
Total number of mentions	37	201	169	408

*Ann Taylor, Donna Karan, Abercrombie & Fitch, Benetton, XOXO Clothing, Eddie Bauer, Arrow.
Source: Appendix 2.1.

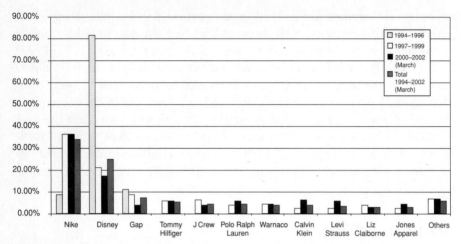

Figure 2.9   Apparel Industry: Distribution of Negative News Mentions
Pertaining to Sweatshops/Human Rights Abuses, 1994 to March 2002
Source: Appendix 2.1.
Note: The bar referring to the period 2000–2002 (March) covers only 27 months as
against 36 months for the first two time periods. Therefore, the time periods are not
strictly comparable.

covered in the database. Wal-Mart was followed by Kmart, which increased its negative news mentions from 17.7 percent in 1994–1996 to 25
percent in 2000–2002 (March). Among the remaining four companies,
JCPenney recorded a small increase over the entire period covered in the
database, while Sears, Nordstrom, and May Department Stores recorded
declines between two time periods (Table 2.12, Figure 2.10).

TOY INDUSTRY

In the toy industry, Disney and Mattel accounted for a majority of all negative mentions, with another three companies, namely Hasbro, McDonald's,
and Chicco, following. An important point to note in the case of the toy
industry is the interperiod fluctuations in negative news mentions for different companies (Table 2.13 and Figure 2.11).

For example, Disney's negative mentions went up from 28.9 percent in
1994–1996 to 37.5 percent in 1997–1999, and 38.7 percent in the period

Table 2.12 Retail Stores: Distribution of Negative News Mentions Pertaining to Sweatshops/Human Rights Abuses, 1994 to March 2002

Company	1994– 1996	1997– 1999	2000– 2002 (March)	Total 1994– 2002 (March)
Wal-Mart	57.29%	46.70%	58.33%	50.54%
Kmart	17.71%	25.47%	25.00%	23.37%
JCPenney	7.29%	13.21%	8.33%	10.87%
Sears	8.33%	5.19%	3.33%	5.71%
Nordstrom	0.00%	6.13%	0.00%	3.53%
May Dept. Stores	5.21%	0.94%	3.33%	2.45%
Others*	4.17%	2.36%	1.67%	2.72%
Total number of mentions	96	212	60	368

*Fred Meyer, C&A, Marks & Spencer, Champion, The Limited.
Source: Appendix 2.I.

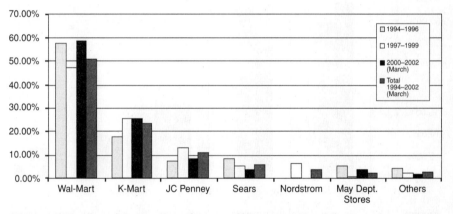

Figure 2.10 Retail Stores: Distribution of Negative News Mentions Pertaining to Sweatshops/Human Rights Abuses, 1994 to March 2002
Source: Appendix 2.1.
Note: The bar referring to the period 2000–2002 (March) covers only 27 months as against 36 months for the first two time periods. Therefore, the time periods are not strictly comparable.

from 2000 to March 2002. In contrast, Mattel's negative mentions declined from a high of 42.2 percent in 1994–1996, to 40.6 percent in 1997–1999 and 29 percent in 2000 to March 2002. Although it is not possible to indicate a causal linkage, all other things being equal, one is tempted to suggest that Mattel's strong code of conduct and independent external monitoring contributed to better compliance at the factory

Table 2.13   Toy Industry: Distribution of Negative News Mentions Pertaining to Sweatshops/Human Rights Abuses, 1994 to March 2002

Company	1994–1996	1997–1999	2000–2002 (March)	Total 1994–2002 (March)
Disney	28.89%	37.50%	38.71%	34.26%
Mattel	42.22%	40.63%	29.03%	37.96%
Hasbro	24.44%	6.25%	16.13%	16.67%
McDonald's	4.44%	12.50%	9.68%	8.33%
Chicco	0.00%	3.13%	6.45%	2.78%
Total number of mentions	45	32	31	108

Source: Appendix 2.1.

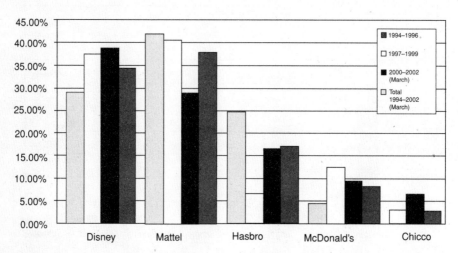

Figure 2.11   Toy Industry: Distribution of Negative News Mentions Pertaining to Sweatshops/Human Rights Abuses, 1994 to March 2002
Source: Appendix 2.1.
Note: The bar referring to the period 2000–2002 (March) covers only 27 months as against 36 months for the first two time periods. Therefore, the time periods are not strictly comparable.

level, an improved climate of public trust, and hence lower negative mentions.

In the case of Hasbro, the proportion of negative mentions declined from 24.4 percent to 6.2 percent between 1994–1996 and 1997–1999, but then went up sharply to 16.1 percent in the following period, 2000 to March 2002. The corresponding numbers for McDonald's were 4.4 percent, 12.5

percent, and 9.7 percent respectively, while for Chicco they were 0 percent, 3.1 percent, and 6.4 percent respectively (Table 2.13).

Concentration among Multinational Corporations of Sweatshops and Human Rights Abuses

During the entire 16-year period covered in Table 2.14, Nike constantly ranked first in terms of negative news mentions with regard to sweatshops and human rights abuses, accounting for a high of 92.5 percent in 1986–1990, 82.9 percent in 1991–1993, 52 percent in 1994–1996, 59.5 percent in 1997–1999, and 61.4 percent in 2000 to March 2002. The decline in the overall percentage for Nike is not an indicator of actual declines in Nike's negative news mentions during this period. On the contrary, they increased from a total of 62 mentions in 1986–1990 to 391 from January 2000 to March 2002, which is a more than sixfold increase in fewer than half as many months. Instead, the percentage decline is attributable to more companies joining the list and thereby distributing the negative news mentions over a larger number of MNCs.

Wal-Mart was the second-ranked company, accounting for 9.3 percent of all negative news mentions during the period 1986 to March 2002. The other three companies among the top five were: Disney (6.6 percent), Kmart (4.2 percent), and Reebok (3.1 percent).

Our findings in this chapter, when combined with case studies presented elsewhere in the book, strongly indicate that MNCs must accept a large part of the blame for the persistence of sweatshops. Available evidence indicates that where MNCs have the ability and resources to take proactive measures, they have done very little to bring about changes that are necessary and desirable. In other areas, where they can exert pressure on the conduct of other actors in the supply chain, notably the local manufacturers, the middlemen, and the local regulatory authorities in the developing countries, they have chosen not to be actively involved except where it is in their economic interest (e.g., relaxation in the enforcement of local laws and regulatory oversight).

The problems of worker exploitation are not the creation of MNCs. However, MNCs cannot absolve themselves of their responsibility to take corrective action when exploitation is apparent; they are one of the principal beneficiaries of this exploitation. They have the technical means and the organizational resources to influence local companies and government

Table 2.14 Distribution of Negative News Mentions Pertaining to Sweatshops/Human Rights Abuses, Top Company Concentrations, 1986 to March 2002

Company	1986–1990			1991–1993			1994–1996			1997–1999			2000–2002 (March)			Total 1986–2002 (March)		
	No.	%	Rank	No.	%	Rank	No.	%	Rank	No.	%	Rank	No.	%	Rank	No.	%	Rank
Nike	62	92.5	1	97	82.9	1	202	52	1	514	59.5	1	391	61.4	1	1,266	61.0	1
Wal-Mart				4	3.4	2	55	14	2	99	11.5	2	35	5.5	3	193	9.3	2
Disney				2	1.7	3	43	11	3	54	6.3	3	41	6.4	2	138	6.6	3
Kmart				1	0.9	4	17	4.3	5	54	6.3	3	15	2.4	4	88	4.2	4
Reebok	1	1.5	3	2	1.7	3	12	3.1	6	36	4.2	4	15	2.4	4	65	3.1	5
JCPenney							7	1.8	8	28	3.2	5	5	0.8	7	42	2.0	7
Adidas							2	0.5	10	14	1.6	7	9	1.4	5	25	1.2	9
Mattel	2	3.0	2	2	1.7	3	19	4.9	4	13	1.5	8	9	1.4	5	45	2.2	6
Gap							4	1	9	17	2.0	6	6	0.9	6	27	1.3	8
McDonald's							2	0.5	10	4	0.5	9	3	0.5	8	9	0.4	12
Coca-Cola							1	0.3	11				3	0.5	8	4	0.2	13
Hasbro	1	1.5	3	1	0.9	4	11	2.8	7	2	0.2	10	5	0.8	7	20	1.0	10
Nestlé				1	0.9	4							2	0.3	9	3	0.1	14
Starbucks										2	0.2	10	9	1.4	5	11	0.5	11
Number of mentions	66	98.5		110	94.0		375	96		837	96.9		548	86.0		1,936	93.3	
Others	1	1.5		7	6.0		16	4.1		27	3.1		89	14.0		140	6.7	
Total number of mentions	67			117			391			864			637			2,076		

Source: Appendix 2.1.
Please note that Nike numbers include negative news stories for footwear, apparel, and equipment. For additional details, please see Chapter 9, Nike, Inc.

authorities to undertake necessary reforms. Moreover, as will be pointed out in other parts of this book, the economic costs of these reforms are quite small and can be easily paid out of the enormous cost savings achieved through the outsourcing processes.

It is distressing to note that the pattern of abuses and their frequency have essentially remained unchanged during this period, strongly suggesting that MNCs have made little overall progress in reducing the incidence of these abuses despite their efforts through their codes of conduct. It provides strong evidence, if indeed such evidence is needed, as to why MNCs and their local partners remain adamantly opposed to independent external monitoring and compliance verification of their conduct in this area.

It should also be apparent that these three issues—wages, working hours, and unhealthy working conditions—are almost entirely under the control of local manufacturers. They are also the issues that form the core of every code of conduct promulgated by the MNCs and their industry-wide associations. These issues are well within the resources and operating agreements of the MNCs with their local partners. The distressingly sad part of this story is that these issues can and should be eradicated completely and expeditiously. None of the so-called explanations offered by the MNCs to date can justify their prolongation. Furthermore, as shall be explained later in this book, the remediation of these issues, or their independent external monitoring and compliance verification, does not incur costs that would materially and adversely impact MNCs' overall costs of acquiring products from their overseas manufacturing partners.

Lest the advocates of unfettered globalization accuse us of protectionism and unwarranted intervention, it should be noted that we are not talking about "living wage" or working conditions similar to those prevailing in the United States or other industrially advanced countries. Our assertions relate to the minimum wages, working hours, and working conditions that are mandated by the labor and environmental laws of the poorer countries, which are all too anxious to keep these laws and their enforcement at a bare minimum so as not to frighten away the badly needed foreign investments and the jobs that they bring with them.

Local manufacturers engage in these practices because there are substantial gains to be made with little downside risk either from their governments or from their principal foreign buyers, namely, the multinational corporations. Local regulations are easily manipulated through bribery and corruption. MNCs appear interested in making a public show of their concerns but are unwilling to put any pressure on their foreign suppliers.

Our data also suggests that the issues of sweatshops and human rights violations are concentrated in a handful of countries and an equally small number of MNCs. The remaining countries and the MNCs are simply "free riders" who would rapidly fall in step as soon as the major players clean up their acts. Thus, corrective action can be focused on these few countries and MNCs in a manner that would enhance, rather than undermine, further growth of globalization.

The issue is maddeningly simple because MNCs can correct these problems with little extra cost and in a manner that would make their supply chains even more efficient and cost-effective. MNCs have the means but lack the will to enforce compliance with their codes of conduct on the part of their foreign suppliers. One can only attribute this inaction to a lack of foresight that would forestall more serious problems for the MNCs in the future. It may also indicate an absence of ethical concern and social responsibility on the part of these custodians of the world's economic resources and standard-bearers of democratic capitalism and free enterprise. In the final analysis, the local manufacturers may have been the instruments of inflicting these abuses on their workers. MNCs are equally culpable because they refused to take corrective action when they had the knowledge of the problem and the means to prevent it from recurring.

APPENDIX 2.1 Distributions of Reports of Sweatshop Conditions and Human Rights Abuses

Data for Tables 2.15 and 2.16 in Appendix 2.1 was derived primarily from Dow Jones Interactive (DJI) and supplemented from other sources (e.g., LexisNexis, *The New York Times*, and *Business Week*). Information contained here should be considered neither comprehensive nor all-inclusive, but as an overall indicator of the news coverage about sweatshops/human rights issues.

This data is based almost exclusively on publications in the English language and from Western sources. To the extent that reports of this type appear in the local language media and are not picked up by the Western news media, the scope of coverage is incomplete. Similarly, certain news stories (e.g., news wires) are often picked up by multiple media and reported in their respective news channels. This tends to inflate somewhat the number of incidents reported, but it is important nevertheless as different news media reach out to different population segments.

Table 2.15 Distribution of Negative News Reports and Mentions Pertaining to Sweatshops/Human Rights Abuses: Companies and Industries, Pre-1985 to March 2002

Industry	Company		Violations over Years					Total Pre-1985–2002
		1985 and Earlier	1986–1990	1991–1993	1994–1996	1997–1999	2000–2002 (March)	
Athletic footwear								
	Adidas				2	14	9	25
	Nike*	62	97	194	353		326	1,032
	New Balance					2		2
	Puma					2	1	3
	Reebok	1	1		12	36	15	65
	Timberland					2	1	3
Apparel								
	Ann Taylor					5	5	10
	Abercrombie & Fitch						2	2
	Arrow			1				1
	Benetton					1	1	2
	Eddie Bauer			2		1		3
	J. Crew					12	6	18
	Jones Apparel					4	7	11
	Liz Claiborne			1		7	5	13
	Levi Strauss			3		4	9	16
	Polo Ralph Lauren					7	9	16
	Calvin Klein					4	10	14
	Tommy Hilfiger					11	9	20
	XOXO Clothing						2	2
	Disney**				30	42	29	101
	Donna Karan					6	1	7
	Gap				4	17	6	27
	Nike*				3	72	61	136
	Warnaco					8	7	15
Automobiles								
	Suzuki					1		1
	Mitsubishi				2		1	3
	Fiat					4		4
Carpets								
	ABC Carpets						2	2
	Carpet One						2	2
	Home Depot						2	2
	IKEA						2	2

(Continued)

Table 2.15   *(Continued)*

| | | Violations over Years | | | | | Total Pre-1985–2002 |
		1985 and Earlier	1986–1990	1991–1993	1994–1996	1997–1999	2000–2002 (March)	
Industry	Company							
Electronics								
	Samsung						1	1
	Sanyo				1			1
	Thompson				1			1
	Siemens						1	1
Food and beverages								
	Coca-Cola				1		3	4
	Dole Food Co.					2		2
	Nestlé			1			2	3
	PepsiCo					1		1
	Starbucks					2	9	11
Retail								
	JCPenney			2	7	28	5	42
	Kmart			2	17	54	15	88
	Wal-Mart			4	55	99	35	193
	Nordstrom					13		13
	Sears				8	11	2	21
	Fred Meyer				4			4
	May Dept. Stores				5	2	2	9
	C&A					2		2
	Marks & Spencer					1	1	2
	Champion					1		1
	The Limited					1		1
Toys								
	Chicco					1	2	3
	Coleco		1					1
	Disney**				13	12	12	37
	Hasbro		1	1	11	2	5	20
	McDonald's				2	4	3	9
	Mattel		2	2	19	13	9	45
Total number of mentions		0	67	117	391	864	637	2,076
Total number of reports		37	77	109	257	698	504	1,682

*News reports on Nike footwear and all-inclusive production are combined in the athletic footwear category (87.9% of all news reports); articles on Nike apparel production are in the apparel category (10.9% of all news reports).

**News reports on Disney toys and all-inclusive production are combined in the toy industry category (43% of all news reports); articles on Disney apparel production are included in the apparel category (57%).

Note: Quite often news stories report on multiple countries, companies, or issues (e.g., child labor, wages, worker abuse). Therefore, the number of issues mentioned will be greater than the number of news reports surveyed.

Table 2.16 Distribution of Negative News Reports and Mentions Pertaining to Sweatshops/Human Rights Abuses: Types of Violations, Pre- 1985 to March 2002

Type of Abuse	1985 and Earlier	1986– 1990	1991– 1993	1994– 1996	1997– 1999	2000– 2002 (March)
Working conditions	38	10	23	142	447	298
Wages	9	75	92	226	410	240
Working hours	3	7	26	111	209	132
Human rights violations	2	10	13	85	197	116
Child labor	5	17	18	89	160	101
Other worker abuse		7	4	40	54	26
Total number of mentions	57	126	176	693	1,477	913
Total number of reports	37	77	109	257	698	504

Note: Quite often news stories report on multiple countries, companies, or issues (e.g., child labor, wages, worker abuse). Therefore, the number of issues mentioned will be greater than the number of news reports surveyed.

Quite often news stories report on multiple countries, companies, or issues (e.g., child labor, wages, worker abuse). Therefore, the number of issues mentioned will be greater than the total number of news reports surveyed.

APPENDIX 2.2   World Wide Web Sites Pertaining to Corporate Responsibility Issues

Asian Human Rights Commission	www.ahrchk.net
Business & Human Rights: A Resource Website	www.business-humanrights.org
Center for Economic & Social Rights	www.cesr.org/programs/dkny.htm
China Labor Watch	www.chinalaborwatch.org
Clean Clothes Campaign	www.cleanclothes.org
Columbia University	www.socialanalysis.org
Co-op America	www.coopamerica.org
CorpWatch	www.corpwatch.org
Essential Information	www.essential.org/links
Global Exchange	www.globalexchange.org

Interfaith Center on Corporate Responsibility	www.iccr.org
International Labor Rights Fund	www.laborrights.org
In These Times: Independent News and Views	www.inthesetimes.org
Lawyers Committee for Human Rights	www.lchr.org
Maquila Solidarity Network	www.maquilasolidarity.org
Misereor	www.misereor.org.de
National Consumers League	www.natlconsumersleague.org
National Labor Committee: In Support of Human and Worker Rights	www.nlcnet.org
The National Mobilization Against Sweatshops	www.nmass.org/nmass/ articles.html
New Economics Foundation	www.neweconomics.org
Nike Watch	www.nikewatch.org
Oxfam Community Aid Abroad	www.caa.org.au
Reseau Solidarite	www.reseau-solidarite.org
Save the Children	www.savechildren.net
Sweatshop Watch	www.sweatshopwatch.org
Third World Network	www.twnside.org.sg
Transnational Corporations Observatory Publishing	www.transnationale.org
University of Massachusetts	www.umass.edu/peri/pdfs
World Socialist Web Site	www.wsws.org/news&analysis
Worker Rights Consortium	www.workersrights.org

PART TWO

Multinational Corporations' Responses to Change

3

Multinational Corporations' Responses to Public Criticism: Failure of Communications Strategies

MNC responses to public criticism and concern can best be described as a flood of public relations rhetoric designed to assuage the public's feelings through statements of commitment that are invariably short on specifics and long on generalities, magnanimous in promises and stingy in accomplishments. The consequences of this failed strategy have been all too apparent, even to corporate representatives. Public distrust of MNC claims has grown. In addition, the pressure on the companies has intensified with further calls for government regulation and mandatory requirements for setting minimum standards of corporate conduct, along with independent external monitoring, verification, and public reporting of corporate compliance.

An inevitable result of this mismatched strategy is that even where companies have taken meaningful remedial actions, these have been generally dismissed as too little and too late, and as essentially self-serving. These halting efforts are seen as victories on the part of corporate critics, providing them with additional incentive to expand and intensify their efforts and to put even more pressure on the recalcitrant companies. This chapter focuses attention on the communications strategies of MNCs as they deal with the crisis of public confidence in corporate conduct. Most of the companies confronting these issues have consistently underestimated the extent of public knowledge of the MNCs' operating practices and have overlooked the public's expectations of what MNCs must do to correct the situation. MNCs have also underestimated the resources of corporate critics to discover adverse information about the companies' conduct and to bring it to the attention of the concerned public for maximum emotional impact.

Elements of MNC Communications Strategy

The MNCs' communications strategy consists of four elements. (1) They cite conditions of market competition to justify their conduct, and (2) they point to the benefits these operations bring to poor people in developing countries, who would otherwise be worse off than before. (3) They accuse critics of creating misinformation and arousing exaggerated expectations of what companies should do to correct problems. And (4) the companies claim that their conduct has been ethically and legally correct and socially responsible.

A major element of the MNCs' communications strategy has been to justify their conduct on the basis of market and competitive factors while also pointing to increased societal benefits through income growth and job creation. This strategy fits in with their own perception of operating in a competitive environment. Investors, bankers, and financial markets often find such claims to be persuasive. However, this tactic ignores the fact that to be effective, competitive markets require equal bargaining power on the part of various factors of production—bargaining power that workers in developing countries almost never have. Corporate critics, however, are quick to point out these obfuscations to the news media and to the public, further eroding public trust in corporate statements.

MNCs have chastised corporate critics—and their portrayal of sweatshops and environmental degradation—as trafficking in romantic self-delusion. Long working hours, low wage rates, and employment of children between the ages of 14 and 16 are presented as the necessary price of progress, conditions that are inevitable in the early stages of economic takeoff and that will pay off in the future through accelerated growth and prosperity.

MNCs contend that they scrupulously adhere to local laws and regulations in their own operations and that they insist that their suppliers also adhere to similar standards of compliance. They put the blame for poor working conditions largely on the shoulders of local manufacturers and local labor authorities. At the same time, they condone lax compliance as a necessary evil when developing countries cannot afford the luxury of enforcing labor and environmental standards similar to those prevailing in advanced industrial countries. MNCs also assert that an increase in local wage rates—beyond prevailing legal requirements and market conditions—would be counterproductive, since it would force companies to increase the retail prices of their products. This would have the effect of reducing aggregate demand. It would also shift production to manufacturers who are even less scrupulous in their treatment of workers.

The current public uproar about the operations of multinational corporations in developing countries will continue to grow as people in the industrially advanced countries become aware of the often abusive and unsafe working conditions in plants making products for MNCs. There are also the issues of disregard for environmental degradation and increased pollution affecting the long-term health and well-being of people in developing countries. And finally, MNCs are charged with bribery, economic corruption, and collusion with despotic governments and corrupt officials to violate human rights. While the extent of many of these charges may have been exaggerated by corporate critics, MNCs have undermined their position by denying these conditions altogether. MNCs have not helped their case when they steadfastly refuse to subject their claims to independent external verification. They also plead lack of power and influence to prevent these abuses and to bring about needed reforms—a plea that increasingly falls on deaf ears.

The goals of the MNCs' current communications strategies fall into the following categories:

- To counteract public hostility to corporate activities by claiming that criticism is based on ignorance or misinterpretation.
- To counter the spread of unfavorable information by calling for the need to further explicate complex issues.
- To counteract inadequate access to and bias in the news media.

The Concept of a Legitimacy Gap

It will help our understanding of the efficacy of MNCs' communications strategies by evaluating these through the yardstick of legitimacy (Table

3.1). Business is a social institution and, therefore, depends on society's acceptance of its role and activities if it is to survive and grow. At any given time, there is likely to be a gap between business performance and societal expectations, a gap caused by certain business actions and by the changing sociopolitical environment. The concept of a legitimacy gap is dynamic, since both corporate performance and societal expectations evolve over time as they respond to a changing external environment and to corporate behavior. A continually widening gap will cause business to lose its legitimacy and will threaten its survival. Business must, therefore, strive to narrow this legitimacy gap in order to claim its share of society's physical and human resources and to maintain maximum discretionary control over its external dealings and its internal decision making. The quest for legitimacy by corporations along with doubts by their critics about the legitimacy of some of their actions are at the core of the controversy surrounding business-society conflicts and the concept of corporate social performance.

Academic literature, business-related magazines and newspapers, and print and broadcast mass media are replete with illustrations of companies fighting to contain public hostility and distrust through educating them on the virtues of free enterprise as a way of absolving themselves of the necessity of justifying their conduct. When this does not work, they seem to justify their conduct by phrasing it in language that downplays the scope of their conduct that is the subject of controversy. Thus during the Arab oil embargo of the 1970s, oil companies tried to justify their conduct by down-

Table 3.1   Business Strategies for Narrowing the Legitimacy Gap

Legitimacy Gap

Business Performance ←——————————————→ *Societal Expectations*

1. Do not change performance, but *change public perception* of business performance through education and information.
2. If changes in public perception are not possible, *change the symbols* used to describe business performance, thereby making it congruent with public perception. Note that no change in actual performance is called for.
3. If strategies 1 and 2 are not working, attempt to *change societal expectations* of business performance through education and information and thereby bring down these expectations to the level of corporate performance.
4. In case strategies 1 through 3 are unsuccessful in completely bridging the legitimacy gap, *bring about changes in business performance*, thereby making a closer match with society's expectations.

playing the absolute level of profits while emphasizing profit margins. Similarly, when confronted with threats of public boycott for the sale of infant formula in developing countries, MNCs shifted the attention of the public away from the abuses by highlighting the use of infant formula in saving the lives of otherwise sick children. The companies omitted the fact that the children who needed infant formula represented less than 2 percent of all children, and that most children are better off with breastfeeding than with any other alternative. Similarly, during the apartheid controversy in the 1970s and 1980s, the foreign companies operating in South Africa downplayed the fact that their local operations were also participating in the apartheid practices mandated by the white government of South Africa and instead highlighted their role in providing more jobs for the blacks of South Africa. In each of these cases, as well as numerous others, it was shown that companies rarely tried to address directly public concerns about their criticized conduct and instead continued to highlight their positive contributions regardless of the tenuous relation of these contributions to the issues of concern to the public.[1]

Communication Channels

Corporate communications dealing with external social issues and affected constituencies invariably have a "window out" bias; that is, they are geared to disseminate information that the company wants its critics to hear. However, in order to track new issues and to monitor emergent groups, corporate communication channels must also contain a large "window in" element. They should tell the company what its critics are saying about it. Emerging issues, by their very nature, are unstable and constantly in flux. They have a high propensity to change in directions that are often unpredictable. By the same token, these issues attract advocacy groups whose life span may be measured in weeks and months rather than years. There is constant motion, and groups change at astonishing speeds as they form alliances, split apart, and shift between strategies of consultation and confrontation.

MNC communications strategy also dictates that these channels filter out information not directly needed for the relevant corporate activity. This process, however, is likely to be counterproductive when applied to emerging issues and new groups. The MNC does not have enough experience with issue groups and cannot determine a priori the parameters of relevant information. Therefore, external communication channels should have a large element of redundancy to allow for a certain amount of static in the system to signal management that something unusual is happening.

To develop effective communication channels, MNCs must be willing to communicate with critics, even with groups whose values may not agree with the traditional values or the position of the company. In their embryonic stages, new institutions and value systems may lack central direction and clear goals. They may even seem destructive, at least in the short run, since they are tied together only in their opposition to a common adversary, the MNC. For the MNCs, it serves no constructive purpose to attack these "opponents." By retaliating against these groups when they are in their embryonic stage, MNCs will not eliminate the causes that gave rise to these groups, but companies may end up preparing the ground for breeding even more militant groups. MNCs can best help achieve social harmony and contribute to social justice by focusing on the problems that have to be dealt with and not on the spokespersons who voice them.

Inadequacy of Prevailing Patterns to Conflict Resolution

When confronted by NGOs and critics of MNC conduct, companies often condemn criticism from any quarter as if it were questioning the legitimacy of the competitive free enterprise system.[2] Companies defend the activities of multinational corporations in developing countries without at the same time explaining or correcting their own shortcomings that were the subject of public criticism in the first place. As part of their initial response, companies deny the legitimacy and competence of the groups that criticize MNCs. They may also resort to a legalistic defense of corporate actions, which meets the letter but not necessarily the spirit of prevailing laws and regulations. When all else fails, companies may have to meet and discuss the issue with their critics, in a spirit of advancing mutual understanding and cooperation. These approaches can be grouped into three broad categories: public relations responses, legal responses, and industrial relations responses. Although these response patterns have a certain inherent merit, companies must not apply them ritualistically. Companies must pay serious attention to the life-cycle stages of an issue. They must understand how important this issue is to the critics' agenda and how important it is within the larger sociopolitical context. Otherwise, these responses can become largely ineffective and even counterproductive.[3]

In the section that follows, the consequences of flawed communications strategies are analyzed. The next chapter will present an analytical framework that will allow us to examine various dimensions of a company's external, sociopolitical environment and to evaluate the saliency of corporate responses.

PUBLIC RELATIONS RESPONSE

The public relations response stems from the belief that corporate critics either are motivated by selfish concerns or are ignorant and uninformed about the economic and social contributions that MNCs have made in the countries of their operations. Companies try to narrow the real or alleged gap between societal expectations and corporate performance through public education and information. This approach is doomed to failure because it is based on two faulty assumptions: (1) corporate critics lack information about the issues, and (2) the relevant data or facts are those that the corporations prefer to disseminate.

The fundamental flaw in this logic is that while the MNC is looking at the issue in narrow economic terms, its critics insist on viewing it in broad sociopolitical terms. The different groups view a given set of events or facts in quite different ways when judging their veracity and deciding how to develop new approaches to resolve conflict. These differences depend not only on the degree of scientific rigor demanded by different groups, but also on how different groups perceive changes in existing approaches that affect their vital interests. Finally, when MNCs confine themselves to merely rejecting the reform proposals of their critics without suggesting alternatives except the status quo, they surrender the initiative and lose the opportunity to play a proactive role in shaping the public policy agenda.

LEGAL RESPONSE

The legal response is used to defend the MNC's legitimate right to engage in activities that are under attack and to question the right of its critics to intervene. When used exclusively or in combination with the public relations response, this approach may reduce the danger of litigation, but it also creates the image of a company under siege that is hiding behind legalities, evasive tactics, and unwillingness to change. It may also increase public distrust and skepticism toward the corporation and give greater credibility to its critics.

INDUSTRIAL RELATIONS RESPONSE

The industrial relations-bargaining response is fashioned after the traditional employer-union negotiations and assumes that even in the area of social conflict, a modus vivendi can be achieved in a spirit of give-and-take where the opposing groups can reach acceptable solutions based on their competing needs, relative bargaining power, and support in the larger community.

This approach, however, fails because it is based on two faulty assumptions. First, the MNC's emphasis is on managing these new stakeholders just as it manages its traditional stakeholders, such as stockholders and employees. In the traditional case, the integrity of the corporation and its mission are not in question. The conflict is based on the allocation of resources and benefits. Second, the external stakeholders are quite different from the traditional ones and do not respond to similar incentives and constraints. The new stakeholders represent people who are affected by corporate actions, but who may or may not be directly involved in influencing those actions. Quite often, these groups represent not simply constituencies of people but rather constituencies of ideas, such as ethical and behavioral norms that may have been downgraded or ignored by the corporation—norms such as environmental preservation or other social issues.

These new stakeholders do not want to be managed within the operational parameters defined by the corporation, but instead may question the integrity of the corporate mission, its operational processes, and its allocation of corporate resources and outputs. The situation is even more difficult when the corporate adversaries are emerging single-issue groups or are advocating causes that are not yet part of a society's mainstream agenda. MNCs usually consider these groups to be of marginal relevance, or worse, part of a lunatic fringe. Companies are unlikely to yield them anything substantial except payment for "nuisance avoidance." These groups, however, make up in intensity and commitment what they lack in numbers and resources.

Realizing that any positive corporate response is a measure of their "nuisance value," the new groups use a strategy of ever-escalating demands and ever-declining compliance. When a company feels that after intense negotiations it has reached an agreement, the opposing group often fails to deliver on its part of the bargain and even escalates its anticorporate rhetoric and broadens the scope of its demands from the corporation. This pattern is all too familiar to companies in the early stages of business-society conflicts, especially when the companies involved are inexperienced in handling conflicts that deal with social issues.

Effectiveness of MNC Communications Strategy: An Assessment

Our analysis of various arguments advanced by a variety of multinational corporations with extensive involvement in overseas production and sourcing suggests that most of them have used some combination of the first three approaches indicated in Table 3.1. The focus of their strategy has been to educate and inform the public about the "real" conditions prevailing in these countries, in order to defend the companies' performance and to downplay the allegations of their critics as isolated instances or misplaced and exaggerated accusations.

The message content is quite general and lacks specifics. It is based on the assumption that the general public—the recipient of these messages—has a low threshold of interest in these issues and is not interested in details. Moreover, companies claim corporate critics lack resources to effectively counteract corporate messages.

History, however, has not been kind to companies that delude themselves into thinking that the public is simpleminded or that critics cannot formulate effective messages that reach a wide audience. The battlefield for the hearts and minds of the public is littered with the companies that followed this approach.[4]

On issues such as sweatshops, the public already distrusts corporations and places little faith in their messages. There is a tendency—especially among the young, affluent, educated, and politically active—to give greater credence to public interest groups whose allegations are often buttressed by reports in the national and international news media of corporate misdeeds. Often, the intensity and extensiveness of corporate messages generate their own negative responses by lending greater credibility to the messages of public interest groups. The fact that companies have been invariably unwilling to provide the public with factual information about their activities compounds MNCs' problems.

The following section is an analysis of some of the assertions MNCs have made in response to the accusations of sweatshop-like conditions in their overseas operations, and shows that most of the arguments made by the companies are easily refuted. It is unlikely that the current communications strategies will be effective, and MNCs must take proactive and concrete actions (Table 3.1, step 4) if they are to reduce the legitimacy gap that currently exists between corporate performance and societal expectations.

Sweatshops Are Good for You!

One of the most egregious, factually incorrect, and morally offensive arguments made by the ardent advocates of globalization is that the "horrible conditions" described by the corporate critics are figments of the imagination. These conditions can be considered horrible, the MNCs claim, only when compared with the conditions prevailing in industrially advanced countries like the United States.[5] When viewed in the context of the poorer countries, it is claimed, these sweatshop-like conditions are a distinct improvement over conditions that existed before and that still prevail in businesses producing primarily for domestic markets. MNCs accuse corporate critics of "cultural imperialism" for insisting on minimum age laws, ridicule them for seeking a "living wage" in developing countries, label them as unrealistic and protectionist, and accuse them of abetting disguised attempts by organized labor in the United States to prevent companies from purchasing from low-wage countries. MNCs point out that even in the United States there were no minimum age limits until the latter part of the twentieth century, and that at the present time young adults regularly work in places like convenience stores and fast-food restaurants where minimum wages are far below any reasonable definition of a living wage.

If sweatshops are such a good idea, why not make them sweatier? If it is acceptable to employ young workers when they are 14, why not give them a chance to become productive citizens and wage earners when they are 12 or even 10 years old? If a country's economic growth is to be accelerated and the cause of free trade furthered, why confine work hours to 10 hours a day when these young workers are healthy enough to work 12-hour days? And while we are at it, why indulge in such luxuries as one day off a week? Couldn't these workers do more for their countries and their families by working 12-hour days and seven-day weeks? And what about working conditions? Certainly, the need for keeping costs to a minimum does not allow for keeping proper air circulation and ventilation or maintaining a clean facility and providing workers with personal safety equipment. These young workers are strong and agile enough to overcome such minor inconveniences.

The proponents of the status quo, in terms of sweatshops, do not offer any cogent explanation as to why they consider the current level of sweatshop conditions to be optimal. When pressured, they revert to the oft-repeated assertion that these countries and their workers cannot afford wages and working conditions that are similar to those currently prevailing in the United States. This is a baseless assertion in view of the fact that there is no evidence that any credible opponents of sweatshops, whether organized unions or other public interest groups, have ever demanded that wages and working conditions in developing conditions must be similar to those in the United States.

For example, Ethan Kapstein, writing in *Foreign Affairs*, states that "forcing the standards of industrialized nations on developing countries and the firms that operate in them could backfire by reducing investment and job creation."[6] In another article, Kristof and WuDunn indicate that workers' wages in China have risen from $50 to $250 a month. Using highly anecdotal data consisting of a handful of emotionally laden human-interest stories, they make gross generalizations about the conditions in China as if they were incontrovertible facts.

Kapstein and his cohorts decry the lack of data and substantive evidence on the part of corporate critics. And yet they themselves stand accused of making conclusive statements without any supportive evidence. Kapstein offers no support for his statement that the changes demanded by corporate critics amount to U.S.-style wage and environment standards. When Kristof and WuDunn state that monthly wages in China have gone up fivefold, they do not offer any verifiable data.[7] Without exception, the supporters of MNCs pay lip service to the need for companies and their local affiliates to comply with local laws and regulations without seeming to realize that MNCs and their local affiliates engage in widespread disregard of local laws on wages, working hours, and working conditions. Consider, for example, Kapstein's statement that companies ought to abide by the laws of the land where they do business.[8] The question is why "ought" and why not "must"? Or should MNCs have the discretion to decide what local laws to obey?

In their visits to China, Kristof and WuDunn cite examples of parents who are grateful that their 15-year-old daughters are working nine hours a day, seven days a week. That may indeed be the case from the perspective of the Chinese parents. However, shouldn't it matter to these authors that the incidents described by them are gross violations of the minimum wage and working hour laws of China?

One marvels at the ease with which the proponents of globalization grab at any information that seems to support their viewpoint without subjecting it to careful scrutiny. Consider, for example, the following story, which was widely circulated in November 2000, about the plight of young workers in Bangladesh.[9] A "Special Report on Globalization" in *Business Week* reported that "soon after a bill was proposed in the U.S. Congress in 1993 to ban imports from countries where children work in factories, garment makers in Bangladesh fired 36,000 workers under age 18, most of them girls. . . . Few of the fired workers ended up in school. Instead, many took more dangerous jobs and became prostitutes."[10]

And what was the source of this information? It came from the association of local owners of apparel factories in Bangladesh, who are among the most notorious sweatshop owners in the world. Factories in Bangladesh have been frequently involved in accidents and fires costing the lives of hundreds of workers in single accidents.[11] Even the internal audits of foreign MNCs show these owners to be notorious in hiring younger workers, keeping false records, and making them work under conditions that border on slavery and human bondage. How is it that suddenly the data provided by these employers—with a vested interest in creating fear among foreign countries—is taken at face value? Does it matter that the children who were said to be under 18 years of age were as young as 14? And where did all the 18-year-olds come from to replace the children who were fired? If all these 18-year-olds had been unemployed, why were they not hired in the first place? Is it also possible that since jobs are so scarce, perhaps a majority of these 18-year-olds were already being forced into prostitution when they were routinely fired from their jobs to be replaced by younger workers? One might also be more generous and argue that the employment of 18-year-olds, at decent wages, would allow them to help their younger brothers and sisters go to school and not be forced to work under slavelike conditions. Rumors also have it that once the foreign news media left and the hoopla died down, those young workers were brought back into the factories through the back door, which is where the local factory owners had always wanted them.

The Job Creation Function of MNCs

The advocates of globalization emphasize the crucial role of MNCs in creating jobs in developing countries. It is suggested that without the activities of the MNCs, these countries will continuously suffer from abnormally high unemployment leading to mass poverty, low life expectancy, high infant mortality, and low level of education. However, these jobs were not created out of some sense of altruism but rather were the result of cold-hearted financial calculations. Profit is the only reason why MNCs choose to operate in one country rather than another.

The issue for us, and for the MNCs, is not what the poor workers with no bargaining leverage are willing to accept in order to keep their jobs, but what the MNCs should be willing to pay as a simple matter of fairness. The cost difference between $5.15 per hour in the United States and $0.25+ per hour is so huge that MNCs could pay even three or four times these wages—if the local workers had any bargaining leverage—and still make enormous profits compared to the alternative of manufacturing these products at home.

If the MNCs were really serious about their role in job creation and bringing prosperity to these countries, they would pay wages that would allow these workers to have enough savings to invest in human capital, such as further education and more training, to make them eligible for more skilled and higher-paying jobs. A decent enough wage paid to an adult wage earner would allow for children and young adults to go to school, receive some education, and perhaps train for a better job in hopes of a better future. Can we really justify inhaling toxic and potentially carcinogenic fumes, eating insufficient and unhealthy food, and living in highly unsanitary and overcrowded conditions as the necessary price of development? How does one account for the damage that we would have done to the health of these young people, which will show up 20 or 30 years down the line?

The irony is that MNCs can afford to accomplish all this at very little extra cost, with very little material difference to their bottom line. All my experience working in these countries has convinced me that the incremental cost of providing fair wages and decent working conditions is minimal and easily affordable, when seen in the context of total wage costs, ex-factory cost of goods, or wholesale prices received by MNCs.[12] The issue, therefore, must be addressed in different terms. To wit, MNCs opt for overseas production because it is tremendously cheaper than production costs at home. Therefore, MNCs must accept some responsibility to minimize and ameliorate the second-order effects of their actions in developing countries. These would include, among others, working and living conditions of the workers, the wages they receive, the extent of voluntariness in their acceptance of overtime including forced labor, avoidance of child labor, and protection from all kinds of harassment. Equally important are the considerations of harm to the environment and pollution that might have long-term negative consequences to the health and well-being of workers and the general population.

MNCs Cannot Afford Paying Higher Wages

This is another of the oft-repeated tactics of the MNCs, which is rarely substantiated but always bemoaned. In various newspaper comments, U.S.-based multinationals, and especially retail chains, have argued that retail prices of, say, men's shirts or women's blouses would go up by 5 to 10 percent if wages of workers in their factories in China, Indonesia, or other countries were to be raised by 5 to 10 percent. Even a cursory examination of data would show that this assertion is preposterous and unsustainable. It is absolutely false that by paying marginally higher wages than current levels (which are often below the level required by local laws) a business would become unprofitable for the MNCs. These companies are loath to publicly reveal any cost or profit data about their operations in developing countries. However, most knowledgeable experts agree that in-country production costs in these countries rarely exceed 10 percent of the end-user prices of these products in MNC major markets, which are usually in industrially advanced countries. It is estimated that direct labor costs range from 2 to 5 percent of the ex-factory cost of the product. A typical branded men's polo shirt retails for between $30 and $50 in the United States, whereas the direct labor cost of manufacturing this shirt in a developing country is less than $1. Similarly, a well-known brand of sneakers may retail for $75 in the United States and contain less than $2 in direct labor costs in Vietnam, China, or other overseas locations.

In a special report, *Business Week* points out that notwithstanding company claims, "workers' pay, even if it's better than average for that country, is still pitiful considering the nearly 40 percent gross profit margins Nike and Reebok earn." For example, Tong Yang Indonesia (TYI), a shoe factory outside Jakarta with more than 8,500 workers, "pays about 22 cents an hour, just over Indonesia's minimum wage. It gets around

$13 for every pair of shoes it makes for Reebok, paying only $1 for labor. Still, TYI says that after paying for materials and overhead, its margins are just 10 percent. It can't just hike its price to Reebok. 'They look for suppliers who sell for the lowest price,' says a TYI manager. 'If we aren't cheap enough, they'll go to Vietnam or somewhere else.' The big profits go to shoe companies and retailers. The shoes typically sell for $60 to $70 a pair."[13]

It should be apparent that a wage increase of even $0.50 to $0.75 per hour, which is two to three times the current wage of $0.25, could not possibly make a material difference in the retail prices of these products. Nor should it affect the overall profitability of the MNC unless this increase in wages is marked up by 100 percent at every level of the supply chain until it reaches the ultimate customer at the retail level.

Another untenable assumption in this argument is that all other elements of a company's cost structure are so finely tuned that no other efficiencies are possible to offset the increased wage costs. Every company can find some fat in the usual overhead and general and administrative expenses to offset such small amounts for local wage increases in developing countries. MNC executives, experienced in overseas operations, would readily agree that field expenses often get out of hand because of distance from the head office and the high cost of maintaining expatriates in foreign locations. These companies also become inefficient in terms of utilization of raw materials and processing costs because labor is so cheap that it can pay for a lot of mistakes in other aspects of the business. Thus, a marginal increase in the wages paid to these workers (a fraction of the 5+ percent in-country production costs) is unlikely to have a material impact on the company's profitability. In case MNCs find these calculations inaccurate, they should help us by providing us with relevant information for independent analysis and verification. We would also agree to data confidentiality to protect the cooperating companies' competitive position and proprietary information.

The aforementioned discussion leads to one inescapable conclusion. Yes, developing countries do need industries that employ masses of workers in low-tech industries. And yes, low wages are a necessary ingredient for creating more employment and income growth. But these industries do not have to operate under sweatshop conditions where people are exploited in virtual human bondage. If this is all we have to offer as an example of the Western way of doing business, then we have no business priding ourselves on promoting human dignity, individual choice, or democratic capitalism.

Development of New Responses

We have seen that traditional corporate responses to outside pressures have not succeeded. Confronted with such pressures, corporations have continued to issue bland public statements that explain their position in ritualized terms of law or public relations, or companies have sought to bargain in an industrial relations manner. Each of these approaches is based on one or more of the following beliefs: that corporations should not become involved in debates with rabble-rousers; that discontent and demands made on the corporations are caused by ignorance and misunderstanding and that education will remove the cause, if not counteracted by foreign ideologies; that the outside groups are adversaries against whom the corporate goals and values must always be defended; that both sides have something to gain and that, consequently, bargaining is a means toward a solution. What MNC managers often fail to realize is that these very assumptions are major barriers to appropriate, meaningful response, and that managers themselves are at least as much in need of education as the outside pressure groups. Before one can expect much improvement in the ways corporations respond to a changing environment, MNC managers must change their perceptions about the role of their corporations in society. The corporation's internal machinery must be adapted to the need for prompt, accurate, and routine consideration of the public interest, especially in matters of environmental change. Only then can decision makers hope to minimize the problems of the future and respond appropriately to the pressures of the present.

We now come to the question of new responses corporations should make to their changing social environment. Our concern is not with specific responses to specific problems, but rather with general patterns of response to general changes in society and with ways of preparing the corporation for the challenges and pressures of the future. The first and foremost requirement is that the corporation take a more positive and less self-centered view of what the public interest is and of how corporations should respond to it. In the short run, this change may take the form of granting some sort of due process to external groups such as NGOs advocating the cause of local workers. Such due process will provide a framework for the development and crystallization of issues that are of concern to society at large and will also suggest avenues for corporate action, individually and in cooperation with other social institutions.

Public concern must be fostered at all levels and not be confined to top management. Policy decisions are likely to founder at the operational level if the intent of top management is not made clear and if operating-level personnel cannot or will not identify their personal goals with those of the corporation. To achieve a continuing congruence of corporate and social goals, the corporation must, therefore, be seen from the inside and from the outside in a system-wide context. Corporate managers at all levels must deliberately bring public interest factors to bear on their policies and decisions. The reason for doing so should not be simple charitable sympathy, but rather a real duty or obligation arising out of the causal interrelation between the corporation and society at large. MNCs must change their frame of mind and be willing to communicate even with those groups whose values do not agree with the traditional values or the position of the company. The spirit should not be one of antagonism, but of willingness to understand and discuss.

MNCs must also change their public response to issues. It does not help the company to keep quiet on important matters or to issue carefully drafted, legally correct, but unresponsive position papers or public relations communiqués. In a charged atmosphere, these strategies are likely to backfire. Silence may be construed as arrogance, while unresponsive communiqués may appear to be implicit admissions of guilt hiding behind the screen of legalism. MNCs should not engage in the essentially useless tactic of attacking their supposed opponents by branding them as socially deviant, destructive, or antisocial. By the very nature of things, new institutions and value systems in their embryonic stages lack central direction and clear goals. Neither the MNC's nor the community's interests are served if the company mobilizes its resources to destroy new institutions before they have a chance to develop. MNCs can retaliate against these institutions when they are in their embryonic stages, but companies cannot hope to eliminate the causes that give rise to these institutions. Early retaliation will instead prepare the ground for breeding more militant and less constructive institutions. MNCs can best help achieve social harmony and contribute to social justice by focusing on the problems that have to be dealt with and not on the spokespersons who voice complaints.

Some of the recommendations made here are concrete, practical, and relatively easy to achieve. Others are abstract, theoretical, and highly speculative, clearly not designed for immediate implementation. In all cases, however, our goal has been to improve the operation of the corporate system and to preserve its fundamental role in society.

Notes

1. For an extensive description of a large number of case studies dealing with the issues of legitimacy gap, please see: S. Prakash Sethi, *Advocacy Advertising and Large Corporations* (Lexington, Mass.: D. C. Heath & Co., 1977); S. Prakash Sethi, *Handbook of Advocacy Advertising: Concepts, Strategies, and Applications* (Cambridge, Mass.: Ballinger Publishing Co., 1987); S. Prakash Sethi, *Multinational Corporations and the Impact of Public Advocacy on Corporate Strategy: Nestlé and the Infant Formula Controversy* (Boston: Kluwer Academic Publishers, 1994); S. Prakash Sethi and Oliver F. Williams, *Economic Imperatives and Ethical Values in Global Business: The South African Experience and International Codes Today* (Boston: Kluwer Academic Publishers, 2000; pap. ed. Notre Dame, Ind.: University of Notre Dame Press, 2001); S. Prakash Sethi and Paul Steidlmeier, *Up Against the Corporate Wall: Cases in Business and Society*, 6th ed. (Upper Saddle River, N.J.: Prentice-Hall, 1997).

2. Ibid.

3. For a more detailed discussion of these response patterns, see S. Prakash Sethi and Dow Votaw, "Do We Need a New Corporate Response to a Changing Social Environment? Part II," from *California Management Review* (Fall 1969), reprinted in Votaw and Sethi, *The Corporate Dilemma* (Englewood Cliffs, N.J.: Prentice-Hall, 1973), 191–213; Sethi, *Advocacy Advertising*, 57–60.

4. Sethi and Steidlmeier, *Up Against the Corporate Wall*; Sethi, *Multinational Corporations*; Sethi, *Advocacy Advertising*.

5. See, for example, "The Case for Globalization," *The Economist* (September 23, 2000), 19–20; "Anti-Capitalist Protest—Angry and Effective," *The Economist* (September 23, 2000), 85–87; Nicholas D. Kristof and Shery WuDunn, "Two Cheers for Sweatshops," *New York Times Magazine* (September 24, 2000), sec. 6; Ethan B. Kapstein, "The Corporate Ethics Crusade," *Foreign Affairs* 80:5 (September–October 2001), 105–119. For examples of other abuse, see John Gittings, "China's Children Labor round the Clock," *The Guardian*, Guardian Foreign Papers (September 26, 2001), 14; Barry Bearak, "Lives Held Cheap in Bangladesh Sweatshop," *New York Times* (April 15, 2001), sec. 1, 1; "A World of Sweatshops," *Business Week* (November 6, 2000), 52; "Report Says Nike Plant Workers Abused by Bosses in Indonesia," *New York Times* (February 22, 2001), C2.

6. Kapstein, "Corporate Ethics Crusade," 106. See also "Case for Globalization"; "Globalization and Its Critics: A Survey of Globalization," *The Economist* (September 29, 2001).

7. Kristof and WuDunn, "Two Cheers," 70.

8. Kapstein, "Corporate Ethics Crusade," 106.

9. "Global Capitalism: Can It Be Made to Work Better?" Special Report, *Business Week* (November 6, 2000), 72–100.

10. Ibid.
11. Bearak, "Lives Held Cheap."
12. "Globalization: Special Report," *Business Week* (November 6, 2000).
13. "Special Report: Global Labor," *Business Week* International Editions (November 6, 2000), 52.

CHAPTER
4

Corporate Codes of Conduct: Parameters and Analysis

A corporate code of conduct consists of a set of activities that a company commits to undertake when a conflict arises between that business and society at large. The effectiveness of corporate responses to these conflicts depends on a number of factors: the sociopolitical environment; public awareness; the emotional intensity generated by the issue; the dynamics of competition and industry structure in which the company operates; and the institutional character, corporate resources, and management style of a particular corporation.

To be effective, a code of conduct must be acceptable to all the relevant stakeholders and must fit within the competitive realities of the marketplace. It must not be static or fixed in a particular time and situation, but must be able to respond to evolving conditions. A specific action can be socially responsible only if it takes account of time, environment, and the nature of the parties involved. The same activity may be considered socially responsible at one time, under one set of circumstances, and in one culture, but may be considered socially irresponsible when any of these factors change. A system for evaluating corporate social performance, therefore, must take into account the cultural and sociopolitical environment, and the criteria used must necessarily be general and flexible.

The framework developed here suggests a rationale by which a social issue and corporate response patterns can be analyzed in terms of their effectiveness in meeting societal goals and MNC objectives. This chapter describes such a framework, and shows how MNCs can apply it to resolve business-society conflicts. Subsequent chapters will show how this framework evaluates sweatshop-related issues and other various MNC strategies and their codes of conduct.

The framework[1] consists of three components: the external environment, a corporation's response patterns, and an institution's objective in selecting particular responses.

1. ***The external environment.*** The external environment deals with the context within which different institutions' strategies are introduced and evaluated. The focus is on the generalized external conditions created by a multitude of actions by various social actors that are essentially similar within a given contextual and temporal frame. The emphasis is on how an issue or a problem reaches successive stages of severity because of its cumulative effect, real or perceived, on the public's consciousness.

2. ***Institutional responses.*** Responses to external sociopolitical forces are influenced by the nature of the institution itself, especially by its value set, mission, and goals; by its leadership style; by organizational structure; by physical and human resources; by its vision of the future; and by ways in which these attributes influence an institution's or a group's strategic choices. This component examines the diversity, adequacy, and effectiveness of strategic responses employed by different groups and institutions to achieve their stated objectives.

3. ***Institutional imperatives and the nature of strategic options.*** The dynamics of social change create an uncertain environment in which an institution must constantly defend its turf and justify its modus operandi. The characteristics of an institution set the limits within which it will act, define its perception of the external environment and the relevant stage of an issue's life cycle, and determine its response modes toward other groups' actions. In a changing sociopolitical environment, the performance of a corporation, or for that matter any other social institution, must be culturally and temporally determined to a large extent. In the final analysis, all organizations depend on society for their existence, continuity, and growth. All institutions, therefore, must constantly strive to fit their activities into congruence with society's overall goals.[2]

This author has examined a large number of business-society conflicts, patterns of corporate responses, and underlying rationales that drive a corporation's top management to opt for a particular strategy of response. This analysis has led me to conclude that in business-society conflicts, management seeks to (1) maximize and protect management's discretionary authority; (2) minimize risk to corporate survival; and (3) avoid conflict with other sociopolitical groups. These goals are hierarchical, that is, top management will not sacrifice its autonomy to minimize economic risk to the corporation or avoid social conflict with other constituent groups. Thus, where trade-offs must be made, they will be made in favor of managerial autonomy and at the expense of the other two goals in descending order.[3]

The External Environment

The impact of the external environment on a problem and the effectiveness of an institution's response can be best evaluated in terms of the life cycle of the problem. Each issue goes through various stages in terms of various factors, such as the public's awareness of its importance, its saliency, its magnitude for potential harm, the scope and time available for corrective action, and the private or government agencies that could undertake remedial action. To facilitate our understanding of how a social conflict can evolve, we will divide the elapsed time between the emergence of a problem and its solution into four categories or stages: (1) preproblem, (2) problem identification, (3) remedy and relief, and (4) prevention. There is some overlap among these categories because social problems do not fall neatly into discrete groups. Nor can they always be solved in distinct successive steps.

PREPROBLEM STAGE

In the process of manufacturing and marketing, firms are constantly engaged in a series of transactions that respond to two kinds of forces: market and nonmarket. In the case of market forces, a firm adapts by varying its product and service offerings to meet changing societal needs and expectations. Adequacy of response is measured by a firm's ability to sell its products and services profitably in a competitive environment.

All market actions, however, have some nonmarket or indirect consequences. These second-order effects are of two kinds. The first type pertains to the normal leakages found in any production and service activity and is unavoidable. The second type pertains to the unintended and unanticipated consequences of a firm's activities on other individuals and groups who were not a party to the market transactions and who were unaware of the potential adverse effect to which they were exposed. These second-order effects, called externalities, have traditionally been borne by society as a whole. Taken individually, each action or incident is not significant in terms of its impact on the corporation or the affected parties. However, when undertaken by a large number of companies and continued over a long period of time, their cumulative effect is substantial. When that happens, a problem is born.

The preproblem stage has both cultural and sociopolitical dimensions. The capacity or willingness of people to accept or tolerate a level of societal degradation may keep a situation from accelerating to the problem-identification stage. In many cases, the time lag between the creation of a problem and the emergence of its negative side effects may be quite long, especially if the problem is too complex to be isolated or identified. In other instances, influential groups may be able to restrict information or prevent government agencies and political organs from recognizing the issue. Conversely, an open communication system, the availability of mass media, and politically active and sophisticated groups can elevate a situation to the level of a crisis before all the necessary evidence is in.

The elapsed time at the preproblem stage is probably the longest of all the four stages, although there is a tendency for the time span to become narrower with increasing public awareness. Most individuals and institutions respond to the problem passively. They aim their efforts at adaptation and treat the problem as a given. The ways in which a problem may escalate to the identification stage vary in different cultures and depend on a number of factors: the relative sociopolitical strength of the affecting and affected groups; the availability of necessary expertise; the relative size of the affected area relative to total area and population; the existence of mass communication systems in the society; and access to media by various groups.

PROBLEM-IDENTIFICATION STAGE

Once a problem has become large enough and its impact significant enough, affected groups strive to define it, identify its causes, and relate it to the source. This period is marked by extreme tension between opposing groups. Corporations try to delay the issue from reaching the problem-identification stage, while their critics seek to classify an issue as a problem as soon as possible. This is one of the most difficult stages in the whole process of resolving business-society conflicts. The causes of the problem may be varied, with each factor contributing only minutely to its overall impact. The definition of the problem necessarily involves conflict between vested interests and value orientations of individual groups. What is a problem to one group may appear to be merely an obstruction to another.[4]

REMEDY AND RELIEF STAGE

Once the causal linkages have been established, the question arises of how to remedy the harm already inflicted on the injured parties and how to impose sanctions, penalties, or restraints on the culprits. This stage is marked by pragmatic negotiations and damage containment. It is not unusual for the previous adversaries to join in new alliances in order to find third parties—for example, the government—to share the financial burden.

During this stage, corporate rhetoric undergoes a sharp change. While admitting the existence of the problem, companies attempt to limit their culpability by pointing to other groups and even to the affected individuals who must bear some responsibility for their condition. Companies also assert that any benefits they gained because of lower costs were transferred to the companies' customers in lower prices, additional taxes to government, and greater employment opportunities for workers. Companies may also suggest that they run the danger of bankruptcy if asked to shoulder the entire burden of remedy and relief. The groups seeking redress generally follow a deep pockets strategy. That is, they pursue any and all entities that have the necessary financial resources and can be tied to the problem.

PREVENTION STAGE

The prevention stage is not sequential, but generally overlaps with the problem-identification and remedy and relief stages. At this point, the problem has achieved a level of maturity. The sources of the problem are well established or easily identifiable. The attempt now is to develop long-range programs to prevent recurrence.

This stage is marked by uncertainty and difficulty in making an accurate appraisal of potential costs and benefits. Any strategies to be pursued by society at large will, of necessity, involve unfamiliar sociopolitical arrangements and unpredictable financial costs. It is not uncommon to find a high degree of self-righteousness in the pronouncements of various groups, which may be long on rhetoric but short on substance. Groups tend to advocate solutions that favor their particular viewpoints and to overstate the potential costs of solutions supported by groups having opposing viewpoints. The conflict is also heightened by the fact that most of the costs and benefits are likely to accrue to future generations. Therefore, in order to bolster their claims and positions, these groups vie for the right to speak for posterity.

The ideological antibusiness bias of certain groups can hinder the development of socially equitable and feasible long-term solutions at this stage. So too can the obstreperous tendency among some businesspeople to resist every demand for change. Preventive measures may also lead to a "new issue cycle" through unforeseen side effects of the solutions that were adopted.

Dimensions of Corporate Social Performance

Historically, business has resisted taking responsibility for the second-order consequences (negative externalities) of its normal business activities. This is changing. There is now increasing societal pressure all over the world for companies to minimize the second-order effects of their activities and to take a more active role as they assume greater responsibility for correcting the social ills that occur. Corporations typically respond to business-society conflicts in four stages: no obligation, social obligation; social responsibility, and social responsiveness.

CORPORATE BEHAVIOR THAT CONCEDES NO SOCIAL OBLIGATION

A corporation following this response pattern refuses to recognize any problem of negative externalities, regardless of the magnitude of available evidence. The company does not admit that it had anything to do with the creation or expansion of the problem or that the company has any responsibility to ameliorate it or help those affected by it.

During the preproblem stage, most companies opt for this posture as a measure of self-protection and to avoid assuming any responsibility until the issue has crystallized and the magnitude of the problem has become apparent. At this point, they may change their stance and admit their social obligation or social responsibility. In many cases, however, this no-obligation stance persists long after other companies facing a similar situation have changed their response patterns. A number of factors influence this choice. These include a company's assessment of the potential costs; internal confidential information indicating the company's culpability to be far greater than the public realizes; the importance of the company's current products and services to the well-being of a country; and a highly self-centered corporate culture, with a dictatorial, top-down management style.

A company may gain considerable short-term advantage by following this strategy, but may also be exposed to heightened economic and political risks in the long run. In the case of a large corporation, this strategy will allow corporate critics, and even other companies in the industry, to focus all their energies in bringing this company in line. If a company does not cooperate with other industry members, it may lose consumer confidence and market share. Such a stance may create a coalescence of political forces to invite regulatory scrutiny with unforeseeable consequences. In the end, the company may be forced to bow to societal pressures, spend more resources to conform its conduct to societal expectations, and gain less in terms of public trust.

CORPORATE BEHAVIOR AS SOCIAL OBLIGATION

When a corporation responds to market and social forces in a manner that meets only the minimally imposed legal constraints, or that is almost totally required by economic necessity, the response mode is one of social obligation. The criteria for legitimacy are economic and legal only. The company meets its legitimacy criteria only through its ability to compete for resources in the marketplace and by conducting its operations within the legal constraints imposed by the social system.

Competition for resources is not always an adequate criterion, however. Market conditions may force other groups to yield to the corporation's will, but they do so unwillingly and under duress. The affected groups will also use other measures—political and social—to bring about changes in the market forces themselves, thereby increasing their bargaining power. Business institutions are not necessarily the most willing players in the competitive arena. Firms constantly strive to free themselves from the discipline of the market through increases in size, diversification, and generation of public support through advocacy advertising and other means of persuasion. Even in an ideal situation, the ethics of the marketplace provide only one kind of legitimacy, which nations have been known to modify for activities deemed vital to the national well-being.

Nor can the legality of an act be used as the sole criterion. Norms in a social system develop from a voluntary consensus among various groups. Under these conditions, laws tend to codify socially accepted behavior and seldom lead to social change. There are three reasons why the legal criterion alone may not be sufficient. First, social norms are dynamic and change over time, whereas legal changes, which are much more formal, are delayed and must await the enactment of a law, regulation, or court decision. Second, specific social values may contradict each other, whereas there is a presumption of consistency in the legal code. Third, the formal nature of the law confers on the legal code a degree of social acceptance that a social system may not be willing to accord to certain activities during a transitional period, although it may tolerate such activities informally or on a small scale.

In addition, the law has left unresolved the adjustment process between duty and responsibility as legitimating factors. A democratic society must have standards concerning the use of power and the process by which wielders of power are selected, evaluated, and removed from their positions. Although the power exercised by corporate managers has vastly increased, legal criteria have not come to grips with these changes. Therefore, the traditional economic and legal criteria are necessary but not sufficient conditions of corporate legitimacy. The corporation that flouts them will not survive, and even the mere satisfaction of these criteria does not ensure its continued existence.

When companies consider their duties to be simply social obligations, corporate response to the external environment is essentially defensive in character. The business entity fights hard to maintain the status quo in the social system and to preserve its decision-making autonomy in areas affecting its behavior.

CORPORATE BEHAVIOR AS SOCIAL RESPONSIBILITY

Corporations may be special-purpose organizations, but the nature and extent of that special purpose may change over time. Society may conclude that the magnitude of negative side effects from an economic activity is unacceptable. Or a society may find unacceptable the manner in which certain business institutions perform their economic functions.

A corporate response mode is termed one of social responsibility when it calls for changes in corporate behavior that bring the firm's performance to a level that is congruent with currently prevailing social norms, values, and performance expectations. In the industrially advanced countries during the past two decades, most of the conflicts between large corporations and various social institutions would fall into the category of social responsibility.

As we shall see in the latter part of this book, the conduct of MNCs is not consistent across all markets. Some corporations are lauded in their home countries, or in other industrially advanced countries, for their social responsibility and even social responsiveness. But when they operate in developing and poorer countries, they routinely deny social obligation or at best admit their social obligations but deny any further claims. Furthermore, even among poorer countries, their stance of social obligation almost always depends on how rigorously a host country's national and local governments enforce labor and environmental laws and how successfully these governments avoid corruption. Moreover, these attitudes are relatively little influenced by cost factors. As we have noted elsewhere in this book, MNCs' sourcing practices and their emphasis on manufacturing processes that require maximum use of unskilled and low-skilled workers with low-tech capital have narrowed intercountry wage rates in dollar terms.

It would seem that our great multinational corporations are not sufficiently motivated by the internal core ethical values of their institutions, at least where their conduct in poorer countries is concerned. Instead, they respond to the pressures that these countries can exert. The unfortunate outcome of the situation is all too apparent, as analyzed in the first chapter of the book.

Social responsibility does not require a radical departure from ordinary corporate activities or from the normal pattern of corporate behavior. The corporation simply keeps a step ahead, making changes before new societal expectations are codified into legal requirements. By adapting to social change before it is legally forced to, a corporation can be more flexible in its response and achieve greater congruence with social norms. The company also gains legitimacy at a lower social and institutional cost. Whereas the concept of social obligation is proscriptive in nature, the concept of social responsibility is prescriptive.

CORPORATE BEHAVIOR AS SOCIAL RESPONSIVENESS

When a corporation is socially responsive, it anticipates the changes that may result from its current activities or from emerging social problems in which the corporation must play an important role. In terms of social responsiveness, the issue is not how firms should respond to social pressures, but what their long-run role in a dynamic social system should be. Business institutions are expected to initiate policies and programs that will minimize the adverse side effects of their present or future activities. They must act, however, before these side effects assume crisis proportions and become catalysts for another wave of protest against business. Companies should also prepare to accept the challenges that society may come to consider appropriate for corporations to tackle. These activities are characterized as examples of social responsiveness.

Table 4.1 presents a grid pattern showing the relationship between the intensity of an issue and corporate response patterns through the stages or the life cycle of an issue's evolution. It is important to note that the speed with which an issue moves from an emerging to a critical stage, from the corporation's viewpoint, is largely determined by an interaction between external environmental forces and patterns of corporate response. This table also summarizes the four types of corporate response patterns.

To apply this framework to the issues of overseas sourcing, sweatshops, and human rights, we have provided an estimate of the time line through which the issue has progressed from the preproblem stage to problem-identification stage and remedy and relief stage. Subsequent chapters will discuss the types of responses used by different groups and individual companies in dealing with this issue.

Selection of Appropriate Corporate Response Patterns

The next stage in our analysis shows how to select an appropriate response pattern to a given social issue. This will depend, to a large extent, on the stage of the issue life cycle of the external environment, on patterns of response adopted by other corporations and industry groups similarly placed, on the nature of constituency groups and the intensity of their advocacy, and on prior public expectations based on a corporation's behavior in similar situations in the past.

As the corporation develops appropriate responses to societal problems and external constituency groups, one of its main objectives is to protect management's discretion to manage corporate affairs in the ways it considers best for the corporation, its dependencies, and society at large. In general:

- The opportunity for maintaining maximum discretionary decision-making authority is greatest in the preproblem stage and lowest in the prevention stage.
- In the remedy and relief stage, as well as in the prevention stage, public perception of how well management used its discretionary power

Table 4.1 Stages of Conflict Evaluation—Sweatshops/Human Rights Issue

Dimensions of Corporate Response Pattern		Preprobblem Stage (Before 1989)	Problem-Identification Stage (1989–1995)	Remedy and Relief Stage (After 1995)	Prevention Stage
Response Mode	Character of Response				
No social obligation	Do not concede existence of the problem. Refuse any responsibility for causation and amelioration.				
Social obligation	Do what is required by law and economic necessity. Response is defensive and proscriptive.				
Social responsibility	Mitigate negative side effects of corporate activities on society. Response is prescriptive and interactive.				
Social responsiveness	Promote social change. Response is proactive, anticipatory, and preventive.				

during the preproblem and problem-identification stages will determine how much flexibility the corporation will be able to preserve.

- If constituency groups succeed during the problem-identification stage in bringing an issue into the judicial and political arena and scoring gains, management's discretion is likely to be minimal in subsequent stages.

- During the remedy and relief stage and the prevention stage, a management's discretion is even more affected by what other corporations are doing than it was in the two earlier stages.

- A social obligation mode of corporate response is likely to yield maximum discretion in the early stages of the issue's life cycle. However, if this response pattern fails, the rate of decline in management's discretionary authority will likely be very steep in subsequent stages.

- In the early stages of the issue life cycle, it is difficult to sell a social responsibility mode of response to the corporation. Resistance may also give rise to additional external constituencies, who may otherwise not have become viable. Such a response could be counterproductive, at least in the short run.

- Development of a social responsibility mode on the basis of good environmental scanning and constituency group analysis—especially in the problem-identification stage—could yield consistently higher degrees of discretionary authority for the management in subsequent stages.

- A social responsiveness mode is most conducive to maintaining management discretion if the response begins in the preproblem stage and becomes the essential core of strategic planning. In other stages of the issue life cycle, management must follow the social responsibility mode to establish credibility. However, corporate critics are unlikely to consider this level of corporate response as adequate because of the company's insistence on a response of social obligation in the earlier stages, namely preproblem and problem-identification.

Activity Domains

The strategic response patterns of organizations in a given societal conflict can be classified into four broad categories: domain defense, domain offense/encroachment, domain expansion, and domain integration.[5]

DOMAIN DEFENSE

The objective of this strategy is to maintain both the sanctity of an organization's activity domain—that is, its raison d'être and the legitimacy of its goals—and managerial autonomy in choosing means to accomplish organizational goals. Domain defense includes both the organization's persona, that is, its right to exist, and its functional mode of operations. The critical element in domain defense is maintaining the integrity of an organization's core values and the means that the organization has traditionally used (historical prerogatives) to maintain and expand those core values. It is not crucial whether these core values have their original legitimization from legal, sociopolitical, or historical bases. These values may even have been acquired through a derivative process, that is, through an affiliation, whether legal or simply implied. Such core values may also derive from a halo effect with another organization possessing societal acceptance of its core values.

In business-society conflicts, a company will go to great lengths to ensure the integrity of its activity domain against all adversaries—whether economic or sociopolitical. Therefore, public interest groups should avoid creating situations in which a corporation's very existence is threatened. The outcome of such a conflict—even where a corporation's opponents can claim victory—is likely to result in aggregate social loss because of unforeseen repercussions after a business ceases operations. The only situation in which such a condition might be justified is when the very existence of the business—and not merely its activities—is considered harmful to society.

DOMAIN OFFENSE/ENCROACHMENT

An organization seeking to create a new activity domain or to expand an existing one has two approaches at its disposal, which it may pursue in any combination: (1) It may stake out an area of activity or a group of people that is not being currently served; and (2) it may displace another group and take over its activity domain. The former may come about because a particular activity/issue or group has not been deemed economically or politically important by existing organizations. However, to make this group or activity viable, the group leadership will have to enhance its influence in the environment, thereby making it more of a threat to the activity domain of another organization. The second approach is designed to remove a particular activity from the domain of an existing organization, such as a public interest group, and thereby threaten its survival and growth or, at a minimum, reduce its potential to damage the corporation's vital interests.

In business-society conflicts, a company might use this strategy by co-opting the values and agenda of its opponent NGOs—without necessarily adhering to the NGOs' specific goals or plans. The company's objective would be to undermine and thereby reduce the influence of the NGO group in areas the corporation considers important to its interests.

Another approach to domain offense is for different companies to organize into a group and offer a combined response to the NGOs. Their objective is to shift the relative balance of power between the companies and those who oppose them. This strategy is likely to succeed where the intention is to combine resources into a more potent response pattern in the form of social responsibility and social responsiveness. However, the strategy is likely to backfire when it is used as a social obligation response pattern and during the preproblem and problem-identification stages.

In the preproblem and problem-identification stages, the companies are likely to suffer from adverse selection in which the most recalcitrant company drives down the combined corporate response to the lowest common denominator. During the remedy and relief stage, this approach will suffer from this "free rider" problem, thus creating an environment where high-performance companies are unlikely to opt for social responsibility or social responsiveness patterns.

DOMAIN EXPANSION

In business-society conflicts, strategies of domain defense and offense often assume that the domain of activity is clearly delineated and that any gain for one group must come at the expense of some other group. The conflict is thus viewed as a zero-sum game by all parties concerned. Domain expansion occurs when opposing groups seek to expand the scope of a particular domain where incrementally added activities offer opportunities for cooperation and coalition building, and thereby devise new and more creative solutions to conflict resolution.

There are two important points to remember about the strategy of domain expansion: First, the organization following the strategy of domain defense (for instance, a corporation) does not surrender any of its domain specifications; nor does it restrict its operational autonomy.[6] Instead, it agrees to cooperate with opposing groups in entirely new areas of activity that had previously not been part of its domain. Second, this domain expansion may consist of marginal or peripheral activities that will not appreciably alter the characteristics of an organization's domain of primary activity. Thus, domain expansion may have more symbolic than substantive value, and the opposing groups may often use it as a face-saving device when the conflict appears unresolvable and the dominant group prefers to minimize the potential for future conflict by creating an aura of amiability or cooperation. Where domain expansion is significant in scope and potential impact, it almost invariably comes at the expense of third parties who are either unaware of this potential assault on their activity domain or are too weak to defend themselves against this encroachment.

DOMAIN INTEGRATION

The strategy of domain integration calls for a proactive approach to conflict resolution in which opposing parties do not seek to enhance their positions and activity domains at the expense of others, either those who are directly involved in the conflict or third parties who are not yet involved. Instead, this approach seeks to incorporate or reconcile conflicting objectives of the opposing groups in a manner that produces a unified set of goals and operational strategies that yields a larger gain for all concerned. It is in a sense a win-win solution. For a domain integration strategy to work, four things are necessary: (1) Opposing groups develop a high level of trust in each other's motives and integrity; (2) they must not seek to challenge each other's core values and must respect the absolute minimum goals necessary for each organization's survival and well-being; (3) they must be willing to yield on less important goals in order to achieve their major aims and to help their opponents maintain their core values; (4) in conflict resolution, the opposing parties must seek innovative solutions that redefine the nature of the problem itself and thereby enable the conflict to be resolved, not only for the groups involved but also for the broader community.

There is an important distinction between compromises and integrative agreements. Compromises are based on specific trade-offs in which opposing parties attempt to match their relative gains and losses to ensure that each one maximizes its relative gain when adjusted for one's bargaining and the risk of loss from delayed or postponed agreements. Integrative solutions, by contrast, attempt to fashion agreements that have the potential of yielding higher combined values while minimizing the losses on issues that are most important to various parties to the conflict.[7] Integrative solutions are preferable where:

- Both sides have a large number of nonnegotiable demands, and conflict resolution is not possible unless a way can be found to reconcile all the parties' interests.

- Compromises have been forced under pressure of time or other factors but without resolving the underlying sources of contention. They become unsatisfactory to both parties and cause issues to resurface at a future date. Domain integration offers greater long-term stability.

- Domain integration creates mutually rewarding arrangements and thereby strengthens relations between parties.

- Domain integration fashions solutions that are least disruptive and that accommodate the interests of parties, both inside and outside the conflict. They have the potential for contributing to the welfare of the broader community.[8]

Notes

1. Adapted from S. Prakash Sethi, "A Conceptual Framework for Environment Analysis of Social Issues and Evaluation of Corporate Response Patterns," *Academy of Management Review* 4:1 (January 1979), 63–74. See also S. Prakash Sethi, *Multinational Corporations and the Impact of Public Advocacy on Corporate Strategy: Nestlé and the Infant Formula Controversy* (Boston: Kluwer Academic Publishers, 1994), 18–24; S. Prakash Sethi, Nobuaki Namiki, and Carl L. Swanson, *The False Promise of the Japanese Miracle* (Marshfield, Mass.: Pitman Publishing Inc., 1984), 149–166.

2. Sethi, "Conceptual Framework." See also Barry D. Baysinger, "Domain Maintenance as an Objective of Business Political Activity: An Extended Typology," *Academy of Management Review* 9:2 (1984), 248–254; Robert H. Miles, *Coffin Nails and Corporate Strategies* (Englewood Cliffs, N.J.: Prentice-Hall, 1982); C. Perrow, *Complex Organizations: A Critical Essay*, 2nd ed. (Glenview, Ill: Scott, Foresman, 1979); J. Dowling and J. Pfeffer, "Organizational Legitimacy: Social Values and Organizational Behavior," *Pacific Sociological Review* 18:1 (1975), 22–136.

3. S. Prakash Sethi and Cecilia Falbe, "Determinants of Corporate Social Performance," paper presented at the Stanford Business Ethics Workshop, Graduate School of Business, Stanford University, Stanford, California, August 14–17, 1985. See also Sethi, *Multinational Corporations*, 28–30.

4. S. Prakash Sethi and Paul Steidlmeier, *Up Against the Corporate Wall: Cases in Business and Society*, 6th ed. (Upper Saddle River, N.J.: Prentice-Hall, 1997).

5. In developing a typology here, I owe a debt of gratitude to Barry Baysinger ("Domain Maintenance") and Robert Miles (*Coffin Nails*) for their work. However, although the nomenclature in the current study is rather similar in important parts to that of Baysinger and Miles, the typologies developed here are substantially different as to their content and applications. For example, Baysinger proposes three types of activity domains: domain management, do-

main defense, and domain maintenance. He makes a distinction between domain defense and domain maintenance in that the former is concerned with defending the organization's goals and purposes; the latter is concerned with the methods by which the organization pursues its goals and purposes. In my analysis, I make no such distinction. Based on an extensive study of a large number of business and society conflicts, I have found that both corporations and their adversaries may use similar tactics while pursuing different strategies. See Sethi and Steidlmeier, *Up Against the Corporate Wall.* Thus in my classificatory schema, domain defense and domain maintenance are merged, thereby making a major departure from Baysinger's typology. Baysinger's concept of domain management is somewhat similar to my category of domain offense, with the difference that I do not make any distinction between offense and domain creation. While his notion of domain defense is quite similar to the one suggested here, his other two categories are quite different. Domain offense, according to Miles, is a competitive notion and incorporates both market displacement and internal efficiencies that would provide the organization with further resources with which to defend its activity domain. In my classification, domain offense is defined primarily in terms of its objective, that is, to attack and encroach on one's adversary's activity domain regardless of means to achieve such a purpose. Miles' concept of domain creation essentially focuses on diversification strategies wherein organizations seek out new areas that offer greater growth potential or a more hospitable operational environment. As has been shown in the text, this concept varies significantly with the concepts of domain expansion and domain integration that have more specific meaning and carry implications for organizational strategies and tactics.

6. Domain expansion, as developed here, shares some apparent attributes with Baysinger's typology for domain management ("Domain Maintenance," 249), with some significant differences. Baysinger visualizes cooperative activities primarily among one type of groups—for example, business organizations lobbying together—while our classification visualizes domain expansion coming through cooperation with opposing types of organizations even while conflict continues among similar organizations. An example of this situation is where one or more companies break ranks from the industry-held joint positions, and instead form alliances with activist groups opposing them.

7. Dean G. Pruitt, "Achieving Integrative Agreements," in Max H. Bazerman and Roy J. Lewicki, eds., *Negotiating in Organizations* (Beverly Hills, Calif.: Sage Publications, 1983), 36.

8. Dean G. Pruitt, *Negotiating Behavior* (New York: Academic Press, 1981), 137–162; see also Pruitt, "Achieving Integrative Agreements," 35–50.

Proactive Corporate Responses: Voluntary Codes of Conduct

O ne of the approaches most commonly used by the multinational corporations to address the concerns of their critics is to promulgate voluntary codes of conduct. These codes have become de rigueur for all MNCs that profess to be good corporate citizens and to conduct their operations in a professional and socially responsible manner.

Corporate codes of conduct can serve an important business and social purpose. From the MNCs' viewpoint, codes provide the corporation with a voluntary and more flexible approach to addressing some of society's concerns. They create mechanisms through which a company can fashion solutions that are focused, cognizant of the corporation's special needs and public concerns, and economically efficient. They also have the benefit of anticipating societal concerns in general and those of important stakeholders in particular. They engender public trust through the reputation effect, while avoiding being tainted by the actions of other companies.

Voluntary codes also serve an important purpose from the public's perspective. They minimize the need for further governmental regulation, which is more expensive and less efficient because governments must deal with political considerations and the need to create regulations that cover all possible situations and contingencies. Codes also allow the moderate nongovernmental organizations among the affected groups to seek reasonable solutions before the issues are captured by more radical elements, who may be more interested in escalating the level of social conflict rather than fashioning feasible solutions that are mutually acceptable.

Current State of Code Formulation and Implementation

Corporations project these codes as a means of assuring important segments of their stakeholder constituencies, and public at large, that they conduct their business in a highly ethical and professional manner that goes beyond prevailing legal standards, and that they are responsive to the needs and expectations of all those who are affected by a corporation's normal business activities.

At present, most codes suffer from three faults that have significantly diluted their potential impact:

1. Codes are presented as public statements of lofty corporate intent and purpose, but are short on specific content.
2. Codes are not taken seriously, even within the company, by either managers or employees. Code compliance is not integrated into the organization's reward structure and operating procedures.
3. Codes lack effective and meaningful monitoring procedures as to verification and public disclosure of a corporation's compliance with the code provisions.

The problem, in our view, is not with the concept of voluntary codes, which is a highly desirable concept because it offers a flexible approach to resolving issues that have not been satisfactorily resolved through existing legal and other sociopolitical mechanisms. The problem lies largely with the MNCs' unwillingness to use this approach in a substantive and meaningful manner.

Multinational Corporations and Codes of Conduct

The situation with regard to multinational corporations and international codes of conduct has assumed greater importance because these companies operate in emerging economies and poorer countries. These countries lack effective legal and regulatory infrastructures. They have a desperate need for economic development and job creation, which makes them and their poor workers easy prey for exploitation with little or no effective venues to seek redress from abusive working conditions, subsistence wages, and environmental degradation with serious adverse long-term effects on their health and well-being. For a variety of reasons, nation-states have been unable to create uniform systems of corporate oversight and accountability. MNCs on their part have sought new markets and production facilities, which offer them distinct cost advantages. In doing so they have often ignored the oppressive working conditions and abuse of worker rights that prevail in these countries. They have also successfully sought a diminution of environment, health, and safety standards, which the host countries are obliged to yield at the risk of losing foreign investments.

International codes of conduct, or more specifically codes of conduct that attempt to redirect and monitor the behavior of multinational corporations in emerging economies, have become the focus of intense public scrutiny and debate. The drive for enactment of these codes is most pronounced in the United States, with other industrialized countries, notably those in Western Europe, following the U.S. lead at a somewhat slower pace. In the United States, the primary drive for international codes has come from public interest groups—religious institutions, human rights activists, antipoverty groups, and groups concerned with third world countries. The activities of NGOs have been reinforced by frequent and extensive reports in the national and international news media about child labor, worker abuse, and unhealthy and unsafe working conditions in the plants in developing countries. These goods are manufactured to fill orders from MNCs and intended for the consumers in industrially advanced countries. Another group of increasing importance to investigate and improve sweatshop-like conditions has been the universities and colleges whose paraphernalia (e.g., college jerseys) are made by licensees in the developing countries. They are closely followed by young and affluent consumers who are both socially concerned and who have substantial discretionary spending power.

To date, MNCs have a poor record of implementing their own codes. Rather than being proactive agents of change, MNCs are often seen as being dragged into action only when public pressure becomes too intense to ignore. A review of MNC efforts, and those of their trade associations, in the sphere of codes of conduct over the past 15+ years indicates that

MNCs, in general, do not see codes of conduct as an opportunity to improve their overseas performance with regard to labor, environment, and other related issues (e.g., protection of human rights, bribery, and corruption). Nor do the companies, as yet, view them as a means of building public trust. Instead, these codes are viewed as a necessary evil and an inconvenient nuisance, which should be handled with minimum cost and as little effort as possible.

The inevitable result of this has been that corporate codes of conduct are treated with disdain and largely dismissed by both the knowledgeable and the influential opinion leaders among various stakeholder groups and even among business organizations and political parties.[1]

MNCs' codes of conduct, as currently practiced, lack credibility because the entire process is shrouded in secrecy and is not transparent. The companies refuse to have their compliance to codes—that they voluntarily created—subjected to independent external monitoring, verification, and public disclosure. Instead, the MNCs insist that people should have trust in the company's statements as to their compliance efforts—a somewhat dubious proposition under the best of circumstances. To wit, why should the companies be so reluctant to open their performance to public scrutiny, if they have nothing to hide and everything to gain where their good performance would engender public trust and enhance corporate reputation?

While the clamor for greater oversight and control over the conduct of MNCs continues to escalate, the companies have yet to come to grips with this phenomenon. Resorting to the old cliché of "sticking to one's knitting"—which in practice they rarely do, particularly when it affects their own bottom line—they have tended to ignore the social consequences of their market actions, especially in the emerging economies of the world.

And yet this situation cannot be left alone. Greater public awareness at home on such issues as environment, workplace safety, protection of workers' rights, and consumer protection has given rise to a variety of groups with enough political and media sophistication to expose corporations to ever-increasing scrutiny and public accountability. This posture of "benign neglect" cannot be sustained. There are increasing and ever more insistent calls on MNCs to help in curbing worker abuse and human rights violations in developing countries where they do business, and especially among their own foreign operations and those of their subcontractors and suppliers. Otherwise they risk boycotts and protests from public interest groups in their home markets.

Bridging the Gap between Promises and Performance

There are currently two approaches used by MNCs with regard to codes of conduct. The first is a group approach wherein a number of companies in a particular region or industry develop a common set of guiding principles and implementation standards that are followed by all members of the group. This approach appears to be the preferred choice of companies when they are first confronted with real pressure into implementing a code of conduct. It offers them a measure of protection as a group in dealing with their critics.

The second approach is for individual companies to develop their own codes of conduct. Individual company codes are created where a group approach does not succeed or is proceeding at a slower pace. Individual codes are offered as a stopgap arrangement or as a complementary effort to the groupwide approach.

A survey of current efforts in code development and implementation on the part of MNCs that are active in manufacturing operations in developing countries reveals a dismal picture. At the group level the code process is often used to retard progress, while at the individual company level code efforts seldom move beyond exercise in public relations and halfhearted efforts at improving conditions that originally prompted the need for code creation.

Group-Based or Industry-Wide Approach

A common refrain among companies under public pressure is to advocate creating industry-wide or areawide standards that would be applicable to all companies in that industry/region. The case for an industry-wide or regionwide approach is based on the premise that companies in an industry or region face similar problems, competitive conditions, and external pressures. Therefore, a coordinated approach should be more cost-effective. An industry-wide approach creates a level playing field and generates cooperation among all member companies toward achieving their common goal.

At first glance this approach appears logical. In reality, it is quite the opposite. The underlying rationale is flawed both in terms of economic reasoning and as a matter of good public policy. The justification offered by the companies goes against the grain of market competition and the creativity it generates toward solving unusual and apparently difficult problems. MNCs contend that too many codes would cause confusion in the minds of the public. A multiplicity of codes would make it hard for others to compare and evaluate performances among different companies. It would make it difficult for local manufacturers to comply with codes from different companies. The proponents of the group-based approach also suggest that it would give the participating companies a united position from which to respond to the concerns of their critics and the public at large.

This line of reasoning, however, is specious and self-serving. It can be demonstrated that a group-based approach, whether driven by a commonality of issues faced by MNCs or creating a combined front against a common adversary, is unlikely to succeed. Instead, it is a used as a pretext under which the participating companies are more likely to retard meaningful action in developing and implementing a code of conduct. Companies all over the world compete with each other in providing products and services to customers. Competition in the marketplace allows consumers to pick the best product-price combination that meets their needs. It is hard to imagine that a company that believes it has a superior product would delay introducing it in the marketplace until all other competitors can also offer similar products.

Why should it be any different in the case of codes of conduct? Different companies may develop codes whose viability would be determined in the marketplace for their relative strengths and weaknesses. The issue of multiple compliance is not that critical. Once the superiority of a particular code has been established in terms of its content and implementation, other companies would be only too willing to accept this code in meeting their own requirements.

There are also other, more substantive, arguments against the group-based approach. For example:

- In the early phases of creating voluntary standards of conduct, when there are few, if any, commonly accepted performance criteria, an industry-wide or group-based approach is likely to deter a company that is willing to take the initiative—and concomitant risk—in seeking more innovative approaches.
- If there are no legal and socially acceptable frameworks for cooperation already in place, an industry-wide or group-based approach may tempt companies to collude against more socially responsive initiatives.

- To be successful, an industry-wide or group-based approach requires the largest possible number of companies in a particular industry or region to join the collective effort. It also requires a consensus before any decision can be taken. This situation plays into the hands of the companies that are least inclined to undertake substantive action. Endless discussions, procrastination, and obfuscation may delay any real action indefinitely, leading to public ridicule and distrust. The current situation of the Fair Labor Association is a case in point and is discussed in detail in Chapter 8 of this book.

- The need to keep the largest number of companies in the group reduces performance standards to the lowest common denominator. The companies with the weakest records can force standards down to what they are willing to live with.

- The major flaw in this approach is that it suffers from the free rider problem. Individual companies have little incentive to improve their performance because the recalcitrant are not interested in doing so in the first place, and the forward-looking have nothing to gain. These industry-wide efforts depend on "voluntary compliance" and rarely incorporate enforcement measures to ensure that all companies will meet their commitments. This situation admirably suits the poorly performing and recalcitrant companies that stand to gain from enhanced public approval—at no cost to themselves—as a result of the time and resources expended by the best-performing companies. At the same time, the best-performing companies suffer from the taint caused by the actions of recalcitrant companies.

- Corporate critics can always point to the weakest company's poor record as symptomatic of all companies in the industry and thus deprive the high-performance companies of public goodwill and credit for their socially responsive conduct.

The proof of this logic is obvious. Despite years of consultation and negotiation, none of the major industry groups associated with sweatshops, human rights abuses, and related issues have developed or implemented meaningful codes. We face the specter of industry associations in toys, apparel, mining and minerals, and a host of other industries that have yet to create meaningful codes—after years of negotiations and consultations.

Individual Company or Go-It-Alone Approach

The go-it-alone approach calls for a company to create a code of conduct that is unique to its needs and may differ, in both content and implementation, from the approach pursued by other companies. The go-it-alone approach contrasts sharply with the group-based or areawide approaches.

With regard to international codes of conduct, the current situation is similar to that of an emerging industry in which there are no established products and markets, where customer needs and expectations are well defined—often in terms of dissatisfaction with current products—and where the customer is ready and willing to try out new products that offer better price-value than those that already exist. Therefore, an enterprising firm has an opportunity to garner greater market share, and earn higher profits, by being in the right place, at the right time, with the right product. This first mover's advantage can be quite important when a fast growing market is still in flux and no companies have a dominant market share.

In terms of corporate or industry codes of conduct, the current product offerings have a low rate of customer (societal) satisfaction. Most companies or industry groups offering codes make similar claims as to performance and yet are unable and unwilling to satisfy customers (society) with credible performance measures. These codes generate nothing of any value to either the companies or society.

The phenomenon is generally described in the economic literature as a problem of asymmetric information and is best illustrated by the example of selling used cars, as discussed by the Nobel laureate economist George Akerlof.[2] In many ways, international codes of conduct are like used cars. In both cases, sellers find it difficult to convince anyone that they are telling the truth. Each seller knows the quality of his/her offerings. Since the products are not similar, the customer must have sufficient, and believable, information about the claims made by each seller. The sellers, however, are unwilling to provide verifiable or trustworthy information. At the same time, each seller immediately matches the claims of every other seller, since the buyer has no means to compare the truthfulness of competing claims. The result is that the buyer treats each seller's information as equally false and thereby debases the quality claims of all sellers.

Buyers may be willing to pay higher prices for superior used cars, but only if they have reason to believe the sellers' claims. Without this information, the buyer has no choice but to regard all claims as suspect and thus pay the lowest price possible. This situation does not serve sellers that have a better car because they cannot get a higher price for it. Similarly, this situation fails to meet the needs of customers who are willing to pay more for a better used car but are unable to find reliable information. The only beneficiaries are sellers of the worst used cars, the lemons, because they will get the price that is proportionate to the quality of the car being sold. The market of used cars also becomes inefficient because it fails to provide good matches between buyers and sellers.

It should be apparent that the analogy of used cars as lemons neatly fits the current state of international codes of conduct. It therefore follows that:

- If a company does not want its international code of conduct to be treated like a lemon it should create a code that is markedly different in quality and provide reliable information, which allows its code to be evaluated in an objective and dependable manner.

- The individually created code provides the company with the flexibility to include issues in the code that are most relevant to the corporation in terms of business-society relations and that the corporation can better control through its actions and performance.

- This approach also avoids the free-rider problem; that is, the company stands to gain or lose only from its own actions and does not suffer from the actions of other companies.

- It can generate direct economic benefits such as increased customer loyalty and enhanced corporate reputation. Public trust in the corporation will grow, which will translate into a more hospitable sociopolitical environment.

- Finally, the argument for a unified approach in terms of economies of scale does not hold because neither the problems nor the solutions have as yet become standardized in terms of societal expectations and corporate performance to create a baseline.

MNCs' Reluctance to Pursue the Go-It-Alone Approach

One might ask why MNCs are not vigorously following the go-it-alone approach, since it has such apparent advantages. Furthermore, why should the companies be so adamantly opposed to engendering greater public credibility for their efforts through transparency, independent external monitoring, and public disclosure of their compliance efforts?

An analysis of the current state of affairs points to various explanations. Notable among these are a widening gap between corporate promises and corporate conduct; industry pressure against individual companies that seek to break the logjam of industry resistance to change; and the reluctance of these companies to stand up to widespread industry or group opposition. Companies are also afraid that a stand-alone approach will intensify public pressure by requiring the company to accept ever greater responsibility for workers in overseas factories.[3] Finally, there is the strong incentive on the part of the company's own field offices to keep pace with their competitors and avoid any risk of increased costs that stricter code compliance might require.

Sins of the Past Will Haunt MNCs

A major problem, which is rarely discussed, is that when it comes to creating codes of conduct and complying with them, most companies have been entrapped by their own misstatements and false promises. Companies have been all too willing to make promises in the form of codes of conduct whenever they are forced to respond to public concern, but they have treated these promises as harmless paper exercises that they will not need to put into practice anytime soon—if ever. A good illustration of this imbroglio can be seen in a case involving Nike. A public interest group in California charged in a civil complaint that Nike had committed a consumer fraud by making false assertions in its code of conduct about the treatment of workers in overseas factories that manufactured shoes for Nike. The company, however, successfully argued that its promises in the code were protected by the free speech provisions of the U.S. Constitution and were not to be treated as binding commitments. The court dismissed the complaint, accepting Nike's contention that its statements were protected under the First Amendment guarantees of free speech.[4] Unfortunately for Nike, the case did not end there. It was reversed on appeal by the Supreme Court of California. Regarding the plaintiff's allegations that Nike, the defendant corporation, "in response to public criticism, and to induce consumers to continue to buy its products, made false statements of fact about its labor practices and about working conditions in factories that made its products," the Court held that "Applying established principles of appellate review, we must assume in this opinion that these allegations are true."[5] Nike is considering an appeal to the U.S. Supreme Court.

With rare exceptions, MNCs have constantly asserted that they follow their codes of conduct, which at the very least require that they abide by lo-cal labor laws with regard to wages, working hours, and working conditions. In reality this has been far from accurate. This author's own experiences ex-amining sweatshop conditions around the world suggest that at best less than 10 percent of these plants are likely to be in full compliance with local laws.[6] And the gap has widened as the years have passed and the promises have become more specific. The problem facing the multinationals is not simply making good on their promises in the current period or committing themselves to do right in the future. They also must take care of years of la-bor law violations and the heavy financial burden—not to mention loss of public credibility—that would be imposed if the companies were required to pay these workers for the wages and benefits that were owed them for prior years.

There is another, more ominous, aspect to this problem in terms of MNCs' local suppliers. Initially, MNCs sought to abrogate their responsibil-ity for the conduct of their overseas suppliers, arguing that these suppliers were independent entrepreneurs and that the companies had no control over them. However, it has been shown that foreign multinationals exert tremendous control over suppliers because of their buying power, which of-ten accounts for a majority, if not the entirety, of the output of these suppli-ers. MNCs also have detailed information about the cost structure of their suppliers and, therefore, have to know the extent to which the suppliers can comply with local labor laws within the price constraints imposed by the MNC. Therefore, when faced with public pressure, MNCs have as-serted that their overseas suppliers were also required to comply with the companies' codes of conduct or they would risk losing business. These empty promises have further widened the gap between promise and perfor-mance and increased the cumulative potential liability of MNCs. The problem, however, is not likely to go away and will certainly get worse if MNCs continue to refuse to face the reality of their conduct and continue to expose themselves to increased public scrutiny, adverse media reaction, and consumer outrage.

The chapters that follow analyze three group-based approaches to code formulation and implementation. These codes are illustrative of most other codes that fall into this category and share similar problems—a compliance gap between promise and performance, and difficulties entailed in the group-based approach to creating and implementing a code.

We also analyze two examples of individual company-based codes. Again, these codes are illustrative of the flaws that currently exist in individual company codes. Our intent is to draw attention to the direction MNCs must take if they are serious in their commitment to create and implement voluntary, but meaningful, codes of conduct. And finally, we discuss in detail the case of Mattel, Inc., which is the only company in the world that has to date met its commitment to subject its code compliance to independent external monitoring, verification, and full public disclosure of the findings of the monitoring group.

Notes

1. Illustrations of various corporate codes of conduct can be found on company web sites—Levi Strauss, Gap, Mattel, McDonald's, Wal-Mart, Walt Disney, Shell, Nike, Motorola, Texas Instruments, and Sara Lee, to name a few.
2. George A. Akerlof, "The Market for 'Lemons': Quality Uncertainty and the Market Mechanism," *Quarterly Journal of Economics* 84 (MIT Press, 1970), 488–500.
3. The experience of this author, working as chairperson of an independent monitoring council, strongly suggests that given good and believable information, responsible corporate critics—the large middle—are quite willing to work with companies that are making a good faith effort in code creation and implementation. See Chapter 13 of this book.
4. *Marc Kasky on behalf of the General Public of the State of California vs. Nike, Inc.*, San Francisco County Superior Court, September 25, 1998. See also "Corporation, Officers Cleared in Public Relations Misrepresentation Case," *Corporate Officers and Directors Liability Litigation Reporter* 15:11 (Andrews Publications Inc., April 3, 2000), 12.
5. *Marc Kasky vs. Nike, Inc. et. al.*, Supreme Court of California, Ct. App. 1/1/A086142, S087859, May 2, 2002.
6. "A World of Sweatshops," *Business Week* (November 6, 2000), 84.

PART THREE

Group-Based Approaches

The Sullivan Principles in South Africa:
A Regionwide Approach
to Codes of Conduct

The best and perhaps the most successful example of a group-based approach is application of an international code of conduct called the Sullivan Principles in South Africa. Unlike most other industry- or areawide efforts currently underway, this was an international code created independently of the companies that became its initial sponsors. This was the first voluntary code of ethical conduct to be applied under realistic operating conditions, involving a large number of corporations and recipient constituencies, and an institutional framework to implement the project and to monitor and evaluate performance.[1] The Principles had a large measure of moral authority to validate corporate actions and, where necessary, to exhort companies to undertake activities they might otherwise not have considered.

The Sullivan Principles came into being on March 1, 1977, when the Reverend Leon H. Sullivan, pastor of the Zion Baptist Church in Philadelphia, who was also a member of General Motors' board of directors, announced that 12 major U.S. multinational corporations with operations in South Africa had voluntarily agreed to abide by a code of conduct that would govern their operations there, especially with regard to black workers

(Exhibit 6.1). The six principles came to stand for (1) the ascendance of moral principles over purely economic interests; (2) the power and influence of religious groups and social activists to change corporate behavior; and (3) the power of multinational corporations, however reluctantly applied, to bring about social and political changes in the host countries of their overseas operations.

Nowhere in the annals of international business, especially in the history of multinational corporations, has there been an experiment so unique, and yet so profound, as the operations of U.S. companies in South Africa under the white-dominated regime that practiced legalized apartheid. The Sullivan Principles created a watershed event in a drive that had been gathering momentum, primarily in the United States, but also in many other industrialized countries. They established the concept of enhanced responsibility on the part of multinational corporations as a result of their worldwide operations.

Exhibit 6.1   Statement of Principles of U.S. Firms with Affiliates in the Republic of South Africa

Each of the firms endorsing the Statement of Principles has affiliates in the Republic of South Africa and supports the following operating principles:

1. Nonsegregation of the races in all eating, comfort, and work facilities.
2. Equal and fair employment practices for all employees.
3. Equal pay for all employees doing equal or comparable work for the same period of time.
4. Initiation of and development of training programs that will prepare, in substantial numbers, Blacks and other non-whites for supervisory, administrative, clerical, and technical jobs.
5. Increasing the number of Blacks and other non-whites in management and supervisory positions.
6. Improving the quality of employees' lives outside the work environment in such areas as housing, transportation, schooling, recreation, and health facilities. Where implementation requires a modification of existing South African *working conditions*, we will seek such modification through appropriate channels.

We believe that the implementation of the foregoing principles is consistent with respect for human dignity and will contribute greatly to the general economic welfare of all the people of the Republic of South Africa.

The operation of the Sullivan Principles during their more than 15 years was not smooth, especially given their unprecedented character, an emotionally charged sociopolitical environment, and a large measure of mutual distrust between the corporations and their critics. Nevertheless, the Principles served an extremely useful purpose, both as a symbolic gesture indicating the moral repugnance of all civilized people against the evil of apartheid, and as a practical measure for providing sorely needed help to South Africa's poor and disenfranchised people.

The Sullivan Principles came out of a unique set of circumstances that engendered particular strengths relating to the manner of their implementation and the magnitude of their success. These circumstances were related to:

- The inherently indefensible character of apartheid on grounds of both moral repugnance and political illegitimacy, especially when viewed in the context of the American political process.
- The widespread public antagonism in the United States and other parts of the world toward the then white-controlled regime of South Africa.
- A widely held belief that corporations were receiving economic benefits through their cooperation, either directly or indirectly, with the white-controlled regime.

The creation of the Principles also benefited from the economic and sociopolitical dynamics that affected the companies with operations in South Africa, especially those that became the founding signatories of the Principles.

- These were large U.S.-based multinational corporations that prided themselves on being responsible economic institutions, for which reputation and public trust were important assets that had to be protected.
- The CEOs of these large corporations put their personal reputations and corporate resources behind the Principles. This minimized the free rider problem.
- The coalition of the original signatory companies came from diverse industries. These companies were the market leaders in their respective sectors and had little incentive in forcing the standards to the lowest common denominator.

The definition and scope of the initial Principles came about as a result of intensive discussions and negotiations between the Reverend Sullivan and the representatives of the companies. The final product reflected the ensuing accommodations and often complementary but just as often conflicting interests of the corporate community.

- The Principles were quite explicit about their intended goals and yet quite vague about how they would be implemented.
- For the first time in any code of conduct, the Principles and their implementation process recognized the need for independent outside monitoring and verification of corporate activities under the Principles and public reporting of corporate compliance efforts. These measures changed the tenor of public debate as well as corporate response to demands for greater corporate social responsibility. Even more important, they brought into the public arena concerns about modes of corporate governance, along with broadly defined notions of corporate accountability.

A fundamental difference between Leon Sullivan and the corporate leaders was rooted in the underlying philosophy or rationales that would justify the Principles. Sullivan advocated the Principles on moral grounds rooted in human rights. He wanted to justify the Principles as transcending narrow economic grounds. Although he understood that economic concerns must play a significant role in corporate decisions, he felt that some issues, like apartheid, simply could not be tolerated in the long run, no matter what the economic costs or benefits might be. The signatory companies had a more conventional and limited agenda. They saw the Principles as a means to limit external pressure on the companies to withdraw from South Africa. They also saw the Principles as providing a protective umbrella under which corporations could undertake some urgently needed reforms.

Paradigm Shift: Ethical Imperatives versus Economic Realities

An important issue to emerge from the Sullivan Principles was that the rationale applied by the advocates of changes in corporate conduct—notably the Reverend Sullivan and those belonging to other religion-based NGOs—was quite different from the rationale offered by the MNCs for their willingness to accept the Sullivan Principles. The Reverend Sullivan and other NGOs argued in favor of the Principles from an ethical viewpoint, declaring that it was the duty of international investors to leave South Africa to avoid aiding and abetting the apartheid regime. What Sullivan had in common with most anti-apartheid activists was his concern for the poor and disenfranchised of South Africa. However, he did not, and would not, separate economic injustice from political injustice. He considered forced economic deprivation as inherently immoral and therefore unacceptable.

Multinational corporations, in contrast, would only discuss their actions to remedy conditions in South Africa in strictly economic terms, within a framework of corporate strategy. They would not directly challenge the otherwise immoral actions of the South African government except to ameliorate those conditions in their own operations. Nor would they assert any moral imperative in explaining their new conduct, even where it was apparent that, at a personal level, business leaders found the treatment of blacks in South Africa to be morally repugnant and even when they undertook actions that went far beyond abolishing economic inequalities between whites and blacks in their own operations.

The Sullivan Principles and their application in South Africa clearly articulated a major paradigm shift in business-society relations in which corporations were expected to justify their actions not only on economic grounds but also on ethical and moral grounds. Unfortunately, the business community failed to recognize this paradigm shift at the time. As a consequence, it paid a large price by abandoning the high moral ground that it had worked so hard to achieve in South Africa and had every right to claim.

MNCs avoided this linkage for fear that demands on their economic conduct would further increase and that they would be hard-pressed to justify their economic, market-driven decisions in ethical terms. They were concerned about the problems of adverse selection and free riders in which they would be tainted by the bad actions of other companies, which they could not control. They also perceived the need to present a combined industry or business position to protect themselves from "unwarranted" demands by outsiders. This corporate reluctance to change robbed the companies of the credit they deserved for their actions. Even worse, it prevented them from taking many actions that, in the long run, would have been far more effective and would have made the Sullivan Principles a shining example of how ethical imperatives and economic conduct do not need to be inimical. Good ethics and good business must coexist in corporate conduct if it is to succeed under the demands of the new paradigm.

It is a tragedy that this lesson was not effectively learned in South Africa. Even today, the MNC finds itself trapped in the old paradigm, in which it continues to defend itself by citing the ineffective premise of competitive markets and the role of open markets in creating economic growth, employment, wealth, and human welfare.

Implementation Phase

From Sullivan's perspective, the Principles were not a static, one-time-only argument. Instead, he considered them to be a dynamic response to changing economic and sociopolitical conditions. It was this conception of the Principles that explains his willingness to compromise on the scope of the Principles during their initial formulation.

From their very inception, the Reverend Sullivan was determined to ensure that the Principles were implemented in a manner that would ensure independent oversight, external monitoring and verification, transparency, and public reporting. He was concerned that in the absence of these measures the Principles would have no credibility with any of his constituencies and would certainly be scorned by anti-apartheid activists. The corporate community also shared Sullivan's concerns and was interested in creating systems to meet these concerns.

The implementation phase of the Principles benefited from extensive involvement of midlevel corporate managers—both in the United States and in South Africa. Having received their marching orders from the top managers, and supplied with sufficient resources, these managers brought extensive operating experience and knowledge of their corporate cultures to the task of implementing the Principles. Implementation involved creating new systems and operating procedures, since there were no preexisting models. Starting with a clean slate, these executives developed systems that assured efficient use of resources, due diligence in the dispersal of funds, proper record keeping to minimize leakage of funds in the pipeline, and accountability for performance. This approach also allowed for coordinated efforts by groups of companies to tackle large projects, as well as flexibility for individual companies to pursue specific projects that were better suited to their operations in South Africa. The full text of an initial amplification, as released on July 6, 1978, appears in Exhibit 6.2.[2] This process continued, and by the end of 1986 there were a total of five amplifications.

Exhibit 6.2   First Amplification of the Statement of Principles

Principle I—Nonsegregation of the races in all eating, comfort, and working facilities.

Each signator of the Statement of Principles will proceed immediately to:

- Eliminate all vestiges of racial discrimination.
- Remove all race designation signs.
- Desegregate all eating, comfort, and work facilities.

Principle II—Equal and fair employment practices for all employees.

Each signator of the Statement of Principles will proceed immediately to:

- Implement equal and fair terms and conditions of employment.
- Provide nondiscriminatory eligibility for benefit plans.
- Establish an appropriate comprehensive procedure for handling and resolving individual employee complaints.
- Support the elimination of all industrial racial discrimination laws which impede the implementation of equal and fair terms and conditions of employment, such as abolition of job reservations, job fragmentation, and apprenticeship restrictions for Blacks and other non-whites.
- Support the elimination of discrimination against the rights of Blacks to form or belong to government registered unions, and acknowledge generally the right of Black workers to form their own union or be represented by trade unions where unions already exist.

Principle III—Equal pay for all employees doing equal or comparable work for the same period of time.

Each signator of the Statement of Principles will proceed immediately to:

- Design and implement a wage and salary administration plan which is applied equally to all employees regardless of race who are performing equal or comparable work.
- Ensure an equitable system of job classifications, including a review of the distinction between hourly and salaried classifications.
- Determine whether upgrading of personnel and/or jobs in the lower echelons is needed, and if so, implement programs to accomplish this objective expeditiously.
- Assign equitable wage and salary ranges, the minimum of these to be well above the appropriate local minimum economic living level.

Principle IV—Initiation of and development of training programs that will prepare, in substantial numbers, Blacks and other non-whites for supervisory, administrative, clerical, and technical jobs.

(Continued)

Exhibit 6.2   *(Continued)*

Each signator of the Statement of Principles will proceed immediately to:

- Determine employee training needs and capabilities, and identify employees with potential for further advancement.
- Take advantage of existing outside training resources and activities, such as exchange programs, technical colleges, vocational schools, continuation classes, supervisory courses and similar institutions or programs.
- Support the development of outside training facilities individually or collectively, including technical centers, professional training exposure, correspondence and extension courses, as appropriate, for extensive training outreach.
- Initiate and expand inside training programs and facilities.

Principle V—Increasing the number of Blacks and other non-whites in management and supervisory positions.

Each signator of the Statement of Principles will proceed immediately to:

- Identify, actively recruit, train and develop a sufficient and significant number of Blacks and other non-whites to assure that as quickly as possible there will be appropriate representation of Blacks and other non-whites in the management group of each company.
- Establish management development programs for Blacks and other non-whites, as appropriate, and improve existing programs and facilities for developing management skills of Blacks and other non-whites
- Identify and channel high management potential Blacks and other non-whites into management development programs.

Principle VI—Improving the quality of employees' lives outside the work environment in such areas as housing, transportation, schooling, recreation, and health facilities.

Each signator of the Statement of Principles will proceed immediately to:

- Evaluate existing and/or develop programs, as appropriate, to address the specific needs of Black and other non-white employees in the areas of housing, health care, transportation and recreation.
- Evaluate methods for utilizing existing, expanded or newly established in-house medical facilities or other medical programs to improve medical care for all non-whites and their dependents.
- Participate in the development of programs that address the educational needs of employees, their dependents and the local community. Both individual and collective programs should be considered, including such activities as literacy education, business training, direct assistance to local schools, contributions and scholarships.

Exhibit 6.2 *(Continued)*

- With all the foregoing in mind, it is objective of the companies to involve and assist in the education and training of large and telling numbers of Blacks and other non-whites as quickly as possible. The ultimate impact of this effort is intended to be of massive proportion, reaching millions.

Period Reporting

The signatory companies of the Statement of Principles will proceed immediately to:

- Utilize a standard format to report their progress to Dr. Sullivan through the independent administrative unit he is establishing on a 6-month basis which will include a clear definition of each item to be reported.
- Ensure periodic reports on the progress that has been accomplished on the implementation of these principles.

Consistent with the desire of the signatory companies to contribute toward the economic welfare of all people of the Republic of South Africa, they are urged to seek and assist in the development of Black and other non-white business enterprises, including distributors, suppliers of goods and services and manufacturers.

There will be a continuing review and assessment of the guidelines in light of changing circumstances.

Independent Oversight Mechanism

The Reverend Sullivan understood that the credibility and viability of the Principles depended on what the companies would actually do to comply and whether corporate critics and the public at large would believe the companies' claims. Sullivan created a not-for-profit organization called the International Council of Equal Opportunity Principles (ICEOP), composed of church leaders and educators who would oversee the overall functioning of the Principles and assess the progress made by the signatory companies. The ICEOP structure was large and deliberately unwieldy. Sullivan wanted this group to be inclusive, so he brought in leaders reflecting different constituencies and viewpoints. Such a large oversight structure, however, ran the risk of becoming splintered and unfocused if different subgroups tried to redirect the Principles' implementation to conform to their particular visions.

Sullivan was able to contain this risk through his strong personality and by maintaining centralized control. This centralization, however, restricted the deliberative process and narrowed input of diverse viewpoints. It eroded the very reason for which the oversight function was created in the first place.

As the implementation gathered steam, the task of monitoring became more elaborate and time-consuming, and Reid Weedon of Arthur D. Little, Inc., the person responsible for creating and implementing the monitoring system, became the de facto policy maker. As Weedon gained Sullivan's trust, he assumed ever greater responsibility for policy-related decisions. Eventually, Weedon would essentially make all the decisions—both major and minor—without prior approval from Sullivan.

The ICEOP was reduced to window dressing and played little, if any, role in the monitoring process, which lost its moral underpinnings. The ICEOP members did not perform their oversight functions and thus unhinged the process from its larger purpose of linking outcomes to the broader moral goals. This deliberate undermining and consequent failure of the independent oversight function had serious negative consequences as the Principles were interpreted and implemented by the companies and as their performance was evaluated and reported to the public.

Objective Performance Measures

A second innovative measure in the Sullivan Principles was the recognition that standards must be created that would objectively measure the performance of individual companies in implementing the Principles. This would minimize the tendency among many companies to exaggerate their claims. It would also limit critics from hurling unsubstantiated charges at the companies. The Sullivan Principles and the signatory companies, though, had a highly favorable environment within which to create objective standards to measure performance. Several factors worked in their favor:

- The participating companies had a large cadre of experienced executives and knowledgeable professionals who could design standards that would meet the highest level of compliance with the Principles and yet remain within acceptable limits of operational efficiency and financial feasibility.

- The signatory companies had the necessary incentive to comply with the Principles and have their performance evaluated in a manner that applied equally to all other companies but would also pass muster with external monitors. This would minimize the free rider problem: The companies would not have to worry about rogue competitors who would gain competitive advantage at the expense of the companies who diligently complied with the standards.

- Corporate critics were deterred from making unsubstantiated charges because of these objective standards and an independent monitoring system and oversight mechanism.

In reality, the system became highly porous as it tried to deliver on its promise because the companies wished it to be so and because Sullivan was unwilling or unable to confront the issue. This was indeed a pity because like so many other aspects of the Principles, the shortsighted and short-term orientation of the companies led them to fritter away this opportunity to elevate their public credibility and to demonstrate the effectiveness of the Principles.

A system of measurement created by the very group whose performance it is designed to measure is likely to fall to the lowest possible level. This is especially so when the system has no independent, outside input. Such a system is prone to pressures from recalcitrant members who plead lack of resources and "gradualism in implementation" and can make the implied threat of walking away if they consider the standards too onerous.

The second reason for the inadequacy of performance standards was Sullivan's willingness to downplay the moral rationale for the Principles and instead view the Principles primarily in the economic context. Both Sullivan and Weedon were apparently overanxious to see the Principles implemented so as to avoid criticism—for lack of progress—from anti-apartheid activists and Sullivan's own supporters. They constantly yielded to the companies' demands about what was to be measured and how it should be measured.

The resultant system of standards suffered from significant shortcomings that made it highly susceptible to manipulation by the companies. In the end, this manipulation undermined their credibility, which they had so ardently sought even while they destroyed the effectiveness of the system. For example:

- Among the most objective and verifiable standards were those pertaining to expenditure of funds. The companies, however, would not be held to any objective measures of outcome, but instead insisted that they be judged by the standards of good faith effort.
- Companies were not required to adhere to any objective, outcome-based standards, even in areas where they had the most control on the outcomes and therefore should have been able to demonstrate compliance.

Coincidentally, these were also the areas that necessitated making painful choices and a proactive deviation from business as usual. The two most obvious, and highly criticized, activities in this area pertained to training and promoting black employees to managerial ranks and to making increased purchases (i.e., corporate procurement) from black-owned enterprises.

Monitoring Performance, Evaluation and Verification, and Public Disclosure

From the very inception of the Principles, Sullivan wanted the task of monitoring performance evaluation and verification to be assigned to A. D. Little, Inc. (ADL), based in Cambridge, Massachusetts, a highly reputable consulting firm with considerable experience in field monitoring, especially in the area of environmental scanning. In particular, he wanted Reid Weedon of ADL to spearhead the effort. This was a tremendous responsibility and a heavy burden in time and resources.

Weedon developed a system that was essentially qualitative and group-oriented, although it appeared to be quantitative. In our opinion, the system was designed with a view to meet certain criteria that were insisted upon by the companies and agreed to by Sullivan. To wit, the companies would not be evaluated in a manner in which they would appear to be competing with each other in performance ratings. Instead, the system would group the companies in three categories: A, B, and C, in which an A rating meant making outstanding progress, B making considerable progress, and C needing to become more active. The system of rating was riddled with subjectivity and qualitative judgments. It appeared to protect individual companies from being accountable for their actions when compared with other companies by grouping more than 150 companies into three broad categories.

The system failed to meet any of the criteria of objective measurement, independent verification, and transparency. The companies' financial contributions were not verified by independent outside monitors but were instead confirmed by the companies' own financial auditors, who would vouch for the spending under the Principles as meeting "generally acceptable accounting standards." One does not have to stretch the imagination to see that these financial auditors would have little incentive to object to their companies' interpretation of expenditures, except perhaps in cases of gross violations. Weedon alone decided how many points a company should receive for undertaking certain activities. The criteria he used were never made public, nor were they open to external examination and validation. And finally, public disclosure did not identify individual companies or their relative performance.

What Did the Principles Achieve?

The signatory companies to the Sullivan Principles spent over $300 million during a period of more than 15 years. This was a substantial sum as an absolute number, even when compared with the amount spent by MNCs from other countries and by South Africa's own large corporations. The companies largely succeeded in abolishing apartheid in their operations. They also instituted wage policies that were far in excess of the pathetically low minimum wages for black workers mandated by the South African labor laws. It was a tacit recognition on the part of the companies that the prevailing wages fell far short of living wages. The companies made a significant contribution to the improvement of living conditions in predominantly black communities, an effort that went beyond looking after their own workers. The companies, however, failed to demonstrate measurable progress in promoting black workers to more skilled and/or supervisory positions. Nor did they make appreciable progress in encouraging black business development through their outsourcing and purchasing policies.

One might ask why it was that despite the support of some of the largest corporations, expenditures of enormous sums of money, the moral leadership of Leon Sullivan, considerable support of the people and institutions in the United States and South Africa, and also the support of the U.S. government, the Principles failed to deliver sufficiently on their stated promise to make the Principles credible in terms of what they intended to achieve. And what if anything did they accomplish in terms of social good and public goodwill?

In our opinion, the problem lies first and foremost with the thrust of the Sullivan Principles and secondarily, but no less importantly, with the U.S. companies. The Principles asked too much of the companies in areas where "no level of *corporate* activity" could possibly be sufficient. In developing the Principles, we believe that Sullivan placed more emphasis in placating his critics, especially in the United States, who advocated withdrawal of U.S. companies from South Africa. In the process, he lost a major opportunity to mobilize the companies in areas where they could have played an important role as agents of change.

Conversely, the Sullivan Principles did not ask enough of the companies in areas where they had the most power to perform, areas such as employment expansion, job training, upward mobility, and small-business development. By emphasizing accountability in dollars spent rather than goals accomplished, the Principles offered the companies a simpler measure of performance accountability. This approach lessened the need for structural changes in the external and internal systems that would have been necessary to achieve most long-term sustainable goals. The structure of the Sullivan Principles, their monitoring mechanisms, and the expectations of the activist constituencies in the United States caused the system to do poorly in those areas where it simply could not do well, and directed companies away from the areas where they could have done better and should have been called upon to deliver more than they did. The Sullivan Principles have provided a plethora of experiences about how to craft a good set of principles to guide business conduct—principles that must be based on a combination of strong moral reasoning and economic feasibility. The Sullivan Principles also provide a rationale for how to create viable and defensible systems and procedures for monitoring and verifying corporate compliance with a given code of conduct, along with the hazards and pitfalls that must be avoided if such a system is to win public trust. The challenge for MNCs and NGOs is to learn from these experiences and to avoid similar mistakes.

The Sullivan Principles also created compliance standards and an independent external monitory system. Although the signatory companies to the Sullivan Principles provided significant inputs in creating performance standards and measurement systems, the final decision was always made by the principles oversight committee and the independent monitor.

During the 17 years of its operation, the companies subscribing to the code spent over $300 million in the areas of health, education, training, and support for black entrepreneurship. These companies were also model employers and operated according to high standards of good corporate citizenship. Unfortunately, these companies and their overseas subsidiaries were often too willing to throw money at problems just to make their numbers for the benefit of the independent monitor, while avoiding harder problems such as training and promoting black employees and increasing corporate purchases from black-owned enterprises. The independent monitor, for his part, more often than not compromised his independence in order to keep the companies in line and to maintain the public perception that the Principles were a success. Notwithstanding, when faced with constant pressure from corporate critics and even the recipients of corporate munificence, an increasing number of companies opted to withdraw from South Africa. Over the period of 1985 to 1992, the number of U.S. companies with activities in South Africa declined from 146 to 52.[3]

Studies show that, despite all the caveats, planning foresight, and built-in checks and balances, the Principles failed to deliver fully on their promise and their potential. A major part of the blame for this failure must lie with the companies, who resisted all efforts to allow public disclosure of the performance of individual companies, as well as group performance on specific measures. This resistance prevented the system from exerting pressure on individual companies and allowed them to coalesce their conduct around broad measures that they could comfortably achieve. Whether or not these were the most important measures was of secondary importance. Another important point ignored was the level of performance and whether it was the best that could be achieved, given the circumstances, and corporate resources and culpability. Nevertheless, the operation of the Sullivan Principles offers an excellent laboratory to examine the efficacy of various modes of corporate actions when confronted with hostile sociopolitical environments, conflicting economic and social goals, and lack of full support from their host country managers.[4] It also points to the tremendous opportunities for creating meaningful codes that would meet both societal expectations and the corporate objective of socially responsible corporate citizenship without making it financially expensive and overly cumbersome in implementation.

Notes

1. This paper is largely adapted from S. Prakash Sethi and Oliver F. Williams, *Economic Imperatives and Ethical Values in Global Business: The South African Experience and International Codes Today* (Boston: Kluwer Academic Publishers, 2000; pap. ed. Notre Dame, Ind.: University of Notre Dame Press, 2001). See also S. Prakash Sethi and Oliver F. Williams, "Creating and Implementing Global Codes of Conduct: An Assessment of the Sullivan Principles as a Role Model for Developing International Codes of Conduct—Lessons Learned and Unlearned," *Business and Society Review* 105:2 (Summer 2000), 169–200.
2. Sethi and Williams, *Economic Imperatives.*
3. Ibid.
4. Ibid. See also Sethi and Williams, "Creating and Implementing."

The United Nations Global Compact:
Corporate Leadership
in the World Economy

The United Nations-sponsored Global Compact is the inspiration of UN Secretary-General Kofi Annan, who challenged the top leadership of the global business community to enact a Global Compact between the United Nations and the private sector to promote human rights, improve labor conditions, and protect the environment. The Compact was an outgrowth of the secretary-general's address at Davos in January 1999.[1] In it, he argued that the globalization of markets, as we have known it for the past decade or so, is unsustainable and likely to trigger a backlash, because the benefits of globalization are distributed too unequally, both within and among countries. Moreover, the current drive toward globalization lacks an adequate social foundation in broadly shared values and practices, without which competitive markets are unlikely to survive and thrive. The secretary-general then challenged the business community to work with the United Nations to rectify this state of affairs. Specifically, he asked companies to embrace and enact in their own corporate practices nine principles drawn from the Universal Declaration of Human Rights, the International Labor Organization (ILO)'s Fundamental Principles on Rights at Work, and the Rio Principles on

Environment and Development—all of which enjoy universal consensus among governments.

The Global Compact, which was formally launched on July 26, 2000,[2] was aimed at mobilizing collective and individual leadership in the business community to take responsible steps to renew a commitment to open markets, while at the same time ensuring a more effective treatment of other emerging societal concerns.[3] It contains nine principles derived from the Universal Declaration of Human Rights, the Declaration of the International Labor Organization on Fundamental Principles on Rights at Work, the 1995 Copenhagen Social Summit, and the Rio Declaration of the 1992 UN Conference on Environment and Development (the Earth Summit). The nine principles were established under their respective headings.

Human Rights

1. Businesses should support and respect the protection of internationally proclaimed human rights within their sphere of influence; and,
2. Make sure they are not complicit in human rights abuses.

Labor

3. Businesses should uphold freedom of association and the effective recognition of the right to collective bargaining;
4. The elimination of all forms of forced and compulsory labor;
5. The effective abolition of child labor; and,
6. The elimination of discrimination in respect of employment and occupation.

Environment

7. Businesses should support a precautionary approach to environmental challenges;
8. Undertake initiatives to promote greater environmental responsibility; and,
9. Encourage the development and diffusion of environmentally friendly technologies.[4]

With the launch of the Global Compact, Kofi Annan put his personal reputation and the prestige of his office on the line in support of this initiative. When viewed in a historical context, this was at best a risky approach. In the past, initiatives involving the UN and the private sector had been generally sponsored by various UN agencies, such as the United Nations Development Program (UNDP), United Nations Children's Fund (UNICEF), International Labor Organization (ILO), World Health Organization (WHO), and United Nations Conference on Trade and Development (UNCTAD). In the present case, in addition to the five UN agencies, the Compact also included workers' organizations, such as the International Confederation of Free Trade Unions (ICFTU) and a number of NGOs including Amnesty International and the World Wildlife Fund.

Most of these initiatives, with the exception of humanitarian efforts such as UNICEF, have not fared well and, in some cases, have generated intense hostility and further widened the schism between the UN and the business community. UN agencies, including many program-oriented agencies, by their very nature are political and must respond to the expectations and political pressures of the member nations in their policies and program initiatives. When it comes to economic issues, especially those pertaining to market intervention mechanisms and free trade, these agencies have been seen as indifferent at best and hostile at worst to the interests of the private sector in general and of multinational corporations in particular. The most notable examples of this attitude can be seen in the UN's aborted attempt to create an international code of conduct for transnational corporations and in the poor implementation of WHO's much ballyhooed International Code of Marketing of Breast-Milk Substitutes, that is, the Infant Formula Code.[5] The drug donations programs of pharmaceutical companies have also not met with much success.[6]

Recent Trends toward Cooperation between UN Agencies and Multinational Corporations

More recently, at the urging of the UN's secretary-general, various UN agencies have initiated a small number of cooperative projects with private sector companies to expand and strengthen the agencies' programmatic missions (Table 7.1). Even these modest efforts have met with strong criticism from the NGOs that have actively participated with the UN agencies in relief work in developing countries. They have questioned the motives of the private sector companies participating in these partnerships because, more often than not, these companies are also seen as major contributors to the problems these UN agencies and NGOs are working to ameliorate.

This should not be surprising. As noted elsewhere in this book, all

Table 7.1 A Partial (Illustrative) List of UN Agency–Private Sector Cooperative Projects

UN Agency	Name of Partnership	Companies Involved	Status
Office of secretary-general	Global Compact UNEP, ILO, OHCHR	Nike, Novartis, Shell, Rio Tinto, BP, DuPont, Daimler Chrysler, ABB, ICC	Launched January 1999, companies joined July 2000
UNDP	GSDF	Rio Tinto, Novartis, ABB, Dow	Abandoned
UNDP	Private Sector Development Program	Chevron, British Petroleum (BP)	Ongoing in Kazakhstan and Angola
UNDP	NetAid	Cisco	Unclear
UNIDO	Competitiveness through public-private partnership	Fiat	Started January 1999—operational for auto industry in India
OHCHR	Business Humanitarian Forum		Held two meetings
UNESCO	Licensing agreements	Boucheron, Mitsubishi, NKK Corporation	Ongoing
UNESCO	Youth Millennium Dreamer Awards	Disney, McDonald's	Gave out awards May 2000
WHO	Global Alliance for Community Health	Placer Dome, Rio Tinto, others	Not available
WHO, UNICEF, UNESCO, UNDP, etc.	UNAIDS Africa Partnership	Boehringer Ingelheim, Bristol-Myers Squibb, Merck, Hoffman-LaRoche, Glaxo Wellcome	Ongoing

Note: Partial list of UN-corporate partnerships, Corporate Watch, September 1, 2000.
GSDF: Ground Self-Defense Force.
UNAIDS: United Nations Program on HIV/AIDS.
UNDP: United Nations Development Program.
UNICEF: United Nations Children's Fund.
WHO: World Health Organization.
OHCHR: Office of United Nations High Commissioner for Human Rights.
UNESCO: United Nations Educational, Scientific & Cultural Organization.
UNIDO: United Nations Industrial Development Organization.

business activities have unintended negative side effects (negative externalities) on the community, arising from their normal activities in the marketplace. The primary goal of private sector companies is to maximize profits by externalizing as much of their costs to the community as possible. The process of economic activity, however, generally creates both positive and negative externalities. Corporations emphasize their creation of positive externalities while downplaying the negative externalities. NGOs and the affected groups, on the other hand, emphasize the negative externalities, while dismissing business claims of positive externalities as so much empty rhetoric.

UN agencies, like other public service organizations, must therefore tread carefully if they are to avoid being ensnared into companies' public relations campaigns. This situation is further exacerbated by the phenomenon of adverse selection; that is, the companies most reviled by the public are also the ones most eager to join the cooperative bandwagon. For example, the UNDP faced the anger of public interest groups in 2000 with its proposed Global Sustainable Development Facility, which was developed under the agency's previous administrator, Gus Speth. The new head of UNDP, Mark Malloch-Brown, has killed the project, but has promoted other partnerships such as a British Petroleum (BP) fishing project in Angola and a business center sponsored by Chevron in Kazakhstan.[7] At the same time, these companies have been engaged in activities that have run afoul of the mission of the United Nations and its various programmatic agencies. Chevron was a major opponent of the UN-brokered Climate Convention on Global Warming, and the company is currently facing a lawsuit for human rights violations in Nigeria. Chevron is also accused of causing environmental problems in places like California, Texas, Nigeria, and Indonesia.[8]

UNICEF is one of the UN agencies that receives substantial funds from the private sector through a variety of cooperative programs. Executive Director Carol Bellamy points out that UNICEF is very careful to "constantly appraise" the companies it deals with and that the agency's guidelines exclude makers of products like infant formula and land mines.[9] At the same time, WHO and UNICEF are part of UNAIDS—a partnership with five leading pharmaceutical companies whose parent corporations are among the violators of WHO's International Code of Marketing of Breast-Milk Substitutes, or the Infant Formula Code. This partnership was so controversial, even within UNICEF, that it led to the protest resignations of two UNICEF officials.[10]

UNAIDS is a program initiative sponsored by various UN agencies (e.g.,

UNICEF, UNDP, WHO), in partnership with five pharmaceutical corporations: Boehringer Ingelheim, Bristol-Myers Squibb, Hoffmann-LaRoche, Glaxo Wellcome, and Merck. The project's goal is to address the AIDS crisis in Africa and to lower the costs of AIDS drugs there. Nevertheless, a number of AIDS groups assert that these companies' involvement is motivated primarily by their need to prevent and forestall the seizure of drug company patents and hence the loss of markets. The most worrisome instances of such seizure are the actions of Thailand and South Africa, which have passed "compulsory licensing" laws allowing for the seizure of AIDS drug patents in the interest of reversing a massive human health disaster.[11]

Initial Public Reaction to the Global Compact

Despite its lofty sponsorship, global ambitions, and extensive efforts at building public support, the Global Compact fared poorly with those who were most knowledgeable and likely to be most involved in activities encompassed by the Global Compact. It also did not escape criticism from among the UN agencies whose support it sought and whose activities the secretary-general was trying to promote through the Compact.[12]

From the perspective of these agencies, the central issues in the debate on UN–private sector partnership are (1) the choice of corporate partners, and (2) the precise definition of the objectives of such projects. There is express concern that companies that are most eager to seek the prestige of UN affiliation tend to be the ones that are known for their actions against such issues as human rights, environmental protection, worker abuse prevention, right of free speech and association, and protection against child labor. In the past, a vast majority of MNCs—and especially those in the United States—have demonstrated extreme reluctance to become entangled with the UN and its agencies, for fear that such involvement, no matter how benign or disinterested, would lead to international regulation of MNCs. This fear is based on both political and practical considerations. Thus, it would seem that the MNCs most likely to welcome UN partnership would be the companies that would make the least desirable UN partners. The phenomenon is known as adverse selection. The critics of Global Compact fear that the eagerness with which the UN has been seeking the cooperation of MNCs will lead it to embrace private sector partners with dubious credibility and poor records of corporate social responsibility. There is a strong sense that corporate influence is already becoming pernicious and will be injurious to the interests of poorer countries and the NGOs that advocate their interests. These UN-corporate partnerships were leading to partial privatization and commercialization of the UN system.[13]

The Global Compact foresaw some of these problems before its launch and worked hard to enlist the agencies' participation. At the same time, it also sought to downplay the role of these agencies for fear of alienating the corporate sector, whose support was paramount if the GC was to have any chance of success. Kofi Annan has emphasized that the nine principles of the Global Compact derive their lineage from various U.S. covenants of UN Agencies. However, some of these agencies have not been supportive of the Global Compact—for reasons of turf and out of concern about compromising their mission. These agencies also saw the Global Compact as the secretary-general's attempt to cozy up to the private sector.[14]

The negative reaction has not been confined to the UN agencies. The UN has also been faced with criticism from other prominent professional groups and from individuals in both the industrialized and the developing countries.[15] These groups have faulted the Global Compact both on general principles and on the choice of private sector partners as seen from the example of the initial group of companies joining the Global Compact. For example, Amnesty International notes that some of the companies joining have been notorious for their violations of human rights and for benefiting from sweatshop working conditions in developing countries.

> First . . . we would like to see companies who join the Global Compact make a public statement that they will be open to independent monitoring. . . . Secondly, it has to be reported publicly . . . [because] all the stakeholders are entitled to have the information resulting from that independent monitoring. And thirdly . . . a sanctions system has to be envisaged . . . so that companies who violate these principles cannot continue to benefit from the partnership. . . . We think that those three steps are absolutely essential if this initiative is to be effective, credible and win the trust of human rights organizations.[16]

In a similar vein, a prominent group of international scholars in law, economics, political science, and other professions, along with leaders of major international human rights organizations and groups advocating the cause of the poor, have expressed their opposition to the Global Compact in a letter to the secretary-general. The complete text of the letter appears in Appendix 7.1 later in this chapter.

The signatory group recognizes the importance of bringing business behavior in line with the universal values and standards represented by the nine principles of the Global Compact. However, the group raises a number of issues challenging the basic assumptions made in the Global Compact. The first assumption implies that there is "universal consensus that open markets are the primary force for development." This, however, is not so, as can be seen from the current "intense debate over the benefits and harms of free trade and market liberalization as currently promoted by the WTO and other institutions." Furthermore, there is no widespread agreement envisaged in the Global Compact's vision of "advancing popular social values as part and parcel of the globalization process." The GC's assertion is highly questionable to the effect that "globalization in its current form can be made sustainable and equitable, even if accompanied by the implementation of standards for human rights, labor, and the environment."

The letter takes issue with the secretary-general's support of the ideology that corporate-driven globalization is the sine qua non of economic development. The current globalization, which provides for unrestricted mobility of capital, but with highly restricted mobility of labor, is far from the ideal of competitive markets, since these conditions rob workers of their bargaining power by shifting the balance of power entirely to the multinational corporation.

The letter indicates that many of the corporations being asked to endorse the Global Compact believe that while corporations *should* be responsible, efforts by governments to hold corporations accountable to international values and standards are harmful to development, innovation, and human progress. This is contrary to all the available empirical evidence. The secretary-general and his professional staff pay some attention to the widespread evidence of human rights violations, sweatshop working conditions, forced child labor, and other instances of worker abuse. Contrary to the assertions of the apologists of new globalization, the authors assert that markets cannot allocate fairly and efficiently without clear and impartially enforced rules, established through open, democratic processes. Asking corporations, many of which are repeat offenders of both the law and commonly accepted standards of responsible conduct, to endorse a vague statement of commitment to human rights, labor, and environmental standards draws attention away from the need for more substantial action to hold corporations accountable for their behavior.

Finally, the authors take issue with one of the most flagrant assumptions made in the Global Compact with regard to its potential impact on the well-being of the poor workers in developing countries. The authors criticize the "purely voluntary nature of the Global Compact, and the lack of monitoring and enforcement provisions. We are well aware that many corporations would like nothing better than to wrap themselves in the flag of the United Nations in order to 'bluewash' their public image, while at the same time avoiding significant changes to their behavior. The question is how to get them to abide by the principles in the Global Compact. Without monitoring, the public will be no better able to assess the behavior, as opposed to the rhetoric, of corporations. Without independent assessment, the interpretation of whether a company is abiding by the Global Compact's principles or not will be left largely to the company itself."

The second letter (Appendix 7.2) takes a narrower approach and questions the credibility and veracity of the companies that have sought to become members of the Global Compact. It argues that they will "threaten the mission and integrity of the United Nations. Some of the companies in the partnership are simply inappropriate for partnerships with the United Nations." The letter offers a number of examples of the companies that it considers unfit to be associated with and benefit from the prestige of the United Nations.[17] It should be noted that many other companies and industry groups seeking affiliation with the Global Compact have been accused of similar misconduct, but are not mentioned in the letter.[18]

In the NGO Panel on Corporate Accountability, held at the UN on February 15, 2001, many NGOs expressed their concerns with the Global Compact and with what they considered to be its fatal flaws. Felicity Hill of the Women's International League for Peace and Freedom (WILPF) stated that her organization had serious reservations. "We worry that the rhetoric and verbal overtures to the NGO community are becoming more profuse and flowery, but our access to the UN is becoming more and more limited. . . . WILPF also questions the tactics of this venture—we feel it sent a very bad signal at a very crucial time."[19] James Paul, executive director of the Global Policy Forum, commented that the Compact embodies "a classically vague statement of principles that does not provide rules for specific situations or complaint procedures of any kind. Nor does it include any form of systematic monitoring. Instead the UN offers corporations an opportunity to exhibit their code-related 'best practices' on a special web site."[20] This allows companies to demonstrate adherence through carefully selected examples. The signatory corporations signing up are able to claim the legitimacy of a wide-ranging code under the prestige of the United Nations, while only having to adhere to it symbolically.[21] Kenny Bruno[22] stated that the "Global Compact assumes the corporate participation as voluntary. There is no monitoring or enforcement or even screening process. With the lack of these dynamics the Global Compact seems to be open to any kind of human, labor or environment rights violations."[23] Kenny Bruno and Joshua

Karliner in their report *Tangled Up in Blue* identified four major flaws which they consider to be fatal in the Global Compact and its partnership programs. These are: wrong companies, wrong relationships, wrong image, and no monitoring or enforcement.[24]

As an alternative to the Global Compact, an alliance of nongovernmental organizations and other groups has invited the secretary-general to join a "Citizens Compact" on the UN and corporations. The Citizens Compact is approved and supported by more than 70 human rights and environmental groups from around the world. It lays out a foundation for cooperation between the UN and nonbusiness, nongovernmental groups to work toward building better relationships between the UN and business, emphasizing the need for monitoring and enforcing a legal framework for corporate behavior.[25]

UN Response to the Critics of the Global Compact

The UN faced a number of challenges in promoting its Global Compact. Kofi Annan realized that the current world economic scene was fundamentally different from the recent past. Given the rise of free trade and emphasis on private markets, MNCs have emerged as important vehicles for expanding economic activity, income growth, and job creation in developing countries. Therefore, the UN must play an important role in this area. And given the character of existing relations between MNCs and UN agencies, it was felt that a clean start, and a direct approach by Kofi Annan, offered the most promising venue for enlisting cooperation from the MNCs. The organizers of the Global Compact, therefore, have played down the active involvement of other UN agencies, for fear that their historical antagonism toward the private sector would make the MNCs unwilling to come aboard.

The Global Compact attempts to use a more cooperative and conciliatory approach toward encouraging MNCs and countries involved—mostly developing countries—to work together in creating systems and procedures that will improve the working and living conditions of the workers and thereby comply with the spirit of the Global Compact. There is also emphasis on working at the local level. Early results in this direction are encouraging. A number of companies from developing countries are participating in Compact-sponsored meetings in which learning is emphasized through exchange of ideas and experiences. It is, however, too early to predict the extent to which local companies will actually take corrective actions in their plants by implementing the Compact's principles.

The experience to date, however, does not offer much hope. NGOs all over the world have been pushing MNCs and their local suppliers to comply with even the minimal labor standards of the countries where their overseas operations are located. While there is some success with regard to the plants owned and operated by the MNCs, this is not the case with regard to local entrepreneurs, who seem to be able to find infinite ways by which to thwart all external pressures to reform working conditions and human rights abuses in their factories.[26]

The organizers of the Global Compact at the United Nations have offered no effective response to the concerns raised by critics and have instead resorted to ambiguous arguments and pleas for patience. In the process, they have drastically changed the meaningful expectations of the benefits of the Global Compact that would be derived by the poorer countries and their people. Instead, the Global Compact at best will be a good old boys club and at worst a support group in which like-minded corporations will share their experiences and encourage each other to do better next time. Speaking for the Global Compact, John G. Ruggie, then assistant secretary-general and now a professor at the Kennedy School at Harvard University, wrote a letter replying to queries from critics. He claimed that the "reaction of the business community was favorable" to the creation of the Global Compact (a questionable assertion, as we shall see in the section that follows). He also stated that "before long, international labor and civil society organizations in human rights, the environment and development joined in the partnership" (an equally dubious assertion, as can be seen from the materials presented herein). With regard to the Citizens Compact, he indicated that the UN cannot associate with it because the measures called for in the Citizens Compact amount to regulation and monitoring, which were not within the purview of the UN. "Thus, the Global Compact is not a code, and it is not about monitoring and assessing corporate performance."

He went on to state: "Instead, ours is a learning model, utilizing the powerful tool of transparency. One of the core commitments companies make within the Global Compact is to go public at least once a year, on our Compact web site, with concrete steps they have taken to implement the principles of the Compact. The idea is to identify and disseminate good practices. Our labor and civil society organization partners—which represent hundreds of millions of people worldwide—will lend their expertise to that process. Indeed, you will be able to see and judge the same actions because all of the information will be in the public domain."[27]

In the opinion of this author, Ruggie's statement seems to beg the question rather than answer it. What is being learned? And how does this learning relate to meaningful transparency? Moreover, even if the UN does not wish to engage in regulating or monitoring practices, there is a great deal more that can be done to make this exercise more meaningful. For example, what is wrong with asking the companies—presenting their case studies of best practices—to indicate how these activities relate to one or more of the Compact's nine principles? Also, what is wrong with creating some sort of standardized benchmarks for various industries where participating corporations can further relate their success stories within a common framework and describe the implementation of the nine principles within each industry, in a manner that is relevant to each industry? In the absence of even the simplest measures of objectivity, consistency, and comparability, the Compact's standards are reduced to giving the companies carte blanche to present whatever evidence they care to provide and claim whatever success they care to ascribe to these "learning models" as meeting the intent of the Global Compact. Even so, the UN would be only too happy to concur.

The Response of MNCs to the Global Compact

Unfortunately for the Global Compact, the corporate response has also been hesitant, sparse, and disappointing. The Compact has faced skepticism from the MNCs whose support is critical to its success. Given the companies' past experience with UN-related initiatives, MNCs have been reluctant to respond favorably to UN-sponsored initiatives, seeing them as the first step toward international regulation of business. Public interest groups have already subjected MNCs to numerous pressures to improve their overseas operations with regard to worker rights and the environment. The question that remains to be answered is whether and to what extent MNCs will respond to the Global Compact in a more positive manner. In a dissenting opinion, Georg Kell responds, "While it is too early to make the point that the GC is motivating sufficient additional companies to join the effort, there are many indications that this indeed will be so." This was apparent from the many meetings held by the Global Compact organizers to bring the corporate sector into its fold.[28]

None of the multinational corporations currently participating in the Global Compact have expressed a willingness to submit their compliance with the Compact to independent external monitoring. Nor are they likely to do so in the foreseeable future. The corporate attitude was expressed in a most forthright manner by a spokesperson of the International Chamber of Commerce and Industry (ICC). As the secretary-general of the International Chamber of Commerce, Maria Livianos Cattui, put it, "Business would look askance at any suggestion involving external assessment of corporate performance, whether by special interest groups or by UN agencies. The Global Compact is a joint commitment to shared values, not a qualification to be met. It must not become a vehicle for governments to burden business with prescriptive regulations."[29]

The Global Compact seeks to gain commitment from the participating corporations to its principles and their implementation. The documents promoting the Global Compact state at some length the benefits and opportunities offered to companies joining the organization. The companies' participation in the Global Compact will help them in building relationships with other companies, government bodies, labor, NGOs, and international organizations, as well as partnering with UN agencies including the ILO, Office of the United Nations High Commissioner for Human Rights (OHCHR), United Nations Environmental Program (UNEP), United Nations Conference Trade and Development (UNCTAD), and United Nations Development Program (UNDP). With this participation, it is suggested that companies will be able to maximize their business opportunities by broadening the corporate vision to include the social dimension and by implementing responsible management policies and practices. Participation in the Global Compact is not difficult because it is not exclusive. All the Global Compact asks is that the participating companies need to "issue a clear statement of support for the Global Compact and its nine principles together with publicly advocating it and to provide a concrete example of progress made or a lesson learned in implementing the principles, for posting on the Global Compact's web site."[30] For the countries, the Global Compact urges them to participate "within the framework of the Compact [and] . . . actively support the principles by initiating and actively participating in projects in partnership with the UN.[31]

The Compact documents further state that "the success of the Global Compact will be measured by how effectively it provokes and stimulates action."[32] Unfortunately, this sums up the irony of the Global Compact, its supposed goals and objectives, and the dismal prospects that it will ever accomplish these goals. The Global Compact emphasizes the "principles" and avoids any mention of performance standards as to how these principles would be implemented. While the GC aims to measure its success through the performance of the participating companies, its own documents specifically disavow any attempt at defining benchmark standards to measure MNCs' adherence to these principles, or to set up any mechanisms, voluntary or otherwise, by which the companies' claims could be verified.

The aforementioned description of the mission and operating philosophy of the Global Compact makes it clear that the organizers of the Global

Compact do not want it to be seen as either setting standards or measuring performance against those standards. Instead, it is a forum to bring together like-minded companies to share ideas. What does one make of the Global Compact and its prospects for improving MNC performance in ameliorating the abusive condition of workers and promoting efforts to further human rights and ensure sustainable development? One can find the answer in a statement by Georg Kell and John Ruggie, the chief UN organizers and advocates of the Global Compact.

> One can readily appreciate why corporations would be attracted to the Global Compact. It offers one-stop shopping in three critical areas of greatest external pressure: human rights, environment, and labor standards thereby reducing their transaction costs. It offers the legitimacy of having corporations sign off onto something sponsored by the S-G—and, far more important, the legitimacy of acting on universally agreed to principles that are enshrined in covenants and declarations. And, the corporate sector fears that future international trade agreements will become saddled with environmental and social standards and collapse under their weight; in comparison, a stronger UN in these areas is far preferable. The NGO community is divided over the approach. The smaller and/or more radical NGOs believe that the UN has entered into a Faustian bargain at best. But the larger and more transnationalized NGOs have concluded that a strategy of "constructive engagement" will yield better results than confrontation, and they are cooperating with the UN. . . . The developing countries, which fully support efforts to keep international trade agreements from restrictions based on working conditions, human rights, and environmental protection, as unwarranted restraint of trade and protectionism, have yet to take a position. But they are also worried that working with MNCs to improve their practices could become a Trojan horse to put pressure on governments of those countries.[33]

The Global Compact: An Assessment

The Global Compact offers the secretary-general a great opportunity and a major challenge. If Kofi Annan can bring the developing countries to work together and develop a common set of policies impacting the issues covered under the Global Compact, he will effect a major paradigm shift in relations between the poorer countries and multinational corporations. It will minimize the self-destructive and "beggar thy neighbor" competition among the developing countries and create a stable and predictable regulatory environment for the MNCs. However, for reasons as yet un-clear, the organizers of the Global Compact, or the secretary-general, have not been explicit in their efforts to persuade the governments of the developing countries to take more positive steps toward enforcing their own laws and to cooperate among themselves to protect their workers and the environment and avoid being pressured by MNCs.

What should we make of the Global Compact or its intended purposes? All the covenants underlying the principles in the Global Compact are already in existence but have not been fully implemented, even by the member nations. Why should one expect that the Global Compact would, somehow, make a major difference in the status quo? After all, human rights, worker rights, and protection of the environment require regulations and enforcement mechanisms at the country level, which have been lacking in large parts of the world where these problems are particularly acute. How would the Global Compact change that?

The UN is superbly situated to play the role of honest broker or to provide a counterbalance between the developing countries and multinational corporations by fashioning benchmarks or minimum standards of conduct that would be followed by both the MNCs and the countries. There should be a common understanding of truly shared values of stable growth, development of internal markets, protection of workers' rights, and the rights of the countries to impose reasonable taxes to provide for investments in human and physical capital. These should be coupled with the rights of ownership, nondiscrimination between domestic and foreign competition, repatriation of profits, and protection from corruption and arbitrary laws and regulations. The gains from the international trade and investments can then be fairly shared for the benefit of all concerned.

The organizers of the Global Compact have anticipated these problems and have worked to minimize their potential adverse impact. This is evident from the documents that outline the activity domains of the Global Compact. They provide for equal opportunity to all companies of joining the Compact as long as they subscribe to its principles and programs. The Global Compact is not designed as a code of conduct. Rather, "it is meant to serve as a [frame] of reference to stimulate best practices and to bring about convergence around universally shared values."[34]

This statement sums up both the strength and the weakness of the Global Compact. To wit, if multinational corporations are *predisposed* in favor of creating a fair, safe, and coercion-free work environment, and to harness physical resources within the context of sustainable development, the Global Compact would support these activities in an environment of trust and mutual cooperation. Conversely, if a large number of multinationals are not inclined to take substantive action in this direction, the Compact will fail to achieve its goals. The drive by human rights and workers' rights groups to persuade MNCs to change their conduct toward workers in the poorer countries is now more than 10 years old, and the lack of success is certainly not for want of effort on the part of both NGOs and even a handful of socially responsible corporations.

Under these circumstances, the influx of corporations to join the Global Compact will suffer from adverse selection, that is, those with least incentive to change will be the most eager to join, so as to gain respectability through their affiliation with the Global Compact. MNCs with meaningful programs already in place will shy away from the Global Compact for fear of being tainted by the bad public image of the poorly performing companies. Supporters of the Global Compact dispute this line of argument by suggesting that many companies with no prior record of worker abuse have joined the initiative, and point to the examples of companies like Nokia, Cisco Systems, Novartis, and DuPont. It is also suggested that enlightened MNCs will want to join to cultivate the first mover's advantage whereby leading companies establish their reputations in early stages of an effort and thus garner greater benefit through enhanced corporation reputation, consumer loyalty, and public trust. Unfortunately, this is more easily said than proven in the case of the Global Compact. The untainted companies may want to join for the sake of goodwill, but they have not made any meaningful commitments to show the extent of their current compliance with the Compact's principles. Nor have they shown how far they need to go to fully comply with them. The Global Compact offers the easiest and most painless way of getting on the side of the angels, where no confessions are called for and no penance is ever necessary.

The negative aspects of this approach are easily predicted and have already become apparent. The initial meetings of the Global Compact attracted corporations that were suffering from adverse public pressure for their poor records in their overseas operations. These corporations were only too eager to gain respect by hanging onto Kofi Annan's coattails. This is the phenomenon of adverse selection discussed earlier. In order to encourage wider participation on the part of the MNCs, the Global Compact specifically disavowed any attempt to hold MNCs responsible for meaningful and measurable efforts in meeting the intent of the principles. It encouraged companies with superficial compliance records to join the bandwagon in the hope they would escape further public pressure and scrutiny of their conduct.

The Global Compact as a Good Fellows Club will probably attract more MNCs to participate in its programs and activities. However, it seems unlikely that it will make much of a contribution toward MNCs' compliance beyond public trumpeting of what they have done. MNCs are more likely to exploit the prestige of Kofi Annan and his office in getting people to look at the companies' public proclamations of their performance but not look too deeply into their actions.

The Global Compact suffers from an ambiguity of goals and inadequate linkages between its purposes and the means to accomplish them. If the primary purpose of the Global Compact is to encourage dialogue and share experiences among different groups for mutual learning, it is quite laudable in itself. In this case, a meaningful and measurable compliance with the Compact's principles will be an intended but second-order effect. However, if the Global Compact is designed to increase meaningful and measurable compliance with its principles as its primary goal, and if the dialogue and shared experiences are the only means to achieve this goal, the Compact is setting itself up for failure. The Compact has disavowed any effort toward setting standards by which compliance with the principles can be uniformly and objectively measured. Nor does it call for systems by which corporate compliance can be verified and made transparent. In the absence of these linkages, the Compact will suffer the fate of all such grand designs in which process becomes all too consuming and the end result becomes lost.

APPENDIX 7.1   Text of a Letter Addressed to Kofi Annan, Secretary-General of the United Nations, by a Group of Eminent Scholars and NGO Representatives from around the World, July 20, 2000

His Excellency Mr. Kofi Annan
Secretary-General
Room 3800
United Nations, NY 10017

Mr. Secretary-General,

We write to you as individuals who care deeply about the United Nations and on behalf of organizations that have worked for years to strengthen and support it.

We are writing to express our concern and reservations about the Global Compact.

On the one hand, we recognize the importance of bringing business behavior in line with the universal values and standards represented by the nine principles of the Global Compact.

However, there are two aspects of the Global Compact that trouble us. First, the text implies a universal consensus that open markets are the primary force for development. As you are aware, there is intense debate over the benefits and harms of free trade and market liberalization as currently promoted by the WTO [World Trade Organization] and other institutions.

Many sectors of society do not concur with the Global Compact's vision of advancing popular social values "as part and parcel of the globalization process," to "ensure that markets remain open." Many do not agree with the assumption of the Global Compact that globalization in its current form can be made sustainable and equitable, even if accompanied by the implementation of standards for human rights, labor, and the environment.

We recognize that corporate-driven globalization has significant support among governments and business. However, that support is far from universal. Your support for this ideology, as official UN policy, has the effect of delegitimizing the work and aspirations of those sectors that believe that an unregulated market is incompatible with equity and environmental sustainability.

Our second concern is the purely voluntary nature of the Global Compact, and the lack of monitoring and enforcement provisions. We are well aware that many corporations would like nothing better than to wrap themselves in the flag of the United Nations in order to "bluewash" their public image, while at the same time avoiding significant changes to their behavior. The question is how to get them to abide by the principles in the Global Compact.

Without monitoring, the public will be no better able to assess the behavior, as opposed to the rhetoric, of corporations. Without independent assessment, the interpretation of whether a company is abiding by the Global Compact's principles or not will be left largely to the company itself.

Many of the corporations being asked to endorse the Global Compact suggest that while corporations *should* be responsible, efforts by governments to hold corporations accountable to international values and standards are harmful to development, innovation and human progress. Many in the NGO community reject this premise. On the contrary, we stress that markets cannot allocate fairly and efficiently without clear and impartially enforced rules, established through open, democratic processes. Asking corporations, many of which are repeat offenders of both the law and commonly accepted standards of responsibility, to endorse a vague statement of commitment to human rights, labor and environmental standards draws attention away from the need for more substantial action to hold corporations accountable for their behavior.

As you are aware, the UN Subcomission on the Promotion and Protection of Human Rights is currently drafting a legal instrument on TNCs [transnational corporations] and human rights. We would look for your support for this initiative.

Although it may take years before we can hope to achieve a binding legal framework for the transnational behavior of business in the human rights, environmental and labor realms, we believe it is necessary to start down that road, and to begin building the political support for that goal now. Therefore, the undersigned groups respectfully request you to re-assess the Global Compact, taking into account the concerns above.

In addition, we offer an alternative, the Citizens Compact, for your consideration. The Citizens Compact stresses the importance of a legal framework for corporate behavior in the global economy. The Citizens Compact also provides suggested guidelines for interactions between the UN and the private sector. We invite your comments on the Citizens Compact and hope you will consider endorsing it.

Again, we believe that bringing corporate behavior in line with the universal principles and values of the United Nations is a goal of extremely high importance. We look forward to working with you and the entire United Nations system toward that goal.

Sincerely,

Upendra Baxi, *professor of law, University of Warrick, UK, and former vice chancellor, University of Delhi (India)*; **Roberto Bissio**, *Third World Institute (Uruguay)*; **Thilo Bode**, *executive director, Greenpeace International (Netherlands)*; **Walden Bello**, *director, Focus on the Global South (Thailand)*; **John Cavanagh**, *director, Institute for Policy Studies (United States)*; **Susan George**, *associate director, Transnational Institute (Netherlands)*; **Olivier Hoedeman**, *Corporate Europe Observatory (Netherlands)*; **Joshua Karliner**, *executive director, Transnational Resource & Action Center (United States)*; **Martin Khor**, *Director, Third World Network (Malaysia)*; **Miloon Kothari**, *coordinator, International NGO Committee on Human Rights in Trade and Investment (India)*; **Smitu Kothari**, *president, International Group for Grassroots Initiatives (India)*; **Sara Larrain**, *coordinator, Chile Sustentable (Chile)*; **Jerry Mander**, *director, International Forum on Globalization (United States)*; **Ward Morehouse**, *director, Program on Corporations, Law and Democracy (United States)*; **Atila Roque**, *programme coordinator, Brazilian Institute of Economic and Social Analysis (Brazil)*; **Elisabeth Sterken**, *national director, INFACT Canada/ IBFAN North America*; **Yash Tandon**, *director, International South Group Network*

(*Zimbabwe*); **Vickey Tauli-Corpuz**, *coordinator, Tebtebba* (*Indigenous Peoples' International Centre for Policy Research and Education*), *and Asia Indigenous Women's Network* (*Philippines*); **Etienne Vernet**, *Food and Agriculture Campaigner Ecoropa* (*France*)

APPENDIX 7.2   Text of the Second Letter Addressed to Kofi Annan, Secretary-General of the United Nations, by a Group of Eminent Scholars and NGO Representatives from around the World, July 25, 2000

His Excellency Mr. Kofi Annan
Secretary-General
Room 3800
United Nations, NY 10017

Mr. Secretary-General,

On July 20th, a number of us wrote asking you to re-assess the Global Compact and to join us in a "Citizens Compact." We are writing again today to express our shock upon learning the identities of the corporate partners for the Global Compact and our disappointment in the Guidelines for Cooperation Between the United Nations and the Business Community.

In the July 20th letter, we expressed concern that the UN is endorsing a specific vision of corporate-led globalization that is opposed by many sectors of civil society. We also suggested that the purely voluntary nature of the Global Compact may distract from the need for a legal framework to hold corporations accountable internationally.

We wrote to you as individuals who care deeply about the United Nations and on behalf of organizations that have worked for years to strengthen and support it.

Now, after reviewing the July 17th Guidelines and the initial list of companies joining the Global Compact, we believe that the Global Compact and related partnerships threaten the mission and integrity of the United Nations.

Some of the companies in the partnership are simply inappropriate for partnerships with the United Nations.

Nike, one of the Global Compact partners and an international symbol of sweatshops and corporate greed, is the target of one of the most active global campaigns for corporate accountability. The company has made announcements of changes to its behavior only after enormous public pressure. It has also aggressively opposed the only union and human rights group supported independent monitoring program—the Worker Rights Consortium (WRC).

CEO Phil Knight withdrew a $30 million donation to the University of Oregon after the University joined the WRC. Nike also cut its multimillion-dollar contracts with the University of Michigan and Brown University after they joined the WRC. Nike became a sweatshop poster child not just through complicity in labor abuses but through active searching for countries with non-union labor, low wages, and low environmental standards for its manufacturing operations. This has made Nike a leader in the "race to the bottom"—a trend that epitomizes the negative tendencies of corporate-led globalization.

Shell is a corporation with a history of complicity in human rights abuses, most infamously in Nigeria. Its operations there are also notorious for environmental contamination and double standards. Shell has adopted sophisticated rhetoric about its social responsibilities, but it has not shown understanding, let alone remorse, about its own role. For example, on its web site, Shell posts a photograph of a pro-Ogoni rally, without acknowledging that the Ogoni people's protests have been against Shell itself.

BP Amoco is another company with sophisticated rhetoric on environmental and social issues. But their actions do not measure up. CEO John Browne admits that climate change is a problem for any oil company, yet his company continues to search for oil and gas even in remote and pristine regions, while investments in renewable energy are a pittance compared with the size of the corporation and its investments in ongoing fossil fuel exploration and production.

Rio Tinto Plc is a British mining corporation which has created so many environment, human rights, and development problems that a global network of trade unions, indigenous peoples, church groups, communities and activists has emerged to fight its abuses. For instance, the company stands accused of complicity in or direct violations of environmental, labor and human rights in Indonesia, Papua New Guinea, Philippines, Namibia, Madagascar, the United States and Australia, among others.

Novartis is engaged in an aggressive public relations and regulatory battle to force consumers and farmers to accept genetically engineered food, without full testing for potential harms and without full access to information. The behavior of Novartis in the area of genetically engineered foods is diametrically opposed to the precautionary principle, one of the principles of the Global Compact.

These are but a few of the corporate endorsers of the Global Compact whose historical and current core activities run counter to the spirit and the letter of the Compact itself.

The Guidelines on Cooperation Between the United Nations and the Business Community which you issued on July 17th raise a further, related set of issues. These guidelines state that "business entities that are complicit in human rights abuses . . . are not eligible for partnership." The inclusion of Shell in the Global Compact violates those guidelines.

The Guidelines also state that a "business entity may be authorized to use the name and emblem" of the United Nations. As the United Nations Development Programme has noted, when a company uses the UN logo, "a mutual image transfer inevitably takes place." It is dismaying to contemplate such an image transfer between Nike, Shell, or Rio Tinto and the UN. The UN logo and the Nike swoosh do not belong together.

The Guidelines state that the use of the UN name may only be used when the "principal purpose is to show support for the purposes and activities of the UN. . . ." This guideline does not take into account the modern practice of branding, by which a corporation sells its image as much as its manufactured products. Nike, one of the Global Compact partners, is a pioneer of modern branding. It is obvious that the use of the UN name and logo by corporations will be not only for short-term profit but for the long-term business goal of positive brand image. The UN must not become complicit in the positive branding of corporations that violate UN principles.

Given that there is no provision for monitoring a corporation's record in abiding by UN principles, the Guidelines' modalities for partnerships are quite susceptible to abuse. For example, a company with widespread labor or environmental violations may be able to join with the UN in a relatively minor cooperative project, and gain all the benefits of association with the UN without any responsibilities. The UN would have no way to determine whether the company, on balance, is contributing to UN goals or preventing their realization.

In short, Mr. Secretary-General, the Global Compact partnership and the Guidelines for Cooperation do not "ensure the integrity and independence" of the United Nations. They allow business entities with poor records to "bluewash" their image by wrapping themselves in the flag of the United Nations. They favor corporate-driven globalization rather than the environment, human health, local communities, workers, farmers, women and the poor.

Again, we urge you to re-assess the Global Compact and its partners. We urge you to re-evaluate your overall approach to UN-corporate partnerships. The mission and integrity of the United Nations are at stake.

Sincerely,

[The list of signatories is the same as in Appendix 7.1.]

Notes

1. Georg Kell and John Gerard Ruggie, "Global Markets and Social Legitimacy: The Case of 'Global Compact,'" paper presented at an international conference, *Governing the Public Domain beyond the Era of the Washington Consensus? Redrawing the Line between the State and the Market*, York University, Toronto, Canada, November 4–6, 1999, 10. See also Sandrine Tesner and Georg Kell, *The United Nations and Business* (New York: St. Martin's Press, 2000); United Nations, *The Global Compact* (New York: United Nations, 2000).
2. It should be noted here that the author of this book worked as a consultant-adviser to the Executive Office of the Secretary-General on issues pertaining to the implementation strategies of the Global Compact.
3. Kell and Ruggie, "Global Markets and Social Legitimacy."
4. United Nations, *The United Nations and Business: The Global Compact* (New York: United Nations, DPI/2074/D, October 1999).
5. J. Davidow, "Multinationals, Host Governments and Restrictive Business Practices," *Columbia Journal of World Business* 15:2 (Summer 1980), 14–19; S. Dell, *The United Nations and International Business* (Durham, N.C.: Duke University Press, 1990); W. J. Feld, *Multinational Corporations and U.N. Politics* (New York: Pergamon, 1980); W. Fikentscher, "United Nations Codes of Conduct: New Paths to International Law," *American Journal of Comparative Law* 30:3 (1982), 577–604; J. M. Kline, *International Codes and Multinational Business: Setting Guidelines for International Business Operations* (Westport, Conn: Quorum Books, 1985); I. K. Minta, "The Code of Conduct on TNCs: In the Twilight Zone of International Law," *CTC Reporter* 25 (Spring 1988), 29–33, 37; P. Robinson, *The Question of a Reference to International Law in the United Nations Code of Conduct on Transnational Corporations*, UNCTC Current Studies, Series A, no. 1 (New York: UNCTC, 1986); W. Sprote, "Negotiations on a United Nations Code of Conduct on Transnational Corporations," *German Yearbook of International Law* 33 (1990), 331–348; UN Centre on Transnational Corporations (UNCTC), *The New Code Environment*, Series A, no. 16 (New York: UNCTC, April 1990); United States Congress, "Status of U.N.

Code on Transnational Corporations," Hearing before the Subcommittee on Human Rights and International Organizations of the Committee on Foreign Affairs, 101st Congress, 1st Session, November 15, 1989; M. L. Weidenbaum, "The UN as a Regulator of Private Enterprise," *Notre Dame Journal of Law, Ethics and Public Policy* 1:3 (1985); S. Prakash Sethi, *Multinational Corporations and the Impact of Public Advocacy on Corporate Strategy: Nestlé and the Infant Formula Controversy* (Boston: Kluwer Academic Publishers, 1994; pap. ed. Notre Dame, Ind.: University of Notre Dame Press, 2001). See also S. Prakash Sethi and B. B. Bhalla, "A New Perspective on International Social Regulation of Business: An Evaluation of the Compliance Status of the International Code of Marketing of Breast-Milk Substitutes," *Journal of Socio-Economics*, 22:2 (1993), 141–158.

6. Reed Abelson, "Crisis in the Balkans: Aid; In a Wave of Balkan Charity Comes Drug Aid of Little Use," *New York Times* (June 29, 1999); "Annan, 18 Nations Retooling Civil Rule in Kosovo; Secretary-General Elicits Pledges of Interim Police to Back U.N. Force There," *Baltimore Sun* (July 1, 1999); Reed Abelson, "Report Outlines Problems with Donated Drugs Sent Overseas," *New York Times* (August 16, 1999); David Pilling, "Up to Two-Fifths of Drug Donations Not Requested: Groups Dumping Old Medicines on Developing Countries, Say Critics," *Financial Times* London Edition 1 (August 16, 1999), 16.

7. Claudia H. Deutsch, "Unlikely Allies with the United Nations," *New York Times* (December 10, 1999), C1.

8. See www.corpwatch.org, "Other Partnerships," Alliance for a Corporate-Free UN.

9. Ibid.

10. "UNICEF Accused of Forming Alliance with Baby Food Industry," *British Medical Journal* (July 15, 2000).

11. Refer supra note 5.

12. Kenny Bruno and Joshua Karliner, *Tangled Up in Blue: Corporate Partnerships at the United Nations*, CorpWatch, www.corpwatch.org (September 1).

13. Sandrine Tesner, *How to Do Business with the United Nations: The 1997 Update* (United Nations Association of the USA, UNA-USA, 1997), 226. See also Sandrine Tesner with the collaboration of Georg Kell, *The United Nations and Business* (New York: St. Martin's Press, 2000), 53.

14. Bruno and Karliner, *Tangled Up in Blue*.

15. Ibid.

16. Excerpts from the statement of Pierre Sane, Amnesty International, June 26, 2000.

17. For details of accusations against these companies please refer to Appendix 7.2. Also refer to web site of CorpWatch (www.corpwatch.org): Asia-Pacific Human Rights Network, "Associating with the Wrong Company," July 13, 2001; Tim Connor of Global Exchange, "Still Waiting for Nike to Respect the

Right to Organize," June 28, 2001; report by CorpWatch, "UN and Corporations Fact Sheet" (under Campaigns: Corporate-Free UN), March 22, 2001.

18. Refer to www.corpwatch.org, "The Global Compact Corporate Partners," Alliance for a Corporate-Free UN, September 1, 2000; this includes articles like: Elizabeth Neuffer, "UN: Aventis Accused of Breaking Global Compact," *Boston Globe*, June 15, 2001; Nityanand Jayram, "Norsk Hydro: Global Compact Violator," October 18, 2001; Corporate Europe Observatory, "High Time for UN to Break Partnership with ICC," July 25, 2001; Nityanand Jayram, "Inconsistencies Galore: A Timeline on Unilever's Mercury Dumping in India," October 4, 2001.

19. Information from Global Policy Forum, which can be found in www.globalpolicy.org, NGO Panel on Corporate Accountability Held at the United Nations, February 15, 2001, under the headline "Global Compact with Corporations: 'Civil Society' Responds."

20. www.unglobalcompact.org.

21. Please refer to supra note 18.

22. Mr. Bruno is a longtime social justice and environmental activist. He is currently associated with TRAC and CorpWatch.

23. Go to supra note 18.

24. Bruno and Karliner, *Tangled Up in Blue*.

25. Ibid.

26. In a communication to this author, the UN's Georg Kell states: "The Compact is embraced by many businesspeople in developing countries. By engaging business leaders from developing countries, we are de facto bringing universal values into countries where governments reject such notions on grounds of principle. This point is quite relevant as it may have far-reaching implications for many related arenas, including international trade. It is in these countries where the learning curve can be steepest and where the UN's comparative advantage is greatest."

27. Excerpts from a letter written by John G. Ruggie, assistant secretary-general, UN, dated July 21, 2000.

28. Communication with the author.

29. Maria Livanos Cattaui, "Yes to Annan's 'Global Compact' If It Isn't a License to Meddle," *International Herald Tribune* (July 26, 2000).

30. The Global Compact, published by the Global Compact Office, United Nations, January 2001. See also the Global Compact web site, www.unglobalcompact.org.

31. Ibid.

32. Ibid.

33. Kell and Ruggie, "Global Markets and Social Legitimacy," 11.

34. Tesner, *How to Do Business*, 226. See also Tesner with Kell, *United Nations and Business*, 53.

CHAPTER 8

The Fair Labor Association: Problems with an Industry-Based Approach to Codes of Conduct

The Fair Labor Association (FLA) is the successor organization to President Bill Clinton's Apparel Industry Partnership (AIP), which was created in 1996 in response to persistent criticism by human rights and labor groups about the use of child labor, slave wages, and sweatshop conditions in factories in Latin America and Asia, which manufactured apparel, shoes, and other low-tech, labor-intensive products for major U.S. brands and retail chains. These groups chided the White House for lack of action on the part of the Democratic president. In 1996, President Clinton and Secretary of Labor Robert Reich created a presidential task force whose goal was to work toward eliminating sweatshops. Known as the White House Apparel Industry Partnership, the task force consisted of companies, trade unions, human rights groups, and religious groups, and convened under the auspices of the White House.[1]

The idea was to organize an association that would set workplace standards for the industry and establish a means of monitoring compliance with those standards. The unions and several of the human rights groups fought hard to set strict criteria that would measurably improve workers' lives. The NGOs and the union representatives demanded that a living wage must be

135

part of the standards, but the companies would not yield on that point. Instead, the companies insisted on keeping the standards loose enough to encourage other companies to join the effort. The group was deadlocked and took nearly a year to produce a draft code of conduct and a framework agreement on monitoring.[2]

Organization of FLA

Consequently, corporate representatives, along with some human rights groups, met in secret, and in November 1998 a subgroup of the AIP announced the formation of a new group called the Fair Labor Association (FLA) to oversee compliance with the code. The Lawyers Committee for Human Rights, the National Consumer League, the RFK Memorial Center for Human Rights, and the International Labor Rights Fund joined Nike, Reebok, Liz Claiborne, Phillips–Van Heusen, Patagonia, L. L. Bean, and Business for Social Responsibility to support the FLA.

As presently constituted, the FLA is a nonprofit organization that includes 13 apparel and footwear manufacturers and retailers: Adidas-Salomon A.G., Charles River Apparel, Eddie Bauer, GEAR for Sports, Jostens Inc., Joy Athletic, Levi Strauss & Co., Liz Claiborne Inc., Nike, Patagonia, Phillips–Van Heusen Corporation, Polo Ralph Lauren Corporation, and Reebok International Ltd. Of these, six are represented on FLA's board: Reebok, Nike, Phillips–Van Heusen, Adidas-Solomon, Levi Strauss, and Liz Claiborne. In addition, approximately 590 companies have affiliations with the FLA in various categories according to the level of participation; for example, collegiate-licensed products are category B licensees.[3] In addition, 160 colleges and universities are affiliated with the FLA to ensure that companies producing goods as their licensees are operating in accordance with FLA principles and the workplace code of conduct. That the FLA includes various human rights and labor rights groups, such as the International Labor Rights Fund, the Lawyers Committee for Human Rights, and the National Consumers League,[4] is a notable feature.

The group's formation was not without controversy. One of the nation's largest unions, the Union of Needletrades, Industrial and Textile Employees (UNITE), and a church-affiliated group, the Interfaith Center on Corporate Responsibility (ICCR), which had participated in the discussions leading to FLA's formation, decided not to join the group because of weak monitoring procedures.[5]

From one perspective, the FLA personifies the advantages of a group-based effort toward code creation and implementation. It has a board of directors that includes major constituent groups. It oversees the FLA's operations, sets policy guidelines, and monitors corporate compliance. A common code, widely applied, offers economies of scale in terms of field audits, thereby lowering the cost of individual audits. It spreads overhead and training costs over a large number of companies and factories. It allows for sharing of information and field experience among participating companies. The combined purchasing power of the member companies also ensures that local manufacturers will have greater incentives to comply with the code or risk being excluded from major foreign markets. The participating companies include a vast segment of the manufacturing sector in developing countries, with over 3,500 factories covering almost 3 million workers in more than 70 countries. The participation of local NGOs in conducting field audits engages in-country community groups and thereby makes effective use of their familiarity with local conditions.

FLA's Mission

The stated mission of FLA is to improve working conditions in factories in the United States and abroad. To this end, the FLA Charter Agreement establishes an industry-wide code of conduct and monitoring system (Exhibit 8.1). The agreement lays the foundation for an independent monitoring system but has not yet been incorporated into the FLA's operations. The FLA accredits independent monitors to inspect factories that manufacture products for its participating companies and for licensees of its affiliated universities, determines whether these companies are in compliance with the FLA's standards, and issues public reports that will give consumers the information they need to make informed purchasing decisions.[6]

Unfortunately, the FLA is also encumbered with all the drawbacks associated with industry-wide approaches,[7] as described in earlier chapters. It has a bureaucratic and highly structured governance system whose overriding concern seems to be protecting the member companies from overzealous NGOs, aggressive members of the community, and the news media. Every element of the process, starting with the content and wording of the FLA code's principles, monitoring protocols, scope of auditing, analysis of data, and issuance of reports for public dissemination, reflects political compromises designed to protect the vital interests and strategies of its most powerful members—the corporations. As a consequence, FLA promises more than it can or ever will be able to deliver. Both the

Exhibit 8.1   Workplace Code of Conduct

Forced Labor. There shall not be any use of forced labor, whether in the form of prison labor, indentured labor, bonded labor or otherwise.

Child Labor. No person shall be employed at an age younger than 15 (or 14 where the law of the country of manufacture allows) or younger than the age for completing compulsory education in the country of manufacture where such age is higher than 15.

Harassment or Abuse. Every employee shall be treated with respect and dignity. No employee shall be subject to any physical, sexual, psychological or verbal harassment or abuse.

Nondiscrimination. No person shall be subject to any discrimination in employment, including hiring, salary, benefits, advancement, discipline, termination or retirement, on the basis of gender, race, religion, age, disability, sexual orientation, nationality, political opinion, or social or ethnic origin.

Health and Safety. Employers shall provide a safe and healthy working environment to prevent accidents and injury to health arising out of, linked with, or occurring in the course of work or as a result of the operation of employer facilities.

Freedom of Association and Collective Bargaining. Employers shall recognize and respect the right of employees to freedom of association and collective bargaining.

Wages and Benefits. Employers recognize that wages are essential to meeting employees' basic needs. Employers shall pay employees, as a floor, at least the minimum wage required by local law or the prevailing industry wage, whichever is higher, and shall provide legally mandated benefits.

Hours of Work. Except in extraordinary business circumstances, employees shall (i) not be required to work more than the lesser of (a) 48 hours per week and 12 hours overtime or (b) the limits on regular and overtime hours allowed by the law of the country of manufacture or, where the laws of such country do not limit the hours of work, the regular work week in such country plus 12 hours overtime and (ii) be entitled to at least one day off in every seven-day period.

Exhibit 8.1 *(Continued)*

Overtime Compensation. In addition to their compensation for regular hours of work, employees shall be compensated for overtime hours at such premium rate as is legally required in the country of manufacture or, in those countries where such laws do not exist, at a rate at least equal to their regular hourly compensation rate.

* * *

Any Company that determines to adopt the Workplace Code of Conduct shall, in addition to complying with all applicable laws of the country of manufacture, comply with and support the Workplace Code of Conduct in accordance with the attached Principles of Monitoring and shall apply the higher standard in cases of differences or conflicts. Any Company that determines to adopt the Workplace Code of Conduct also shall require its licensees and contractors and, in the case of a retailer, its suppliers to comply with applicable local laws and with this Code in accordance with the attached Principles of Monitoring and to apply the higher standard in cases of differences or conflicts.

Source: Fair Labor Association web site, www.fairlabor.org.

governance structure and operating procedures guarantee that the FLA's potential and mandate will largely remain unfulfilled.

Governance Structure

FLA's board of directors consists of six industry representatives, six labor/NGO representatives, and three university representatives. The first university member was included in June 1999, and in October 2001 university representatives were increased from one to three.[8] Except for the university members, the board structure was inherited from AIP. The industry representatives were elected by the participating companies, while the NGO members were elected by the labor/NGO members of the initial AIP members. The board also has a chairperson who is jointly selected by the current members. All future board members are to be selected by their respective groups. The practical impact of the process is that industry representatives will come from only member companies, while labor/NGO members may come from outside the current group, but are unlikely to do so. In any case, to date no outside NGO member has been elected to the board. Even a cursory knowledge of board structure and dynamics should make it obvious that this board is unlikely to represent the public interest over that of the FLA and its constituent members.

The representative character of the labor/NGO members is even more dubious. These members represent only the NGOs that are part of the FLA. This group cannot be said to represent the broad and highly diverse NGO community involved in labor and human rights issues. As board members, they are put in a difficult position. They must represent their broader constituencies to protect their legitimacy. And yet they must constantly make compromises in order to meet the demands of industry members to ensure the FLA's survival. The relative weakness of the labor/NGO board members is already evident when the substance of the FLA's code of conduct, its monitoring procedures, and the public dissemination of its findings are examined.

Analysis of FLA's Code of Conduct

The FLA's code of conduct is a brief document consisting of nine principles covering work-related issues. In general, the code's proscriptions apply to violations of legally mandated provisions of local laws. In addition, the code contains provisions protecting employees from harassment, discrimination, and forced labor. It also requires employers to recognize workers' rights to freedom of association and collective bargaining. While the code provides for a safe and healthy work environment, it fails to provide even a broad definition of the subjects that should be covered under this principle. The code is also silent in the area of dormitories and food. These rank among the more serious problems regarding the plants and workers that are the focus of the code.

In general, the code is quite similar to the multitude of codes that have been promulgated by companies and industry groups that generally employ low-skilled or unskilled workers abroad, in such industries as apparel, toys, and shoes. Similarly, the FLA code is suffused with statements of high intent. It lacks specifics as to the scope of the issues encompassed by these principles, and the objective, quantifiable standards by which compliance with these principles shall be measured. It leaves large areas of compliance and performance evaluation to the discretion of field auditors and monitors. Given next is a brief discussion of various items in the code and the issues they raise in terms of their interpretation and implementation.

WAGES

The FLA's code calls for the member companies to pay the local minimum wage, which may be quite low, even allowing for local cost of living conditions. For example, in Indonesia, Reebok (a founding member of the FLA) pays workers a base wage of $23 per month, while a recent study commissioned by Global Exchange[9] found that the bare subsistence wage for one person was $35 per month. According to the National Labor Committee, Liz Claiborne, another founding FLA member, is paying assembly line workers in El Salvador $134 per month, which is just 51 percent of the cost of the basic basket of essential goods and services for the average Salvadoran family.[10]

The FLA initially attacked the living wage concept, saying that it is difficult to define. However, it later changed its stance when a Living Wage Summit for the Garment Industry, organized by Sweatshop Watch and Global Exchange in July 1998, produced a working definition of the concept.[11] The FLA has since requested the Department of Labor to undertake a study of wages and basic needs data. It will then review the data "to consider their implications, if any" on FLA standards. The FLA does not, however, mention what action, if any, it will take when it receives the findings of the study. It should be noted that any changes in the FLA's stance in this area would require a supermajority vote, which makes such modifications highly unlikely.

EXCESSIVE OVERTIME AND INADEQUATE OVERTIME COMPENSATION

The FLA's Workplace Code of Conduct allows employers, where it is not in violation of local laws, to mandate a six-day, 60-hour workweek (48 hours with 12 hours of overtime) and even more in the case of "extraordinary business circumstances"—a term that is left undefined. In addition, the FLA's standards call for employees to be compensated at the legal rate or, where none exists, at a rate at least equal to their regular hourly compensation. In other words, in the absence of legally mandated overtime rates, the FLA's standards would allow the member companies to require their workers to work overtime (even in excess of local laws) at regular and *not* overtime rates. In most countries, overtime rates are generally considered to be 150 percent of regular wages on normal days, and 200 percent on weekends and holidays.

WORKERS' RIGHT TO ORGANIZE

The FLA's code provisions in this regard are quite similar to those found in a variety of other industry-based and individual company codes. Although we would expect that the FLA's code would contain more specificity, given the blue chip character of its member companies and the participation of human rights and labor groups, the FLA's code does not provide for any standards or actions where there is a clear or extreme human rights violation, or where workers' right to organize is suppressed, as in Myanmar or China. Commenting on the clause, UNITE's Alan Howard said, "This presumably means you can let the army in the factory to put down a strike, as long as you don't pick up the phone to call them."[12]

Compliance Procedures and External Monitoring

The code requires member companies to establish internal procedures to implement the code, inform and educate workers about the code, and create channels of communication between workers and management. It also requires companies to train internal monitors to ensure code compliance.[13]

The code provides for the training and certification of external monitors, who would then undertake on-site audits of local plants. During the first three years, the FLA will partially subsidize the cost of field audits on a sliding scale, from a $600,000 grant from the U.S. State Department. Thereafter, each company will bear the entire cost of external monitoring.[14]

During the first year, the participating companies will be reimbursed 50 percent of their external audit costs; these will be reduced to 45 percent in the second year, and 30 percent in the third year—all subsequent audits will be paid for in full by the companies. Furthermore, if there is a complaint about a particular factory, the executive director of the FLA can call for additional monitoring, in which case the FLA will reimburse the participating company for the cost of such additional external monitoring.

Presumably, this is being done to encourage the companies to initiate third-party audits, which these companies may be reluctant to do because of the cost burden. However, as discussed in Chapter 12 of this book, the costs of such audits are insignificant when they are viewed as a percentage of the annual wage costs, the number of workers involved, and ex-factory cost of goods produced. These costs are also eminently justified, in their own right, when one considers the number and magnitude of local labor law violations found in a majority of plants, and the consequent loss of wages by the workers.

External Monitors

Participating companies can choose their own monitors, provided they are accredited by the FLA. Although many of these monitors are NGOs, this is not necessarily the case in all instances. It stands to reason that a company will strive to find a monitoring group that is likely to be flexible and appreciative of the company's concerns. As the Interfaith Center on Corporate Responsibility said in rejecting the agreement, "we are concerned that large auditing firms will become the FLA's 'independent monitors,' marginalizing participation by NGOs who know the local context and are more likely to have the trust of workers."

This situation is further complicated because the monitors must initially submit their findings to the company, and only secondarily to the FLA.[15] In this scheme of things, the companies become the de facto clients. The arrangement runs the risk of compromising the independence of external monitors.

Selection of Companies to Be Audited

The FLA monitoring standards call for auditing 30 percent of a participating company's vendors. These vendors are to be selected by the participating company, although the FLA's board chairperson has the final authority as to selection. This is a serious flaw in the system and undermines the credibility of the monitoring process.

The FLA does not offer any explanation as to how the 30 percent will be selected and about the company's right to select them. The system is rigged to the advantage of the companies. Since the companies have the best information about their vendor base, it stands to reason that they will choose vendors that are most likely to meet the code standards. Otherwise, why would the companies care which vendor is audited? The veto power of the executive director is more imaginary than real. At best, the executive director will affect selection at the margin where there is clear misuse of the selection privilege on the part of the company. To wit, the executive director must have added information—which is independently obtained and not received from the participating company—about a particular vendor. This scenario is likely only in rare cases. And what about the 70 percent of vendors that were not included in the first place? What type of data would the board chairperson have about these companies? The FLA argues that it has access to internal audit reports of all the vendors, and not just those that are to be included in the group to be externally monitored. Again, there is a large gap between theory and reality. It is highly unlikely that a handful of FLA staff members will have the necessary resources and expertise to examine the internal reports of more than 3,500 vendors (a conservative number) and make informed decisions about the choice of companies to be audited. In reality, they would have little choice but to approve the selections made by the participating companies.

The problem with this process is information asymmetry that leads to adverse selection. Since the companies will almost always have more information, they will choose those vendors that are most likely to have complied with the code. And yet the primary objective of the FLA is to find vendors that are not in compliance with the FLA code and to induce them to improve their performance.

If the FLA and the participating companies are serious about achieving their stated objectives, why not use the random sample selection process? A random sample, scientifically selected, offers a number of advantages:

- The sample represents the entire vendor population. If properly implemented, a random sample of under 10 percent may be sufficient to reflect the compliance character of a company's entire vendor population. This will significantly reduce the cost of external monitoring and allow for more intensive audits of the vendors chosen for such audits.

- Since every vendor has an equal chance of being audited, there is strong incentive toward self-improvement by all vendors.

Flaws in the Monitoring System

On paper, the plan appears to be quite comprehensive. However, a close examination shows the plan to be deficient in objectivity and specificity as to measures of performance. The code lacks substantive measures to penalize companies that are found to have committed gross violations or demonstrated repeated noncompliant behavior. When combined with the severely limited scope of disclosure, the FLA loses most of its supposed power to effect reforms by bringing recalcitrant and noncompliant companies to the light of public scrutiny. In the absence of meaningful internal control measures, and with sufficient disincentive from public disclosure, the FLA and its entire enforcement and monitoring structure is reduced to a thin patina of legitimacy that does more to shield the participating companies from adverse publicity than to make the improvements in the working and living conditions of the workers. As stated earlier, the result should have been expected, given the limitations of the group-based approach and the governance structure and operating procedures enshrined in the FLA's charter.

The FLA's "Monitoring Guidance and Compliance Benchmarks" together with its training manuals provide details as to how the code's principles shall be interpreted and the company performance measured.[16] Unfortunately, these standards are defined in qualitative terms whose acceptable quantitative equivalence is left to the discretion of the external auditors. In other words, given a particular condition, it is quite likely that different auditors will draw different conclusions. The external monitoring system is further weakened by lack of auditing protocols about the sampling standards that should be followed in choosing the types and numbers of company records to be selected for detailed examination and in determining the sample size and composition of the workers to be interviewed—including the details and scientifically rigorous structure of the worker interview questionnaire. The situation is fraught with the potential for lax monitoring as the result of monitor inexperience, susceptibility to pressure by plant management, and financial considerations.

Weak Enforcement of FLA Standards with Poor Record of Compliance

The FLA's approach to encourage participating companies to implement the code makes it difficult for the FLA to discipline companies with poor compliance records. When a company fails to comply with FLA standards, it can be placed under special review for an indefinite period. There is, however, no public disclosure of these actions, nor is there any specific procedure or time framework that would determine whether a company should be expelled from the FLA. Many FLA decisions, including the decision to certify a company's compliance, are determined by a simple majority vote of the board, which is composed of six industry and six NGO representatives. However, a decision to terminate a company's participation can only be made by a supermajority vote, which takes at least two-thirds of all the industry board members and two-thirds of the NGO board members. Given these constraints, a recalcitrant company faces little danger of being expelled or its actions made public. This further undermines the integrity of the entire monitoring and verification process.

Problems with the Brand Certification as Opposed to Individual Plant Certification

Under FLA procedures, there is no disclosure on the compliance of individual plants. Instead a participating company (i.e., brand) is certified as having complied with the code. The process seriously undermines the integrity of the entire FLA effort when we realize that (1) vendors are not randomly selected and instead are nominated by the participating company, and (2) public disclosure is severely limited and is reduced to the FLA's assertion that the brand is in compliance with the code. This has the effect of projecting the findings of 30 percent on the remaining 70 percent of the vendor population. As we have previously argued, because of faulty, nonrandom sample selection this claim cannot be sustained. The public report does not provide any information as to the extent and range of noncompliance among the vendors or what, if any, measures were taken by the company to punish noncompliant vendors.

In the end, the entire process is reduced to a house of cards, where each flimsy and unsustainable assertion is used to justify the next level of equally flimsy and unsustainable assertion. We are left with the distressing observation that after all the expense and efforts of a large number of well-intentioned groups and individuals, the current structure and operation of the Fair Labor Association is unlikely to make significant and observable improvement in the working and living conditions of workers.

Notes

1. "About the FLA," on the web site of the Fair Labor Organization (www.fair labor.org). The participating companies in the AIP were: Nike, Reebok, Liz Claiborne, Phillips–Van Heusen, and L. L. Bean, among the more prominent corporate members.
2. Ibid.
3. Information supplied by FLA.

4. "About the FLA."

5. David M Schilling, director, Global Corporate Accountability Programs, Interfaith Center on Corporate Responsibility, in letter to editor, *New York Times* (November 18, 1998), A30. See also "Two More Unions Reject Agreement for Curtailing Sweatshops," *New York Times* (November 6, 1998), A15.

6. Online home page of FLA (www.fairlabor.org).

7. See Chapter 5 in this book.

8. "Increased University Representation," *FLA Update* 1:11 (October 25, 2001).

9. Global Exchange is a nonprofit organization that received a major part of its funding from Nike to undertake this study.

10. Media Benjamin, "What's Fair about the Fair Labor Organization," *Global Exchange* (February 1999).

11. The living wage is defined as a take-home or net wage, earned during a country's legal maximum work week—but not more than 48 hours. A living wage provides for the basic needs (housing, energy, nutrition, clothing, health care, education, potable water, child care, transportation, and savings) of an average family unit divided by the average number of adult wage earners. The formula takes into account the average number of adult wage earners in order to exclude child labor. For actual formulas and additional information see "Workers and Advocates Demand Living Wage," *Sweatshop Watch* 4:2 (Summer 1998).

12. The priorities of the participating companies, and the relative importance they put on the sweatshop-related issues in developing countries, should be apparent when one compares Nike's contribution of $100,000 to FLA with the company's $200 million sponsorship of the Brazilian soccer team.

13. *Charter Document of FLA*, Section III, "Participation Criteria for Companies," and Section VII, "Monitoring Process," Fair Labor Association, Washington, D.C. 20005, January 24, 2001.

14. "Costs of Inspection by External Monitors," *Charter Document of FLA*, Section D of Monitoring Plan, Fair Labor Association, Washington, D.C. 20005, January 24, 2001.

15. See "Reporting Requirements" under Monitoring Process of FLA Charter.

16. "Monitoring Guidance and Compliance Benchmarks," manual of FLA, Fair Labor Organization, Washington, D.C. 20005; also available on web site of FLA (www.fairlabor.org).

PART FOUR

Case Studies

CHAPTER
9

Nike, Inc.: Missed Opportunities for Effective Code Compliance

Nike is the world's largest marketer of athletic footwear, athletic apparel, and athletic equipment, with annual revenues of a little over $9.488 billion in fiscal year 2001 (ending May 31). Out of this total, $435.9 million are other brands that are not included in regional numbers. Of the remaining revenue of $9.053 billion in fiscal year 2001, footwear represented 62.1 percent; the remaining 37.9 percent was divided between apparel (30.53 percent) and equipment and other products (7.37 percent). The company's largest market is in the United States, which accounted for 53.2 percent of total revenues, followed by Europe (28.6 percent), Asia-Pacific (12.3 percent), and the Americas except U.S. (5.9 percent).[1]

Nike has been a highly entrepreneurial and innovative company in more than one way. It took what used to be a relatively inexpensive, utilitarian, all-purpose (one-type-fits-all) sports sneaker and transformed it into high-tech, high-performance, specialty footwear suited to the needs of athletes in different sports—from tennis to soccer, from sprinting to marathon running, and from golf to baseball.

This would have been a tremendous achievement in itself, but this was not all. Nike had a flair for marketing. Using star athletes to endorse its products, it also made these shoes cool, must-have items. Star athlete endorsements did not originate with Nike, but the company developed endorsements as the centerpiece of its marketing strategy. Nowadays, neither

Nike nor any of its competitors could imagine selling sports products without athlete endorsements. This strategy requires Nike to spend hundreds of millions of dollars in payments to sports stars for promoting these endorsements and related products through various advertising channels. In fiscal year 2001, Nike's total advertising and promotion expenses amounted to a little over $1 billion, representing approximately 9.5 percent of the company's total revenues for that year. These expenses were an increase of 10.2 percent over the previous year.[2]

Clearly, professional athletes and even sports-oriented segments of the general population are not a large enough market to justify such intensive marketing efforts. In fact, a majority of these shoes are sold to the general population, who buy multiple pairs of expensive shoes and replace them even before they are worn out, just to remain "with it." One sees inner-city youth, in the poorest neighborhoods, sporting Air Jordans as must-have accessories along with earphones plugged into their CD players.

Converting an essentially utilitarian product into a fashion item has its downside, too. The shelf life of a fashion item is relatively short and notoriously fickle. It suffers from extreme highs and extreme lows, depending on what's in and what's out. It was, therefore, only natural that once Nike's reputation came under attack on the sweatshops issue Nike was no longer cool, and its sales took a plunge in 1998 and 1999, by which time Nike had become the poster boy of sweatshop outsourcing. It was even the target of a Doonesbury cartoon series.[3]

Another major innovation by Nike appeared in the area of manufacturing. From its very beginning, Nike did not own any of its manufacturing factories. Instead, it specialized in product design and marketing. Just as in the case of athletic endorsements, outsourcing did not originate with Nike, but Nike made it the core element of its procurement strategy. Everything designed and sold by Nike is made in factories owned by other entrepreneurs, who are spread all over the world. At the end of fiscal year 2001 (May 31), Nike had a total of 556,722 contract workers worldwide. Of these, the largest proportion (83.9 percent) was in Asia; followed by Europe, the Middle East, and Africa (6.9 percent); the Americas outside U.S. (6.8 percent); and the United States (2.4 percent). Nike also had the largest number of its factories in Asia (401), followed by the United States (131); Europe, the Middle East, and Africa (103); and the Americas outside U.S. (101).[4]

This approach gives Nike the flexibility to adjust supply with demand, and shift production among different factories and regions of the world to take advantage of lower costs. Nike can be used as a barometer to gauge a country's progress on the development life cycle. As soon as a country has advanced and built a socioeconomic infrastructure, Nike moves to the next country where labor costs are still cheaper and regulatory and environmental infrastructures are weaker. For example, Nike started by outsourcing its footwear in Japan. However, it soon moved its business to Taiwan and South Korea to take advantage of lower labor costs. By 1982, 86 percent of Nike sneakers came from these countries, where Nike helped create a large supplier network.

Nike, however, was constantly looking for new countries with lower production costs, which it found in China and Indonesia when Taiwan and South Korea moved into electronics and other high-value-added products. By 1990, Nike's first-rank suppliers were in China and Indonesia, where many of the same vendors who had previously supplied Nike from Taiwan and South Korea established factories to stay on Nike's vendor list.[5] And the process has continued and expanded to Nike's other product categories—apparel and equipment.

As of 2001, there were a total of 736 factories that employed over 556,000 people worldwide making Nike products.[6] Of those, over 200,000 (36 percent) are employed in the footwear factories. Among those factories, an overwhelming majority (79 percent) make apparel, 12 percent are involved in the manufacture of equipment, and the remaining 68 factories (9 percent) are engaged in the manufacture of footwear. Of the 68 footwear factories, 40 are totally dedicated to Nike's products while the remaining 28 share production facilities with other brands.[7]

Nike has the best of both worlds. By not owning its factories, the company is spared enormous capital investments in low-cost countries where the company might suffer from unstable governments and shaky political and economic conditions. At the same time, by controlling its markets, it exercises enormous leverage over foreign producers, who must compete among themselves for the business of a single buyer with a powerful brand name. This enables Nike to extract maximum cost advantage from its local manufacturers and also protect its gross margins by preventing competition from low-cost producers. Nike has used a similar strategy by expanding into the manufacture and sale of sports-related apparel and equipment such as gloves, swimwear, soccer balls, baseball bats, and so forth. Again, following the fashion analogy, these products are often sold as a part of design collections or matched fashion items.

If imitation is the sincerest form of flattery, the success of this strategy can be seen in its adoption by MNCs from all over the world that market labor-intensive consumer products. This strategy has radically altered the character of international trade and investments. Moving production to low-wage countries has caused tremendous shifts in employment-, country-, and region-based production specialization. This is a prime example of globalization with its concomitant sweatshops, worker abuse, pollution, and environmental degradation.[8]

The Outsourcing World of Nike

Nike's footwear production is concentrated in China, which accounted for 40 percent of all Nike brand footwear in fiscal year 2001. This was followed by 31 percent in Indonesia, 13 percent each in Vietnam and Thailand, and 1 percent each in Italy, Taiwan, and South Korea.[9] In other words, 97 percent of all Nike's footwear products are made in four countries, which are among the world's more repressive regimes with widespread corruption and lax or nonexistent enforcement of their own labor and environmental laws.

Of the 68 footwear factories, the largest number (17) are located in China, where Nike has been manufacturing footwear since 1981. China is followed by Indonesia with 11 factories (Nike's entry date 1988), Thailand—9 (1981), Korea—8 (1974), Brazil—5 (1994), Vietnam—5 (1995), and Taiwan—4 (1971). Many of these factories and their owners have been part of Nike's family of suppliers from the very start of their operations—some of them for more than 20 years. Even in the case of newer factories, a large number are owned and operated by the companies that were already running factories fully dedicated to the production of Nike footwear.

The story is quite different when it comes to apparel and equipment. None of the factories making apparel or equipment are exclusive to Nike. These factories manufacture for a variety of companies, originating in the United States, the European Union, Japan, and other nations. Another point worth noting is that Nike footwear manufacturing is concentrated in a handful of countries, as opposed to apparel and equipment, which are acquired from factories that are widely dispersed all over the world.

This long-term relationship with a small group of owners, whose facilities are totally dedicated to Nike's products, offers Nike tremendous advantages. Nike's relationship with these owners is symbiotic—one of mutual dependence and trust, a fact that is further affirmed from Nike's preference to work with the same group of owners when it seeks expansion in the footwear manufacturing capacity in other countries.

Nike must possess intimate knowledge about the operations, cost structure, and management philosophy of these plant owners. Furthermore, given the long-term relationships, it stands to reason that the partnerships are of mutual benefit. That is, Nike ensures that these owners are successful and profitable and remain committed to Nike. By the same token, these owners would have the best incentives in the world to cooperate with Nike in meeting the company's expectations with regard to product quality, price, and delivery schedules. It also stands to reason that these owners would want to be in total compliance with Nike's code of conduct, since Nike's corporate reputation and public trust depend on such total compliance.

Nike and Sweatshops

It would be unfair to say that Nike created sweatshops. Nor did any of the scores of other large MNCs that manufacture toys, apparel, rugs, furnishings, household goods, and a host of other products that are labor intensive and require low-skilled and low-wage workers to manufacture and export products. But the business model used by Nike and other companies could not have succeeded so well if these companies had not been able to shift the costs and risks of manufacturing their products to the bottom level of the supply chain, which must suffer the most and benefit the least in the latest wave of globalization.[10]

The worker profile in the plants making Nike's products is similar to those of other major U.S. MNCs who are sourcing products in these countries under similar circumstances. An overwhelming majority of these workers are young (16 years and above) and female (over 80 percent). They work more than 10 hours a day for minimum wages, and quite often live and eat in the facilities provided by the factory owners or managers.

In Nike's own words, a composite profile of Nike's overseas workers is as follows:

> You are 22 and single. You are in your third year of your first job. You were raised on a farm. Your supervisor is a woman, four years your senior. Your section leader is a foreigner. He doesn't speak your language very well.
>
> This is the "Nike worker." She works in one of more than 700 factories making Nike products in more than 50 countries around the world. Let's assemble a statistically valid sample of 100 Nike workers from around the world. The youngest should be 16, most are in their early 20s, but many are above 40. Of those 100, 80 are women, 83 are from Asia, 7 are from Europe/Middle East/Africa, and 10 are from Americas.[11]

Our analysis in this section is based on an extensive review of over 1,260 news reports and investigative stories by public interest and labor rights groups both in the United States and in other countries where these issues were raised in reference to Nike. In the process, we also reviewed Nike's own press releases and public comments made by Nike's executives and reported in the news media (Appendix 9.1).

News reports and NGO investigations about sweatshop-like working conditions in plants making Nike footwear and other products correlate with Nike's outsourcing activities. Our study of the news reports on the issue of sweatshops and human rights from all over world showed that Nike-related stories were by far the largest number of news stories attributed to a single company.[12] During the period 1988–2002, 51.6 percent of the 1,263 news stories referred to more than one product category, while 36.3 percent referred to footwear, 10.9 percent apparel, and 1.2 percent equipment (Figure 9.1).

We also compared Nike-related news stories for two contiguous and most recent periods, 1995 to 1997 and 1998 to March 2002. The data are not encouraging in their reflection of Nike's efforts to improve its vendors' compliance with the company's code of conduct (Figure 9.2). A comparison between the two time periods showed that while there was a small increase in the numbers of general complaints in Nike's vendors' plants, there was a small decrease in negative stories pertaining to shoes. The number of negative stories, however, recorded a sharp increase in the case of apparel and and in equipment as well. It would seem that Nike's efforts in its newer product categories are following a pattern similar to athletic footwear with regard to sweatshops and human rights violations.

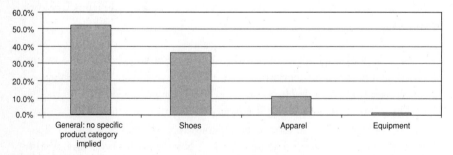

Figure 9.1   Distribution of News Stories Regarding Nike and Sweatshops/Human Rights Abuses: Product Categories, 1988 to March 2002
Source: Appendix 9.1.

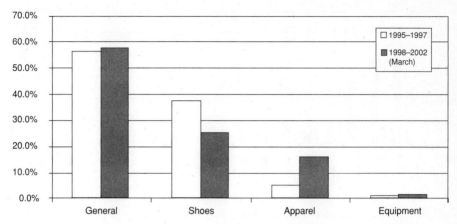

Figure 9.2   Distribution of News Stories Regarding Nike and Sweatshops/Human Rights Abuses: Product Categories, 1995 to 1997 and 1998 to March 2002
Source: Appendix 9.1.

Figures 9.3 and 9.4 indicate a direct connection between the magnitude of Nike's production and the number of negative news stories. Thus, China, Indonesia, Vietnam, Mexico, and Thailand recorded the highest number of negative news stories. It is disappointing to see such little progress on the part of Nike in factories where Nike controls 100 percent of the plant output, has long-term and well-established relationships with the plant owners, and thus has tremendous leverage to ensure compliance

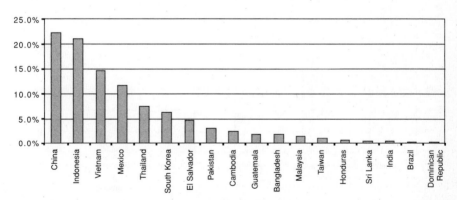

Figure 9.3   Distribution of News Stories Regarding Nike and Sweatshops/Human Rights Abuses: Countries, 1988 to March 2002
Source: Appendix 9.1.

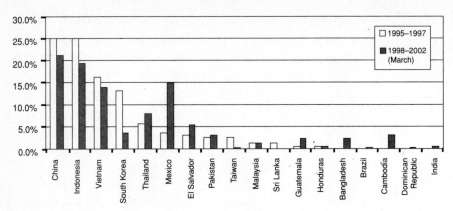

Figure 9.4   Distribution of News Stories Regarding Nike and Sweatshops/Human Rights Abuses: Countries, 1995 to 1997 and 1998 to March 2002
Source: Appendix 9.1.

with the company's code of conduct. While the rate of negative news stories has declined somewhat in China, Indonesia, Vietnam, and South Korea, it has actually increased in Thailand, Mexico, El Salvador, and Pakistan (Figure 9.4).

Figures 9.5 and 9.6 analyze data pertaining to specific issues within the broad definition of sweatshops and human rights. It would seem that during

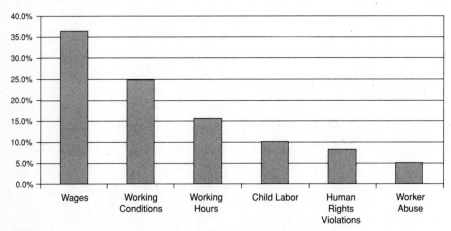

Figure 9.5   Distribution of News Stories Regarding Nike and Sweatshops/Human Rights Abuses: Types of Violations, 1988 to March 2002
Source: Appendix 9.1.

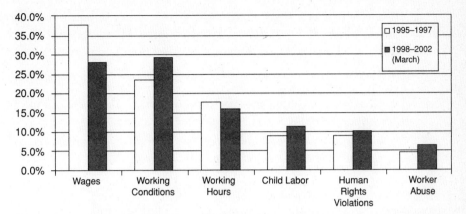

Figure 9.6 Distribution of News Stories Regarding Nike and Sweatshops/Human Rights Abuses: Types of Violations, 1995 to 1997 and 1998 to March 2002
Source: Appendix 9.1.

the period 1988 to March 2000, the largest number of negative stories pertained to wages (i.e., nonpayment of legally mandated wages for regular and overtime hours). This was followed by negative stories pertaining to working conditions, excessive working hours, child labor, human rights, and worker abuse.

Figure 9.6 provides a comparison of data for 1995 to 1997 and 1998 to March 2002. There was a reduction in negative reports with regard to wages and working hours. However, there was an increase in the number of negative stories with regard to working conditions, child labor, human rights abuses, and worker abuse.

Nike and the Sweatshop Issue

The story of Nike and how Nike has dealt with the issues of sweatshops and human rights abuses illustrates the entire spectrum of problems, confrontations, and response strategies pursued by MNCs. This issue evokes highly emotional and confrontational reactions among many groups in the major markets of MNCs, groups such as consumers, university and college students, religious groups, advocates for the poor, the news media, and even governmental agencies. Moreover, the intensity of public reaction has continued to increase, forcing MNCs to be on the defensive and pressuring them into taking corrective measures.

Nevertheless, in many significant ways, Nike's response patterns have been radically different from those of other large MNCs operating in these countries. The reasons for the uniqueness of Nike's responses can be traced to two factors:

1. The intensity of external pressures on Nike and Nike's perception of the accuracy, relevance, and legitimacy of the charges.
2. Nike's corporate culture, management style, and the personality traits of its top management, including most notably the CEO.

To assess Nike's strategies in responding to the sweatshop and human rights issues, we will use the framework of issue life cycle and corporate response patterns presented earlier, in Chapters 3 and 4.

Figure 9.7 describes the perception of issue life cycle from the viewpoints of Nike and the company's critics. The sweatshop issue and its association with Nike had become a significant event in its own right early in 1989, when Nike's operations first became identified in the news media with some regularity. These reports pertained to worker abuse, unsafe and unhealthy working conditions, and failure to pay proper wages for regular and overtime work in the plants that were totally dedicated to the manufacture of Nike footwear.

Analysis of the data suggests that from the time of the first news reports until 1995 or 1996, Nike insisted that there were no widespread problems of sweatshops and that Nike and other MNCs were increasing employment

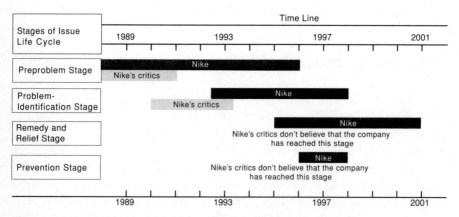

Figure 9.7   Life Cycle of Sweatshops/Human Rights Abuses: Nike's Perception of the Issue Life Cycle as Contrasted with the Perception of Nike's Critics

and reducing poverty in these countries. Where such problems did exist, Nike claimed, they were likely to be isolated cases, tied to prevailing business practices and cultural conditions in those countries.

There was some shift in this public posture starting around 1994, when Nike recognized that these problems were more pervasive than previously realized. Nevertheless, Nike unequivocally refused to accept any responsibility for these conditions, arguing that since Nike did not own any of the overseas factories, it could not be held responsible for these conditions, which were beyond the company's control. Nike's critics, however, contended that the problem had become quite apparent to anyone who cared to observe and that Nike's posture was an abdication of its responsibility.

This process of initial denial and subsequent acceptance in the face of overwhelming evidence has been Nike's response mode throughout the controversy and has not materially changed to the present day. Nike has asserted that it has been taking more substantive actions to respond to these issues, such as its code of conduct, which was originally created in 1992 and has since been revised and expanded every year. Nike's critics have largely rejected these claims as more hype than action.

Three things stand out in our detailed review of these materials.

1. Nike has consistently underestimated the character and scope of the critics' assertions and the emotional intensity with which these assertions have resonated with the public at large and especially with the educated youth in colleges and universities, which are a major market segment for Nike's products. More often than not, the company dismissed the critics' accusations as unfounded and unwarranted, and responded with messages that could not stand the test of logic or practical reality. Nike considered its critics, at least in the early stages of the controversy, to be unsophisticated and lacking in credibility. The company thought it could manage them through adroit use of public relations. Furthermore, the company underestimated the expertise of its critics on the substantive aspects of the sweatshops and human rights issues. Nor did the company expect that critics would be so tenacious in confronting Nike and keeping the issues alive in the public's consciousness.

2. Nike also seemed to underestimate the importance of negative signals from its external environment. Instead, it relied on information from within the company or from the company's own resources, which necessarily lent support to the corporate viewpoint. Similarly,

in evaluating its adversaries, Nike felt comfortable within its corporate self-image of a savvy company that was highly successful in marketing and public relations. Nike's responses, in both content and the manner of their communication, were loaded with public relations imagery. They focused more on what Nike wanted people to hear than on what people wanted Nike to explain.

3. Throughout the entire controversy Nike's responses have been too little and too late. The company confronted the issue only when it could not be avoided and then tried to overwhelm critics with public relations rhetoric. The company was repeatedly forced to reverse itself and concede the validity of its critics' assertions, since the company's own arguments appeared to be flawed and ultimately indefensible.

Table 9.1 presents our analysis of Nike's actions in response to the sweatshop issue and resultant public controversy. During the period 1986–1995, Nike responded by accepting no responsibility for the labor conditions in the overseas factories that made its products. The company continued to insist that the issue was in the preproblem stage. That is, it needed more study, since issues were involved for which Nike had no responsibility. The company claimed that criticism was unfair and unwarranted. At the same time, Nike argued that it had no social obligation to do anything to ameliorate the problem, even if the problem did exist as claimed by the corporate critics. Through all this, Nike was trying to defend its domain, that is, its right to do business in a manner of its own choosing and without any additional obligation to external constituencies.[13]

Communications Strategy

Chapter 3 presented the notion of legitimacy gap and suggested that the credibility of a corporation's communications depends to a large extent on the size of the gap between the public's perception of the corporation's actions and society's expectations. A corporation must narrow this gap to gain public trust. When there is a large and persistent legitimacy gap, the public is not likely to believe the company's messages and is liable to take a dim view of its actions.

Throughout the controversy, Nike suffered from a large legitimacy gap. In order to narrow this gap, Nike had two options.

Table 9.1 Stages of Conflict—Sweatshops/Human Rights Abuses and Nike's Response Patterns

Dimensions of Corporate Response Pattern		Preproblem Stage (Before 1989)	Problem Identification (1989–1995)	Remedy and Relief Stage (After 1995)	Prevention Stage
Response Mode	Character of Response				
No social obligation	Do not concede existence of the problem. Refuse any responsibility for causation and amelioration.	**Nike's Assertion** Using Domain Defense and Domain Offense as Strategies			
Social obligation	Do what is required by law and economic necessity. Response is defensive and proscriptive.	**Nike Critics** Nike Uses Domain Offense Strategy			
Social responsibility	Mitigate negative side effects of corporate activities on society. Response is prescriptive and interactive.			**Nike's Assertion** Domain Offense Strategy	
Social responsiveness	Promote positive social change. Response is proactive, anticipatory, and preventive.				

1. It could create messages that had a direct relation to the public's expectations and create the means by which the content of these messages could be independently verified by external sources whose credibility was higher than that of the corporation.

2. It could deliver substantive action that would, on the face of it, meet societal expectations of a change in corporate behavior. Furthermore, this behavior would have to be independently verifiable by sources with higher public credibility than that of the corporation.

Nike took neither of these two approaches. The company's initial response was that the events for which Nike was being accused were outside its control and responsibility. The company inundated the media with messages through press releases and through pronouncements by its executives.[14] The Nike strategy of communication was as simple as it was fruitless: "Do not change performance, but change public perception of business performance through education and information."[15] The critics were quick to ridicule this strategy as logically flawed and contrary to reality as it existed in the field.[16] A company that as a customer accounts for 100 percent of a plant's output exercises tremendous leverage on the local manufacturer. Would Nike make similar arguments if it were a question of product quality, price, or delivery schedule? Nike's communications strategy and its lack of concrete action failed to assuage the company's critics. The inevitable result of this strategy was a further diminution in Nike's public credibility. Nike then took another action, which seemed to be a positive response to the sweatshop issue as framed by the critics. In November 1992, Nike introduced its first code of conduct. Written in folksy terms, Nike stated that it was determined to "build our business with all of our partners upon trust, teamwork, honesty and mutual respect. We expect all of our business partners to operate on the same principles" (Exhibit 9.1). The code included a memorandum of understanding that all Nike's partners would agree to abide by the code and would so indicate by signing the document. They were also expected to maintain appropriate documentation, which would be made available for Nike's inspection. The code thus absolved Nike from any and all responsibility beyond asking its partners to sign the agreement. There was no provision for what Nike would do to enforce compliance.

Once again, Nike's remedial actions failed to meet minimal expectations. The company acted as if its critics knew nothing about plant operations in these countries. It was widely known, for instance, that no amount

Exhibit 9.1 Nike's Corporate Code of Conduct, 1992

Code of Conduct

NIKE Inc. was founded on a handshake.

Implicit in that act was the determination that we would build our business with all of our partners upon trust, teamwork, honesty and mutual respect. We expect all of our business partners to operate on the same principles.

At the core of the NIKE corporate ethic is the belief that we are a company comprised of many different kinds of people, appreciating individual diversity, and dedicated to equal opportunity for each individual.

NIKE designs, manufactures and markets sports and fitness products. At each step in that process, we are dedicated to minimizing our impact on the environment. We seek to implement to the maximum extent possible the three R's of environmental action: reduce, reuse and recycle.

We seek always to be a leader in our quest to enhance people's lives through sports and fitness. That means at every opportunity—whether in the design, manufacturing and marketing of products; in the environment; in the areas of human rights and equal opportunity; or in our relationships in the communities in which we do business—we seek to do not only what is required, but, whenever possible, what is expected of a leader.

There Is No Finish Line.

Memorandum of Understanding

Wherever NIKE operates around the globe, we are guided by our Code of Conduct and bind our business partners to those principles with a signed Memorandum of Understanding.

1. **Government regulation of business.** (Subcontractor/Supplier) certifies compliance with all applicable local government regulations regarding minimum wage; overtime; child labor laws; provisions for pregnancy, menstrual leave; provisions for vacation and holidays; and mandatory retirement benefits.
2. **Safety and health.** (Subcontractor/Supplier) certifies compliance with all applicable local government regulations regarding occupational health and safety.
3. **Worker insurance.** (Subcontractor/Supplier) certifies compliance with all applicable local laws providing health insurance, life insurance and worker's compensation.
4. **Forced labor.** (Subcontractor/Supplier) certifies that it and its suppliers and contractors do not use any form of forced labor—prison or otherwise.

(Continued)

Exhibit 9.1   *(Continued)*

> 5. **Environment.** (Subcontractor/Supplier) certifies compliance with all applicable local environmental regulations, and adhere to NIKE's own broader environmental practices, including the prohibition on the use of chloro-flouro-carbons (CFCs), the release of which could contribute to the depletion of the earth's ozone layer.
> 6. **Equal opportunity.** (Subcontractor/Supplier) certifies that it does not discriminate in hiring, salary, benefits, advancement, termination or retirement on the basis of gender, race, religion, age, sexual orientation or ethnic origin.
> 7. **Documentation and inspection.** (Subcontractor/Supplier) agrees to maintain on file such documentation as may be needed to demonstrate compliance with the certifications in this Memorandum of Understanding, and further agrees to make these documents available for NIKE's inspection upon request.

of signed codes of conduct would make any difference unless the MNC made a commitment to ensure compliance on the part of its suppliers.

Local manufacturers often kept a double set of books, and poor record keeping was the norm. It was implausible for Nike to behave as if it did not know about such practices. Skeptics were right to assume that Nike was only going through the motions of creating a code of conduct. This was borne out by field experience when plants making Nike footwear were constantly being exposed for worker abuse in different parts of the world.

In terms of the communication model presented in Chapter 3, Nike had moved to the second type of communication to narrow the credibility gap, namely, "If changes in public perception are not possible, change the symbols used to describe business performance, thereby making it congruent with public perception. Note that no change in actual performance is called for."[17] Nike's response strategies also moved to the second stage. It expanded from domain defense to domain offense, claiming to occupy the same territory as its critics. Furthermore, as part of its domain offense strategy, Nike publicly took its critics to task, claiming that critics were unfairly zeroing in on Nike while ignoring other companies with worse records.[18]

Nike made a slight shift in its strategy by acknowledging that it had some obligation to look after the workers in the overseas plants that made Nike footwear, but it didn't accept any responsibility to ensure that this obligation was fulfilled. Despite its failure, Nike has continued to pursue this strategy because the company's management was unwilling to accept the alternative.

In an attempt to gain public credibility, Nike tried another high-profile public relations gimmick by asking Andrew Young, the well-known civil rights leader, to visit Nike plants overseas and to see for himself that workers were well treated. The tactic had all the characteristics of a high-profile star athlete promotion. The spectacle of Andrew Young flying around the world accompanied by the corporate entourage was dismissed by Nike's critics and even its sympathizers as a misplaced attempt to buy credibility.[19]

Nike's next attempt at meeting public criticism came in the form of a revised code of conduct (Exhibit 9.2) in March 1997 in which Nike expanded on some of the provisions made in the earlier code. Nike, however, did not commit itself to any type of responsibility for noncompliance on the part of its vendors. One example of this approach can be seen in a lawsuit filed by a public interest law firm in San Francisco, charging Nike with consumer fraud because it failed to meet its commitments under its own code. Nike argued that the case did not have any merit because the code was not a contract, but was instead a political/commercial communication, which was protected under the free speech guarantees of the U.S. Constitution.[20] Although the lower Court agreed with Nike's position, the case was upheld on appeal in the California Supreme Court.[21]

Independent of the code content, Nike took a few tentative steps to audit some of its plants. This effort was not systematic, nor was it conducted on a regular basis. Instead, different groups produced ad hoc reports, which were not comparable with each other, either over time or along prespecified criteria. The result was a plethora of information that attempted to form an overall picture of Nike's efforts and successes in changing conditions in the overseas plants. Its scope was so limited, however, that there seemed to be an inverse relationship between the quantity of information available and its quality.

By this time, Nike realized that it had to take some action that the public would take seriously. The company needed to dampen the incessant public criticism and avoid further tainting of its corporate reputation. Nike established a full-fledged corporate compliance department, which currently has 58 people, including 12 people in the head office. The location and responsibilities of these professionals varied in many respects. They might be assigned to one country, a handful of plants, or an entire region. They might conduct internal audits, train local managers, and help in the assessment of code compliance. Thus they did not fit the

Exhibit 9.2   Nike's Corporate Code of Conduct, 1997

Code of Conduct

NIKE Inc. was founded on a handshake.

Implicit in that act was the determination that we would build our business with all of our partners based on trust, teamwork, honesty and mutual respect. We expect all of our business partners to operate on the same principles.

At the core of the NIKE corporate ethic is the belief that we are a company comprised of many different kinds of people, appreciating individual diversity, and dedicated to equal opportunity for each individual.

NIKE designs, manufactures and markets products for sports and fitness consumers. At every step in that process, we are driven to do not only what is required, but what is expected of a leader. We expect our business partners to do the same. Specifically, NIKE seeks partners that share our commitment to the promotion of best practices and continuous improvement in:

1. Occupational health and safety, compensation, hours of work and benefits.
2. Minimizing our impact on the environment.
3. Management practices that recognize the dignity of the individual, the rights of free association and collective bargaining, and the right to a workplace free of harassment, abuse or corporal punishment.
4. The principle that decisions on hiring, salary, benefits, advancement, termination or retirement are based solely on the ability of an individual to do the job.

Wherever NIKE operates around the globe, we are guided by this Code of Conduct. We bind our business partners to these principles. While these principles establish the spirit of our partnerships, we also bind these partners to specific standards of conduct. These are set forth below:

1. **Forced Labor.** (Contractor) certifies that it does not use any forced labor—prison, indentured, bonded or otherwise.
2. **Child Labor.** (Contractor) certifies that it does not employ any person under the minimum age established by local law, or the age at which compulsory schooling had ended, whichever is greater, but in no case under the age of 14.
3. **Compensation.** (Contractor) certifies that it pays at least the minimum total compensation required by local law, including all mandated wages, allowances and benefits.

Exhibit 9.2   *(Continued)*

4. **Benefits.** (Contractor) certifies that it complies with all provisions for legally mandated benefits, including but not limited to housing; meals; transportation and other allowances; health care; child care; sick leave; emergency leave; pregnancy and menstrual leave; vacation, religious, bereavement and holiday leave; and contributions for social security, life, health, worker's compensation and other insurance.

5. **Hours of Work/Overtime.** (Contractor) certifies that it complies with legally mandated work hours; uses overtime only when employees are fully compensated according to local law; informs the employee at the time of hiring if mandatory overtime is a condition of employment; and, on a regularly scheduled basis, provides one day off in seven, and requires no more than 60 hours of work per week, or complies with local limits if they are lower.

6. **Health and Safety.** (Contractor) certifies that it has written health and safety guidelines, including those applying to employee residential facilities, where applicable; and that it has agreed in writing to comply with NIKE's factory/vendor health and safety standards.

7. **Environment.** (Contractor) certifies that it complies with applicable country environmental regulations; and that it has agreed in writing to comply with NIKE's specific vendor/factory environmental policies and procedures, which are based on the concept of continuous improvement in processes and programs to reduce the impact on the environment.

8. **Documentation and Inspection.** (Contractor) agrees to maintain on file such documentation as may be needed to demonstrate compliance with this Code of Conduct, and further agrees to make these documents available for NIKE or its designated auditor's inspection upon request.

Nike Inc., 1997

mold of either internal auditors or external auditors. Instead, they appeared to be corporate support staff, helping the local manufacturers improve their performance in all aspects of their operations.

In one area, Nike did make significant progress that has been recognized even by its critics. This was a concerted effort to introduce water-based solvents in its footwear manufacturing process. This not only made the plants safer and provided a healthier work environment, it also generated significant cost savings.[22]

However, when it comes to issues pertaining to workers, such as wages, forced overtime, and harassment, Nike remains mired in a quagmire of ambiguous answers about current performance and noncommittal answers about its future performance. This is confirmed by analysis of the published news reports on Nike's operations, as presented earlier in the chapter. A recent report by Global Alliance—although unsystematic—revealed numerous serious problems in most of the plants where Nike had been in operation for the longest period of time—China, Vietnam, and Thailand.[23] When I questioned Dusty Kidd, Nike's vice president for compliance, he could not definitely state how many plants would be in substantial full compliance with all the major provisions of the Nike code in five years. He could not guarantee whether even one of the Nike plants, randomly selected, would currently be in substantial compliance with Nike's code. Nike's statement contained no recognition of the fact that all these violations represent real money in terms of unpaid wages that are owed to the workers.

The cost of manufacturing shoes includes labor costs. We presume that Nike pays its vendors on the basis of cost calculations that include labor costs that conform with legally mandated minimum wages—which are also required under Nike's own code. Since the violations by factory owners deny workers even these minimum wages, Nike should find a way to make these workers whole by paying back wages to the most vulnerable of its stakeholders.

Nike's Corporate Social Responsibility Report—FY 2001

Nike's latest attempt to communicate with the public at large is the company's "Corporate Social Responsibility Report—FY 2001," published by the company in October 2001. This is perhaps the first proactive report in which Nike has laid out its accomplishments, the process by which the company achieved its goals, and its plans for the future. According to Nike, it is "our first attempt to assess" progress in eliminating and ameliorating multiple issues involved in overseas sourcing (e.g., environment, labor practices, and community affairs). Collected under the overarching concept of "sustainability," the report states: "We run Corporate Responsibility like any other piece of business. We have business plans, goals, action plans, time-lines and measurables. We're driving issues out into all areas of the organization instead of keeping everything housed in a corporate function."[24]

Given the importance ascribed to the report by Nike, it was felt that a brief summary and analysis of the report would be appropriate to explain Nike's corporate philosophy and modus operandi, so that the public could see how the company planned to comply with its own code of conduct and what might be expected of the company in the foreseeable future.

The first and most important point to note about this report is that it is a "self-assessment" and not an independent, externally monitored study of Nike's progress to date and what it entails for the future. The report suffers from the flaws of the proverbial "self-graded" exam. Since the exam taker and the examiner are one and the same company, Nike is guaranteed at least a decent pass when "all the circumstances are taken into account." Moreover, it is not surprising that any shortfalls the company concedes are attributed to circumstances beyond its control. The report tends to claim that problems that have arisen have been so enormous that the company's best efforts have not been enough and that it has been easy for outsiders to find fault with the company's performance with the benefit of hindsight.

This caveat is not designed to cast doubt on the company's veracity or the accuracy of the facts it has presented. Nevertheless, the facts presented may not be enough, and there may be other facts or factors that should be considered to better assess the situation. In addition, the facts may not necessarily lead to the conclusions the company has drawn.

A careful reader of the report will notice a number of important points:

1. Most of the efforts described started in 1998. Given the fact that Nike has been operating in some of these countries since 1981, why did it take Nike so long to begin addressing some of these issues? The question is even more pertinent because Nike has been the subject of intense criticism since the early 1980s with regard to poor working conditions and worker abuse. Nike can't plead ignorance.

2. From the data provided in the report, it would seem that Nike has made a concerted effort to remove harmful substances from its products. It has also created safe operating conditions in plants by using water-soluble adhesives. Again, it should be noted that this effort started in earnest in 1998.

3. The report presents Nike's rebuttal to the often-made accusation that the company makes enormous profits at the expense of workers in poor countries and that it can afford to pay these workers higher wages, since the sum total of these increments would have minimal impact on the company's overall revenues and profitability. The rebuttal comes in two forms. Using standardized data, Nike argues

that it does not enjoy high margins and that large amounts paid for advertising and star athlete endorsements are justified because of pressures of competition. It also argues that paying higher wages beyond the competitive rates would be counterproductive and result in loss of employment.

We find these arguments unpersuasive. In the first place, Nike will present only numbers that yield the conclusions the company wants. Furthermore, the report's underlying assumptions and conclusions cannot be accepted at face value without being audited and verified by independent outside experts. Nor can we accept the argument that any wage increase paid to these workers would be counterproductive.

The rationale offered is theoretical and has no practical relevance.[25] Wages for these workers are not determined in the marketplace except under conditions of monopsony or oligopsony in which one large buyer or a small group of large buyers exercises enormous leverage and extracts maximum advantage from a substantial number of sellers who must compete among themselves to gain business from the dominant buyers. Moreover, the argument cannot explain the fact that one of the accusations against Nike's vendors is that the workers are not being paid even the minimum wages mandated by local labor laws, and are often forced to work excessive overtime without receiving appropriate overtime wage rates.

By its own admission, Nike's record leaves a great deal to be desired. It has not done enough to prevent worker harassment or curb demands for excessive overtime. Nor has Nike taken sufficient steps to ensure payment of correct wages for regular and overtime work. These statements are based on a handful of factories audited by the International Youth Foundation's Global Alliance project and corroborated by other more independent reports, such as a documentary aired by the BBC in 2000.[26]

These reports are presented more by way of mea culpas. This is unacceptable when the plants under question are totally dedicated to producing Nike footwear. Moreover, some of these plants have had a continuous relationship with Nike for more than 15 years. They are totally dependent on Nike, and the company has enormous leverage on these plants' owners to operate their facilities in compliance with Nike's standards and its code of conduct. Would Nike tolerate the conduct of these operators if they continuously failed to meet its product quality and safety standards? Why should it be satisfied with such flagrant violation of its standards with regard to hours, wages, and working conditions?

Independent External Monitoring

Nike's initiatives in setting up an independent external system to monitor the adequacy of its internal compliance and verification efforts are particularly weak when compared with the initiatives of other companies facing similar problems in the countries where Nike's vendors operate. They are also deficient, given the scope of Nike's problems. And finally, they fail in meeting a minimal level of transparency. They will not engender public trust in Nike's claims about the efforts it claims to be making. These shortcomings are especially puzzling, given the continuous reports in the news media about sweatshop conditions in Nike's factories all over the world.

Nike has recently endorsed its participation in the UN's Global Compact and has also agreed to participate in FLA's external monitoring process. However, as discussed in Chapters 7 and 8, both of these initiatives are seriously flawed and cannot purport to deliver monitoring that is adequate, representative, and transparent.

APPENDIX 9.1 News Reports Pertaining to Nike's Outsourcing Operations and Sweatshops/ Human Rights Issues

Data for Table 9.2 was derived primarily from Dow Jones Interactive (DJI) and supplemented from other sources (e.g., LexisNexis, *The New York Times*, and *Business Week*). Information contained here should be considered neither comprehensive nor all-inclusive, but as an overall indicator of the news coverage about sweatshops/human rights issues.

This data is based almost exclusively on publications in the English language and from Western sources. To the extent that reports of this type appear in the local language media and are not picked up by the Western news media, the scope of coverage is incomplete. Similarly, certain news stores (e.g., news wires), are often picked up by multiple media and reported in their respective news channels. This tends to inflate somewhat the number of incidents reported, but it is important nevertheless as different news media reach out to different population segments.

Quite often news stories report on multiple countries, companies, or issues (e.g., child labor, wages, worker abuse). Therefore, the number of issues mentioned will be greater than the total number of news reports surveyed.

Table 9.2 News Reports Pertaining to Nike's Outsourcing Operations and Sweatshops/Human Rights Issues, 1988 to March 2002

		Number of Reports					Type of Labor Rights Violation					
Year	Country	Total	General	Shoes	Apparel	Equipment	Child Labor	Wages	Hours	Conditions	Worker Abuse	Human Rights Violation
1988	China	1		1				1				
	South Korea	1	1					1				
	Taiwan	2	2				1	2				
	Thailand	2	2				1	2				
		6	5	1	0	0	2	6	0	0	0	0
1989	China	7		7				7				
	Indonesia	3		3				3				
	Malaysia	2		2				2				
	South Korea	9		9			1	9				
	Taiwan	7		7				7				
	Thailand	8	1	7				8				
		36	1	35	0	0	1	36	0	0	0	0
1990	China	6		6				6		1		
	Indonesia	3		3				3				
	South Korea	4		4				4				
	Taiwan	2		2				2				
	Thailand	4		4				4				
	General	1	1					1				
		20	0	20	0	0	0	20	1	0	0	0

174

1991											
China	9	4		5			2	8	1		0
Indonesia	3			3			1	3			0
South Korea	4			4				4	2		
Taiwan	4			4				4	1		
Thailand	6	2		4			1	6			
General	1			1				1			
	27	6	0	21	0	0	4	26	4	0	0
1992											
China	5	4		1			2	5	1		0
Indonesia	6	2		4				6	1		0
South Korea	6	1		5				6	2		
Taiwan	5			5			2	5	1		
Thailand	5			5				5			
General	4			4				4			
	31	7	0	24	0	0	4	31	5	0	0
1993											
China	11	2		9			1	11	5	3	0
Indonesia	8			8			1	8	1	2	0
South Korea	6			6				6		4	
Taiwan	2	1		1				2			
Thailand	6	1		5				6	1		
General	6	5		1				6	2		
	39	9	0	30	0	0	2	39	9	9	0
1994											
China	6	2		4			1	6	2	2	0
Indonesia	14	5		9			1	10	8	4	0
Thailand	3	3						3			
Vietnam	6	4		2			2	4			
South Korea	4	2		2			2	4	2	1	
Mexico	4	2		2			1	4			
General	11	2	1	8				8	2		
	48	20	1	27	0	0	7	39	13	8	0

(Continued)

175

Table 9.2 (Continued)

Year	Country	Number of Reports					Type of Labor Rights Violation					
		Total	General	Shoes	Apparel	Equipment	Child Labor	Wages	Hours	Conditions	Worker Abuse	Human Rights Violation
1995	China	11	4	7			2	7	4	4	1	4
	Indonesia	9	3	6			2	8	2	7	1	2
	Mexico	2	2					2	2	2		
	South Korea	6	1	5				6		1		
	Thailand	3	3				1	3				
	Vietnam	12	8	4			4	10	8	2		
	General	26	14	11	1		2	14	9	11	2	2
		69	35	33	1	0	11	50	25	27	4	8
1996	China	17	12	5			7	11	5	12	3	4
	Honduras	1	1					1				
	Indonesia	13	4	9			1	12	4	7	1	5
	Mexico	4		3	1			4	3	3		
	Pakistan	4	2			2	4	1				1
	South Korea	8		8				8	2	2		
	Taiwan	2		2				1		1		
	Thailand	2		2				2	2			
	Vietnam	6	4	2			3	6	4	6	3	3
	General	28	19	6	2	1	3	17	7	11		
		85	42	37	3	3	18	63	29	42	7	14

(Continued)

	1	2	3	4	5	6	7	8	9	10	11
1997											
China	12	5	7		2		8	6	7	2	2
El Salvador	5	2					5	1	4	1	2
Guatemala	1	1		3			1		1		
Honduras	1	1					1		1		
Indonesia	18	8	8	2	2		15	11	14	4	8
Malaysia	2	2			1		2	2			1
South Korea	7	5	2				7	2	4	1	
Sri Lanka	2	2			1		2	2			
Taiwan	2	2	2				2	2	2		
Thailand	4	4			1		4	2	4	2	1
Vietnam	8	5	3	6	4		8	4	17	2	1
General	69	49	14		6		31	7			8
	131	84	36	11	17	0	86	39	54	12	24
1998											
China	18	10	8	11			16	10	16	3	4
El Salvador	8	8		2			5	3	8	2	2
Guatemala	2	2					2		2		
Indonesia	13	5	8	8			10	12	7	4	7
Mexico	14	6	2	1	2		8	5	10	2	4
Pakistan	3	1		3			3	3		2	
Philippines	1	1		1		2	1	1	3	1	
South Korea	3	3		1			2	2	4	1	1
Thailand	6	1	4				6		4	1	
Vietnam	21	19	17	2	6		17	12	19	6	3
General	86	65		4	4		22	13	37	2	11
	175	121	39	13	2	37	92	61	107	23	32

Table 9.2 (Continued)

		Number of Reports					Type of Labor Rights Violation					Human Rights
Year	Country	Total	General	Shoes	Apparel	Equipment	Child Labor	Wages	Hours	Conditions	Worker Abuse	Violation
1999	Bangladesh	1	1					1		1		
	Cambodia	6	2		4		1	3	3	6	2	1
	China	19	10	7	2		6	8	7	11	1	4
	El Salvador	6	3		3		2	4	3	6	3	2
	Guatemala	5			4	1		4	2	2	1	
	Honduras	1	1					1		1		
	Indonesia	23	14	7	2		8	12	9	10	3	6
	Malaysia	5			4	1		4		1		2
	Mexico	15	3	6	6		4	6	5	9		2
	Pakistan	3				3	3	3		3		2
	South Korea	5	1		4			4	2	2	1	3
	Thailand	14	8	1	4	1	2	7	2	9	1	2
	Vietnam	11	6	4	1		4	7	1	3	1	3
	General	94	48	32	14		7	34	23	28	2	8
		208	97	57	48	6	37	98	57	92	15	35
2000	Bangladesh	3	3					1		1		1
	Brazil	1	1									1
	Cambodia	5	1		4		4	3	2	4	2	
	China	24	17	7			5	14	10	12	5	8
	El Salvador	6	4		2			2	3	3	1	1
	Guatemala	2	1		1			2				
	Honduras	1	1					1				

178

Indonesia	19	11	5	3			10	5	9	1	7
Mexico	9	9		5			5	2	4	2	2
Pakistan	4	3			1		1	2	3	1	
South Korea	5	3	2	2			2	2	3		
Thailand	10	7	1	2			4	2	7	1	
Vietnam	9	5	3	1			5	2	4	1	
General	117	75	22	17	3	10	42	12	48	5	6
	215	141	38	32	4	19	92	40	98	19	26
2001 Bangladesh	5		5		2	2	1	3		1	
Cambodia	1		1								
China	17	13	2	2	13	9	8	8	3	2	
Dominican Republic	1		1		1						
Indonesia	13	8	4	1		1	7	4	7	4	4
Mexico	19	4	1	14		7	3	3	9	5	2
Taiwan	1		1				1		1		
Thailand	1		1								
Vietnam	13	4	9		10	6	3	6	1	6	
General	72	41	27	4	11	20	8	16	6	11	
	143	70	45	28	0	44	49	27	51	19	26
2002 China	3	2	3			1	3	1	3	1	3
India	2	2					2		1		
Indonesia	6	2	4			1	4	4	4	2	2
Pakistan	2	2					2		1		
General	17	8	8	1		2	8	6	8		2
	30	14	15	1	0	2	19	11	17	3	7
	1263	652	458	138	15	205	746	321	508	102	172

Source: Please see Chapter 2 for an explanation of the source of this data.

179

Notes

1. Source: Nike's Form 10-K filed with Securities and Exchange Commission, 2–4.
2. Ibid., 28.
3. The Doonesbury series appeared in late 1997.
4. Unless otherwise specifically stated, all the information contained in this section is drawn from a Nike publication entitled "Corporate Social Responsibility Report—FY 2001" (Beaverton, Ore.: Nike, Inc., 2001).
5. Jennifer L. Burns, "Hitting the Wall: Nike and International Labor Practices" HBS Case 9-700-047 (Boston: Harvard Business School, 2000), 3. See also Philip M. Rosenzweig and Pam Woo, "International Sourcing in Footwear: Nike and Reebok" HBS Case 394-189 (Boston: BHS Press, 1994), 2–5, cited in Burns, "Hitting the Wall."
6. Unless otherwise specifically stated, all the information contained in this section is drawn from the Nike "Corporate Social Responsibility Report—FY 2001."
7. Nike's communication to the author.
8. For a further discussion of these issues please refer to Chapters 1 and 2 of this book.
9. Source: Nike's Form 10-K filed with Securities and Exchange Commission.
10. For a further discussion of this phenomenon, please see Chapters 1, 2, and 8.
11. Nike "Corporate Social Responsibility Report—FY 2001."
12. See Chapter 2 of this book. For some examples of these news reports, please see: "Indonesia: Update—Nike, Adidas Factories Still Sweatshops—Report," Reuters English News Service (March 7, 2002); "Rights Group Says Nike Isn't Fulfilling Promises to Reform Sweatshops," *Wall Street Journal* (May 16, 2001); "Nike's Enemies: the Usual Suspects," *Asian Wall Street Journal* (May 7, 1997).
13. The notion of activity domains as part of corporate strategy is discussed in Chapter 4.
14. See for example: "Report Rips Nike Labor Conditions, Alleges Widespread Abuse at Viet Plants," Associated Press (March 28, 1997); "Indonesians 'Just Do It' Sweating for Nike," *San Francisco Examiner* (August 30, 1992).
15. See Chapter 3, Table 3.1, "Business Strategies for Narrowing the Legitimacy Gap."
16. See for example: "Indonesia: Update—Nike, Adidas Factories Still Sweatshops—Report," Reuters English News Service (March 7, 2002); "Rights Group Says Nike Isn't Fulfilling Promises to Reform Sweatshops," *Wall Street Journal* (May 16, 2001); "Nike's Next Move, The Company Has a Long Way to Go in Improving Workers Compensation," *Pittsburgh Post-Gazette* (May 25, 1998); "Nike in Asia: This is Prosperity?," *Wall Street Journal Europe* (June 17, 1997).

17. See Chapter 3, Table 3.1.
18. See for example: "Nike's Image under Attack, Sweatshop Charges Begin to Take Toll on Brand's Cachet," *Buffalo News* (October 23, 1998); "Nike's Enemies: The Usual Suspects," *Asian Wall Street Journal* (May 7, 1997).
19. See for example: "Hired Consultant Gives Nike's Labor Practices Good Review," Associated Press Newswires (June 24, 1997); "Report: No Widespread Abuse of Workers in Nike's Factories," Associated Press Newswires (June 24, 1997).
20. *Marc Kasky vs. Nike, Inc., Complaint for Statutory, Equitable and Injunctive Relief.* In the Superior Court of the State of California in and for the City and County of San Francisco, April 20, 1998.
21. *Marc Kasky vs. Nike, Inc. et al.* In the Supreme Court of California, Ct. App. 1/1/A 086142, S 087859, May 2, 2002.
22. Nike "Corporate Social Responsibility Report—FY 2001," 6–24.
23. Ibid, 34–35.
24. Nike "Corporate Social Responsibility Report—FY 2001."
25. A more detailed rationale against these arguments has been provided in other parts of this book. See, for example, Chapters 1 and 3.
26. "Gap and Nike: No Sweat?" BBC News Programme Panorama; Paul Kenyon, reporter; Fiona Campbell, producer; aired by BBC October 15, 2000.

The Walt Disney Company: A Progressive Approach to Monitoring Compliance

In many ways, Disney is an American icon. Recognized and respected all over the world, it is associated with children, family values, and clean wholesome fun. The Disney brand is perhaps the most valuable asset of the corporation. It is, therefore, logical that the company makes every effort to protect the reputation of its brand and continually enhance public trust in products and services carrying the Disney name.

In 2001, Disney's worldwide operations generated over US$25 billion in revenues. The Walt Disney Company conducts its operations through a number of subsidiary business units, including ABC, Inc., ESPN, Walt Disney Parks and Resorts, Disney Consumer Products, The Walt Disney Studios, and Walt Disney Internet Group.[1] Disney's main operations are divided into four groups: Media Networks (38 percent), Parks and Resorts (28 percent), Studio Entertainment (24 percent), and Consumer Products (10 percent). Disney's theme parks and related services (e.g., hotels, entertainment complexes) are located in Florida and California (United States), Paris (France), and Tokyo (Japan). In addition, the company is also developing a theme park in Hong Kong. The Walt Disney Studios combines resources of Walt Disney Pictures, Touchstone Pictures, Hollywood Pictures, Miramax, and Dimension to produce and offer to the general public various films. Each studio works closely with the company's Media Networks to promote individual film projects. Disney's television groups include: ABC Television, Buena Vista Television,

Walt Disney Television, ESPN, Disney Channel International, and Fox Kids Europe. Disney cable television now comprises 12 channels, reaching 15 million subscribers in 56 territories, with Brazil and Portugal added in 2001. Radio Disney operates primarily in the United States. In 2001 it started to go abroad by launching a radio station in Argentina.

The Disney Stores operation has about 700 locations in nine countries. The Disney Stores are currently in a consolidation phase, and Disney expects to reduce the number of North American stores to between 300 and 400. With regard to the production and distribution of goods inspired by Disney's characters, Disney Consumer Products, a subsidiary of The Walt Disney Company, leads the charge. Besides brick and mortar stores, Disney Company offers distribution of its products through the Disney Catalog and Disney Store web site. The range of Disney products includes hardlines, toys, apparel, and publishing products. Under an agreement with Disney, Gillette Company announced the development of a specialized line of oral care products for children, including manual, battery, and rechargeable toothbrushes featuring Disney characters.

Disney licenses Mattel, Inc., Hasbro, Inc., TOMY, and other toy manufacturers to produce toys for kids, which are distributed through domestic and international retailers, including Wal-Mart and Toys 'R' Us. Kids' and adults' apparel featuring Disney characters is sold through Kmart, JCPenney, and other retailers across the United States, Europe, Latin America, and Canada. In addition, the company distributes audio and computer software products for the entertainment market, as well as film, video, and computer software products for educational markets.[2]

Disney's Licensing Activities, Overseas Manufacturing and Procurement Practices

Disney's licensing revenues are consolidated within its Consumer Products (DCP), which recorded $2.6 billion in sales in fiscal year 2001 (September 30). According to Disney's 2001 annual report, DCP's licensing business showed improvement over the previous year as Disney realigned its licensing business into three distinct categories (i.e., hard goods, toys, and apparel).

This case study is confined to the manufacture and procurement of products in developing countries—mostly toys and apparel—and the extent to which Disney is exposed to the problems associated with manufacturing conditions and labor practices prevailing in the plants that make these products under the Disney brand and logo. Disney's overseas manufacturing and licensing operations, although quite sizeable in terms of units and dollars, differ significantly from other large U.S.-based multinational companies (e.g., Nike, McDonald's, Wal-Mart, Gap, Hasbro, and Mattel).

Disney does not own or operate any manufacturing plants. Given a large and ever-changing product mix and a continuous stream of new toys and games based on Disney characters, production runs for each item tend to be fairly short. Disney also has a large number of licensees and vendors (parties who source merchandise sold in Disney operations such as The Disney Store and Parks and Resorts) with considerable turnover among them. Licensees and vendors invariably use multiple manufacturing facilities. Therefore, the total number of manufacturing facilities making Disney products is quite large. This manufacturing base has rapid turnover and is difficult to identify on a real-time basis. The twin factors of short product life cycle and rapid turnover among licensees, vendors, and manufacturers results in Disney products accounting for a small proportion of a plant's total output. It also limits Disney's leverage in inducing local manufacturers to comply with Disney's standards for working and living conditions in the plants.

Notwithstanding the general conditions described above, there are other factors that provide Disney with unique leverage to influence the conduct of its licensees and their manufacturing facilities. For example, Disney counts among its licensees some of the world's major producers and sellers of toys, apparel and accessories, and other products aimed at children. Among the most notable of these is Mattel, the world's largest toy company. Disney is a highly prestigious and popular brand where new and popular toys—based on Disney's movies and videos—are constantly added to the list. Therefore, most licensees and manufacturers prefer to keep Disney products in their portfolios. Similarly, a meaningful portion of Disney products is manufactured in mainland China, making it possible to craft solutions to the sweatshop problem that are applicable to a large number of licensees and manufacturers in a single country, thus making implementation both efficient and cost-effective.

Families, and especially children, are Disney's primary market. Disney is therefore quite sensitive to protecting its image as a purveyor of wholesome products. The company does not wish to be seen as part of a system where children and young adults are exploited in the manufacturing and selling of Disney branded products. The corporate culture and ethos put a premium on family values and engender "trust" in the company's integrity in all its activities. Thus, unlike many other companies, Disney is not defensive about taking action to correct any shortcomings in its field operations, which carry the Disney logo.

Disney and the Sweatshops/Human Rights Issue

In the early and mid-1990s, ethical issues linked with offshore operations in developing countries became a critical topic in public discussions. Child labor was ranking at the top of this agenda together with other major problems such as toxic waste and product safety. According to a survey by a Boston investment firm, only a few retailers in the United States were tracking ethical issues abroad. Less than 10 percent of corporations had policies in place, relying totally on the laws of the countries in which they operated and placing the entire responsibility on subcontractors.[3]

A series of publicized events during 1995 and 1996 reinforced a growing concern of Disney management that a more direct, proactive approach to addressing labor standards issues was required. These events, such as the growing public debate on the working conditions in Nike's Vietnam footwear factories, were accompanied by additional disclosures and investigative reports in newspapers and television documentaries involving a number of other nationally and internationally known brands from major companies based in the United States and in England and other European countries. The products included apparel, toys, carpets, and household goods. These products involved unskilled and low-skilled workers in poorer countries of Asia and Latin America.[4]

Like most other companies, Disney was caught unprepared when the first reports appeared with regard to sweatshop-like conditions in a plant that manufactured Disney toys. As one Disney spokesperson stated at the time these reports first emerged (early 1995), Disney had no full-time compliance officer in the organization whose sole responsibility was to monitor working conditions and compliance with national labor laws in the factories and countries where Disney branded products were being manufactured.[5] There was a presumption that regulatory oversight for labor law compliance should primarily be the responsibility of the governments of those countries. Chuck Champlin, spokesman at the time for Disney Consumer Products, said, "The law is the mechanism through which a country will express its concern for its people. The country should be the primary agent of change." And such change, according to Chuck Champlin, cannot be made overnight—"It's not like you wave a magic wand and make the world right," he said.[6] The company also relied on its licensees and vendors to self-police themselves in a manner consistent with contractual terms, which required appropriate labor standards to be maintained in the manufacture of its branded product.

It would appear that Disney's antenna, like those of other U.S. companies, was not tuned to detecting the problem, which from their perspective was in the preproblem stage. This was soon to change when the public pressure on the companies continued to increase with ever more reports of worker abuse appearing in the news media. Furthermore, these reports were not confined to any particular company or country, but seemed to be permanently linked with the entire sourcing movement to developing countries.[7]

Antecedents to the Creation of International Labor Standards

From its very start, Disney's response to the sweatshops/human rights issue was proactive and systematic, and had the support of the company's top management. The deliberate character of its response pattern may also have been helped by a low level of public hostility and corporate criticism when compared with other companies like Nike, which practiced an aggressive form of public relations, or others that were caught in the investigative net and were poorly prepared to deliver an articulated and reasoned response. Disney was also less visible in the overseas factories because its products represented relatively small percentages of these factories' output. This was in sharp contrast to other MNCs, such as those involved in the manufacturing of toys, footwear, and computer chips, where plants often employing workers in excess of 5,000, were dedicated to the manufacturing the products of a single MNC.

Table 10.1 provides our analysis of the news stories pertaining to Disney that appeared in the news media around the world. It would appear that the two-year period of 1996–1997 coincided with the highest number of negative reports about Disney, with 88 percent of these reports associated with a single country, Haiti. In terms of issues, the reports covered the waterfront of the problems associated with sweatshops. These were: wages (35 percent), working conditions (21 percent), child labor (17 percent), and human rights violations (14 percent). There was a significant decline in the number of these reports during the two subsequent time periods of 1998–1999 and 2000–2002. This improvement in the situation may have resulted from Disney's success in implementing the company's International Labor Standards (ILS) program.

Disney realized that sweatshops had become a significant issue in its overseas operations. It was also evident that public scrutiny of these operations would increase in scope and intensity in the United States and other industrially advanced countries, which were its prime consumer market. Furthermore, even in developing countries, efforts by the local NGOs, advocates of the poor, and labor activists had expanded their investigative role and brought public attention to wages and working conditions.

Table 10.1 Negative News Stories Concerning The Walt Disney Company, 1994 to March 2002, Distribution According to Country and Issue

	1994–1995	*1996–1997*	*1998–1999*	*2000–2002*
Countries				
Haiti	0	37	6	1
China	1	0	0	11
Thailand	1	0	1	0
Others	5	5	16	2
Total	7	42	23	14
Major Issues				
Wages	1	39	22	14
Working conditions	7	24	20	10
Child labor	1	19	10	0
Human rights violations	5	16	8	7
Working hours	3	8	6	12
Worker abuse	0	6	3	3
Total	17	112	69	46

Note: Data for this table was derived primarily from Dow Jones Interactive (DJI) and supplemented from other sources (e.g., LexisNexis, *The New York Times*, and *Business Week*. Information contained here should not be considered either comprehensive or all-inclusive, but as an overall indicator of the news coverage about Disney and sweatshops/human rights issues. This data is based almost exclusively on publications in the English language and from Western sources. To the extent that reports of this type appear in the local language media and are not picked up by the Western news media, the scope of coverage is incomplete. Similarly, certain news stories (e.g., news wires) are often picked up by multiple media and reported in their respective news channels. This tends to inflate somewhat the number of incidents reported, but it is important nevertheless as different news media reach out to different population segments.

Quite often news stories report on multiple issues (e.g., child labor, wages, worker abuse, etc.). Therefore, the combined number of issues reported will be greater than the total number of news reports—86—surveyed for this study.

Therefore, as a result, Disney initiated a number of efforts in 1996 to address the need for a formalized, disciplined approach to strengthening its endeavors with respect to international labor standards. An immediate step was taken to identify the existence of any industry-wide approaches, which could expedite the introduction of an acceptable level of labor standards all over the world using the combined purchasing power of the companies involved. The only significant effort underway at the time was the White House Apparel Industry Partnership (AIP). While participation in this effort was originally considered, the company was concerned about the initiative's early lack of tangible progress.[8] Disney then decided to follow a "go-it-alone" approach and developed its own ILS program, including a governing code of conduct.

Therefore, in 1996, as a long-term response to correct and control the situation, Disney established a Code of Conduct for Manufacturers. In announcing the code, Disney stated that the company was committed to the promotion and maintenance of responsible international labor practices in its licensing and direct sourcing operations throughout the world. Toward this end, the company implemented a wide-ranging ILS program that included policies, practices, and protocols designed to protect the interests of workers engaged in the manufacture of Disney merchandise, whether for licensees or for direct sale at Disney properties.[9]

Initial Organizing Effect

Disney created an executive-level committee of senior executives representing the company's corporate and business operations throughout the world. This group was charged with the responsibility of devising ways by which Disney would create a meaningful set of labor standards and a viable plan of monitoring to ensure compliance. Reflecting on the company's early efforts, one Disney executive commented: "In developing our plans, we were not driven by cost considerations except in terms of efficiency. Our focus was to ensure that the process would yield a specified level of performance in improving conditions in the factories making our products." According to another executive, "We were motivated by corporate culture which emphasizes a thorough, well-prepared approach to problem solving and frowns on media-hyped quick fix solutions." The executives also agreed that there was "an issue of the ethical context of our conduct and that the company has a moral obligation to ensure that workers are treated fairly and not subjected to unsafe and abusive working conditions."[10]

Disney's Code of Conduct for Manufacturers

Disney's code emulated, in large measure, the principles embodied in the Workplace Code of Conduct developed by the White House Apparel Industry Partnership.[11] The Disney code has since been translated into 50 languages and distributed to tens of thousands of licensees, vendors, factories, and individual workers (Exhibit 10.1).

Disney's ILS program code and implementation standards are quite specific. In general they require, as a minimum, compliance with the host country's labor and environmental laws and regulations. Where these laws

Exhibit 10.1   The Walt Disney Company Code of Conduct for Manufacturers

At The Walt Disney Company, we are committed to:

- A standard of excellence in every aspect of our business and in every corner of the world;
- Ethical and responsible conduct in all of our operations;
- Respect for the rights of all individuals;
- Respect for the environment

We expect these same commitments to be shared by all manufacturers of Disney merchandise. At a minimum, we require that all manufacturers of Disney merchandise meet the following standards:

Child Labor. Manufacturers will not use child labor. The term "child" refers to a person younger than 15 (or 14 where local law allows) or, if higher, the local legal minimum age for employment or the age for completing compulsory education.

Manufacturers employing young persons who do not fall within the definition of "children" will also comply with any laws and regulations applicable to such persons.

Involuntary Labor. Manufacturers will not use any forced or involuntary labor, whether prison, bonded, indentured or otherwise.

Coercion and Harassment. Manufacturers will treat each employee with dignity and respect, and will not use corporal punishment, threats of violence or other forms of physical, sexual, psychological or verbal harassment or abuse.

Nondiscrimination. Manufacturers will not discriminate in hiring and employment practices, including salary, benefits, advancement, discipline, termination or retirement, on the basis of race, religion, age, nationality, social or ethnic origin, sexual orientation, gender, political opinion or disability.

Association. Manufacturers will respect the right of employees to associate, organize and bargain collectively in a lawful and peaceful manner, without penalty or interference.

Health and Safety. Manufacturers will provide employees with a safe and healthy workplace in compliance with all applicable laws and regulations, ensuring at a minimum, reasonable access to potable water and sanitary facilities, fire safety, and adequate lighting and ventilation.

Manufacturers will also ensure that the same standards of health and safety are applied in any housing they provide for employees.

(Continued)

Exhibit 10.1   *(Continued)*

Compensation. We expect manufacturers to recognize that wages are essential to meeting employees' basic needs. Manufacturers will, at a minimum, comply with all applicable wage and hour laws and regulations, including those relating to minimum wages, overtime, maximum hours, piece rates and other elements of compensation, and provide legally mandated benefits. Except in extraordinary business circumstances, manufacturers will not require employees to work more than the lesser of (a) 48 hours per week and 12 hours overtime or (b) the limits on regular and overtime hours allowed by local law or, where local law does not limit the hours of work, the regular work week in such country plus 12 hours overtime. In addition, except in extraordinary business circumstances, employees will be entitled to at least one day off in every seven-day period.

Manufacturers will compensate employees for overtime hours at such premium rate as is legally required or, if there is no legally prescribed premium rate, at a rate at least equal to regular hourly compensation rate.

Where local industry standards are higher than applicable legal requirements, we expect manufacturers to meet the higher standards.

Protection of the Environment. Manufacturers will comply with all applicable environmental laws and regulations.

Other Laws. Manufacturers will comply with all applicable laws and regulations, including those pertaining to the manufacture, pricing, sale and distribution of merchandise.

All references to "applicable laws and regulations" in this Code of Conduct include local and national codes, rules and regulations as well as applicable treaties and voluntary industry standards.

Subcontracting. Manufacturers will not use subcontractors for the manufacture of Disney merchandise or components thereof without Disney's express written consent, and only after the subcontractor has entered into a written commitment with Disney to comply with this Code of Conduct.

Monitoring and Compliance. Manufactures will authorize Disney and its designated agents (including third parties) to engage in monitoring activities to confirm compliance with this Code of Conduct, including unannounced on site inspections of manufacturing facilities and employer-provided housing; reviews with employees. Manufacturers will maintain on site all documentation that may be needed to demonstrate compliance with this code of Conduct.

Publications. Manufacturers will take appropriate steps to ensure that the provisions of this Code of Conduct are communicated to employees, including the prominent posting of a copy of this Code of Conduct, in the local language and in a place readily accessible to employees, at all times.

The Walt Disney Company, 1996

and regulations are less stringent than Disney's code, Disney requires that local factories observe Disney's standards.

While Disney's standards are specific, implementation can be a challenge in cases where differing legal interpretations exist at various levels of governmental authority. For Disney and other companies, China represents this type of challenge. In China the national labor laws provide limits on maximum number of working hours—both regular and overtime—and rest days, which all employers must obey. However, these limits are widely flouted by factories that receive exemptions from local authorities. These exemptions, which can vary from city to city and even among factories in the same city, allow these factories to greatly exceed national labor law provisions in terms of regular and overtime hours, rest days, and other limits on working conditions. The legality of these local waivers is questionable and of dubious validity. However, it is widely and openly practiced and to date the Central Government in Beijing has not taken any action against the offending local municipalities.

Disney supports increased government oversight of labor law, including a unified interpretation and application of labor law at the local, provincial, and national levels, in every country. Until then, for conflicting positions regarding jurisdiction and law interpretation in China, Disney, like most other MNCs, currently recognizes such local waivers only to the limits of its existing ILS standards (which also exceed the limits incorporated in the Chinese national labor laws). Disney believes that until such time that a unified approach to the interpretation of local laws has been established in China, it is necessary to accept local bureaus' exemptions (subject to Disney's ILS standards) as these local labor bureau exemptions exercise enormous influence over the governance of the factories operating within their regions.

Organization Structure and Resource Allocation

Disney believes that a sound approach to the promotion of responsible working conditions must involve cooperation and communication among all constituencies interested in this important area. Further, such an approach offers the best long-term prospects for successful implementation of positive labor conditions. Accordingly, the company encourages broad-based efforts to develop ways to strengthen global labor standards.

From its inception, Disney has given top priority to its ILS program. The oversight of the company's activities rests in a group consisting of senior executives from Disney's corporate and business operations, and the personnel directly responsible for the day-to-day conduct of the ILS program. The group's responsibilities include the overall direction of the ILS program, as well as assessment of ongoing educational, monitoring, and remediation efforts by the company's own ILS team, and by the company's licensees and vendors. In addition, the group makes recommendations with respect to the development and strengthening of policies and procedures on a company-wide basis, including cooperative efforts with interested nongovernmental organizations. Finally, ILS activities are subject to review by the audit committee of the company's board of directors.

Disney has a well-developed organizational structure to implement its ILS compliance program. The formal dedicated organization is called Corporate Compliance. It is staffed by dedicated full-time employees located in offices throughout the world. This staff provides a variety of services designed to maintain and enforce the company's commitment, including education, communication, monitoring, remediation, and collaboration activities.

Internal Monitoring System for Compliance Assurance

Disney faced a major challenge in creating a monitoring system to ensure licensee compliance with its International Labor Standards (ILS). Disney does all its business through licensees and vendors. These licensees and vendors manufacture goods in their own factories as well as contract with other factories. Thus, in assuring International Labor Standards (ILS) compliance at the factory level, Disney is a number of steps removed from exercising authority over plant managers.

To manage the process, Disney decided to create a database, which would be constantly upgraded on a real-time basis. It would also be interactive and provide access to all parties involved in the compliance process on a need-to-know basis. This is an important managing tool and is vital to the efficient management of the ILS compliance program. The database includes over 30,000 plant entries. However, given the high turnover among the factories, the active universe at any one time is approximately 10,000 factories. The important components of the database include:

- Details of factory location, and its linkages with one or more licensees and vendors.
- Factory characteristics, types of products manufactured, characteristics of workforce, dormitories, canteens, and other facilities.

- Complete audit history, compliance status, remediation plans for correcting deficiencies (if required), and schedule of follow-up visits for compliance assurance.
- Details of when and how a factory was terminated, reasons for termination, and any provisions for reinstatement.

The real-time character of this database allows Disney's compliance organization as well as operating divisions to have direct access to this information prior to making any decisions with regard to a particular facility.

Training Programs

As part of its ILS compliance effort, Disney has developed an elaborate training program that encompasses all facets of ILS. These include: training that focuses on building competence at the licensee, vendor, and factory levels in implementing the ILS program, accurate record keeping, and continuous improvement. Another facet of the program deals with the training of field auditors—Disney as well as contract auditors—in applying specific standards in auditing a factory's ILS compliance, outlining detailed procedures by which the field audits would be conducted, the step-by-step approach to a phased audit schedule from initial audit to subsequent follow-ups, and an outline of how the final audit would be prepared for submission to the Disney headquarters. The third element of the training program details review procedures to be followed at the headquarters and in the local offices in reviewing field reports for quality assurance of ILS compliance, and the process by which a factory may be dropped from Disney's list for allowable manufacture.

A review of the program points to its comprehensiveness as to content and the thoroughness with which it is implemented. If the training program is as good in practice as it appears on paper, it has the potential of continuously maintaining Disney's strong overall effort in the company's ILS compliance effort.

Monitoring for Compliance Assurance

Disney recognizes that simply promulgating a statement of principles is not enough and that a code must be rigorously enforced. Toward this end, Disney undertook direct factory monitoring activities in 1997, using professional independent auditors. This effort was further augmented in 1998 with the addition of Disney's own internal monitors to ensure the consistency and quality of the company's ILS-related monitoring activities. To date, the company has conducted more than 25,000 factory audits in more than 50 countries around the world. Each audit involves a close inspection of a factory to examine working conditions, a review of compensation and benefit records, and private interviews with factory workers.

Monitoring Process

Disney's target is to audit every plant in countries the company has determined to present a high risk of noncompliance at least once a year with additional follow-ups where necessary. Audits are conducted both by Disney's own staff of internal auditors as well as outside firms that have been approved by Disney.

Each audit takes approximately one day and involves a two-person team. It covers an examination of the plant's records with regard to payroll, worker injury, and environment, health, and safety (EHS) standards. A sampling of 25 workers are interviewed on a confidential, one-on-one basis. Upon the completion of the audit, the audit team has a meeting with the factory management with regard to deficiencies that need to be corrected. Where a plant is found to be in violation of ILS standards considered "zero tolerance" standards, the plant is immediately terminated from making any Disney branded products. There is no appeal of this decision.

The ILS staff at the company's headquarters in Burbank, California, receives all audit reports and exercises quality control and oversight over the entire audit process. Reports are continually monitored for thoroughness, and sent back to auditors when information is insufficient. Appropriate remediation actions and time frames are communicated to all business partners involved.

Remediation

When Disney's factory audits, or information otherwise brought to the company by third parties, reveal noncompliance with its code, the company first seeks to work with the factory concerned to remedy the situation. Disney encourages the facility to develop a remediation plan to bring its operations into compliance with the code so that manufacturing of Disney merchandise can continue. In cases where the operators of a particular facility do not develop such a plan, or fail to implement it, the company terminates its authorization for the use of the particular factory to manufacture Disney merchandise. Except in cases of egregious violations, Disney's preference is to try to bring a facility into compliance, rather than terminate it.

There is, however, one flaw in this approach. While Disney requires that plant management must henceforth correct all violations of minimum wage and overtime work, it has so far not always required the violating plants to pay back wages to the workers who were improperly denied them. This approach rewards the plant managers by allowing them to keep their ill-gotten gains while penalizing the workers who are the lowest paid and most vulnerable members of the supply chain. The principle and corporate responsibility of making the workers whole through payment of all back wages is unequivocal. However, it would be difficult to enforce such a condition in a country like China given the current business climate. Therefore, as a matter of good faith effort and also compliance with the company code, I believe that Disney and other companies should at the very least insist that local factory owners must pay "all back wages" for the entire period to those workers who are currently on the factory payroll or those who had been on the factory payroll during the previous 12 months.

In Disney's view, however, insistence on full remediation of past noncompliance needs to be balanced against the primary goal of ensuring compliance on a going-forward basis and continued production in the facility. Therefore, if a factory is found to be in repeat violation, the company terminates its relationship with the violating factory.

Other Initiatives

In 2000, Disney further advanced its monitoring efforts by launching a cooperative monitoring project with a group of religious and other institutional investors. This project is designed to provide an assessment of the company's monitoring program and the potential role of nongovernmental organizations in support of the ongoing efforts.

The company is also working on a project whereby it would identify a factory to use as a test case. This factory would assiduously implement and comply with all the provisions of the ILS program. The objective of the exercise would be to evaluate, under realistic conditions, the feasibility of implementing ILS provisions and the economic viability of the plant under real-time competitive market conditions.

Independent External Monitoring and Public Disclosure of ILS Findings

To date, Disney has not made any substantive public disclosure of the company's progress in implementing its ILS program. The company believed that the first phase of its ILS program should focus on development and implementation of an effective effort rather than public promotion of its activities. The current approach now contemplates increasing public transparency of the company's activities, involvement of outside social responsibility organizations and labor rights groups, and public reporting.

Notes

1. The Walt Disney Company annual report, 2001.
2. The paragraph refers to Disney annual report 2000, p. 63
3. "Saving the Brand Name," *Maclean's* 108:50 (December 11, 1995), 30.
4. Rachel Sylvester and Joe Saumarez Smith, "Exposed: Shame of Gap's Child Labor Sweatshops," *Sunday Telegraph* (January 21, 1996), 1; Raynier Maharaj, "Gifts of Love, Made in Hell," Editorial, *Toronto Sun* (January 8, 1996), 12; William Branigin, "Honduran Girl Asks Gifford to Help End Maltreatment," *Washington Post* (May 30, 1996), A29; Stephanie Storm, "A Sweetheart Becomes Suspect: Looking behind Those Kathie Lee Labels," Editorial, *New York Times* (June 27, 1996), 1; D'jamila Salem, "Human Rights Group Targets Disney, Kathie Lee Apparel Lines; Labor Tells Congress That Imported Clothing Were Made by Abused, Underage Workers," *Los Angeles Times* (April 30, 1966), Business Section, Part D, 1; James Lawless, "Child Labor Protested, Wal-Mart Denies Charges," *Plain Dealer* (May 6, 1993), Metro, 1B; "Celebrities Sweatshops," Editorial, *Denver Rocky Mountain News* (June 30, 1996), 67A; "State Charges Eight McDonald's Restaurants with Violating Pennsylvania Child Labor Laws," *PR Newswire* (February 8, 1989), 0208012; Frank Swoboda, "Burger King Accused of Child Labor-Law Abuse," *Washington Post* (March 9, 1990), A11.
5. Interview with the author.
6. "Saving the Brand Name," *McLean's* 108:50 (December 11, 1995), 30.
7. See Chapter 2.
8. For more details please refer to Chapter 8, "Fair Labor Association."
9. http://disney.go.com/corporate/compliance.
10. Interview with the author.
11. It should be noted here that the White House Apparel Industry Partnership was the predecessor organization to the Fair Labor Association. These principles also form the foundation of FLA's code of conduct, which was discussed and analyzed in Chapter 8.

PART FIVE

New Approaches to Viable Codes of Conduct

Guidelines for Creating Multinational Codes of Business Conduct

Imperatives for Multinational Codes of Conduct

The discussion in the previous chapters should not lead us to conclude that voluntary codes of conduct are a hopeless proposition. Quite to the contrary, I strongly believe that despite all the difficulties and problems, these codes offer perhaps the best, if not the only, way to bridge the gap between MNCs' performance and societal expectations in developing countries, especially in the areas of sweatshops, human rights violations, and environmental degradation. The problem does not lie with the concept of voluntary codes, which is quite sound. It rests with MNCs and the manner in which they currently create and implement these codes. Therefore, we should hope for and expect positive changes given the right kind of external pressures and inducements on the one hand, and proactive responses from socially responsible and forward-looking MNCs and their leadership on the other hand.

We have seen the futility of creating universal standards at the international level, as in the UN's Global Compact. It also does not appear imminent that industrially advanced countries will enact laws and regulations—except as a last resort—that will protect workers in developing countries. Besides being susceptible to domestic political pressures, such measures are also prone to being rigid and highly bureaucratic. And the attempt to make one size fit all means that such regulations are likely to be inefficient and expensive. Nor do developing countries themselves seem to have the necessary means or the will to protect their own workers under conflicting pressures from home-country producers, foreign MNCs, and not the least, pervasive corruption and bureaucratic inertia.

MNCs certainly can, and a vast majority of them currently do, exploit this lack of oversight in developing countries. However, there are serious risks attached to short-term exploitation, where companies have ignored the opportunity to undertake modest, proactive reforms during the preproblem and problem identification stages; later, companies may pay a tremendous price in the remedy and relief and the prevention stages—in terms of corporate reputation, compensatory and punitive awards in lawsuits, stringent regulation, and loss of markets.[1]

History repeats itself precisely because we have short memories. We are doomed to repeat our mistakes if we ignore the lessons of history. Our future actions, therefore, must be imbued with vision and creativity, and guided by our experiences of the recent past. MNCs should not look upon these codes with trepidation or fear them as instruments for creating further intrusion into corporate affairs. Instead, by setting clear and mutually agreed upon criteria—where current standards are weak or nonexistent—companies assure themselves of external accountability within the limits of economic feasibility and competitive reality.

The present disparity between the rhetoric and practice of corporate codes of conduct is not unique. It invariably occurs when business-society conflicts are in the early stages of evolution, that is, in the preproblem and problem-identification stages. As an issue evolves, it is simultaneously affected by three sets of forces: past history and antecedents, current contextual framework of the problem, and anticipated future implications. These factors act as crosscurrents, pulling an idea in different directions until a common understanding is reached among various elements, thereby defining the parameters of the issue and giving it a structure.

Voluntary codes of conduct, sponsored by MNCs, are here to stay. When properly developed and implemented, they provide MNCs with a voluntary and more flexible approach to addressing some of society's concerns about MNC actions in their overseas operations. In the process, codes can serve both corporate interest and public purpose, and can strengthen free market institutions. They will also restore public faith in the market economy as the best avenue for enhancement of human welfare, regional economic advancement, and a strengthening of democratic institutions.

Antecedents to Creating a Viable Multinational Code of Conduct

To be viable, and acceptable to both the corporation and its external critics, a code of conduct must narrow the credibility gap between societal expectations and corporate performance. We should expect societal expectations to continually evolve, in keeping with changes in the scope of the issues involved, the level of performance delivered by the MNCs, and the public's trust in the corporations' performances. Society will also change its expectations as to the best that can be expected of a corporation, given the sociopolitical and economic-competitive conditions under which it must operate.

In the interest of honesty, we must face the fact that corporations operate abroad to make money. All else is secondary. We should not expect them to contribute to the overall health of the local economy and well-being of the local people if by doing so they imperil their own survival. Nor should we expect them to justify their conduct by claiming that they support democratic institutions.

Codes of conduct that impact operational costs, productivity, and output must take into account the economic environment and competitive constraints. Minimum standards, whether they govern operating costs or working conditions, must take into account alternative opportunities of employment available to workers and competitive conditions confronted by employers.

What we should expect, and must receive, from the multinationals is accountability for their conduct in their own operations and the operations of their local suppliers and strategic partners. They must demonstrate that they are not abusing their bargaining leverage against their workers. They must ensure that workers live and work under safe and healthy operating conditions, are not forced to work excessive overtime hours, and are paid wages that, at a minimum, meet local labor laws. Workers should not be treated as mere appendages to machines.

It follows that to have any reasonable chance to meet the expectations of the parties involved, a code of conduct must:

- Be economically viable for the corporation, given the dynamics of competition, the industry structure, and the economic and sociopolitical realities of the developing countries where its operations are located.

- Provide for a fair share of gains from improved productivity to workers who are responsible for major contributions to productivity and profitability. Lacking effective bargaining power and suffering from lax enforcement of local labor laws, these workers must depend on the integrity of the MNCs to help them improve their lot. It therefore behooves MNCs and their local suppliers not to exploit them in a manner that is injurious to their long-term health and well-being.

- Address substantive issues that are important, first of all, to the workers themselves and to the corporation's various constituencies, including foreign governments and other affected groups.

Furthermore, the multinationals themselves must:

- Engage important constituencies when formulating the code and the implementation process.

- Be specific as to performance standards that can be objectively measured.

- In order to engender trust, be transparent in their actions and share information with their workers as to costs.

Creating a Code of Conduct

A corporate code of conduct is in the nature of a "private law" or a "promise voluntarily made" whereby an institution makes a public commitment to certain standards of conduct. The nature of voluntariness, and by implication the flexibility afforded to a corporation, depends on the basic premise that MNCs and their critics share a common interest in improving the underlying conditions of the affected groups and regions and that it is in the interest of all parties to resolve the underlying issues within the realistic constraints of financial resources and competitive conditions.

The private law character of voluntary codes of conduct gives the corporation a tremendous opportunity for discretionary action. It also imposes a heavy burden to create independent systems of performance evaluation, monitoring and verification, and public disclosure. This voluntary approach provides the MNC with the opportunity to define the conditions and establish the standards by which the corporation wishes its performance to be measured. However, the scope of the code and the MNC's performance standards must meet an acceptable level of societal expectations.

The MNC, therefore, must not only create a set of laws—a code of conduct; it must also provide a system by which its performance will be measured, evaluated, and verified. The private law character of the code does not reduce the obligations of the MNCs. It increases the burden of the MNC to ensure that its skeptical critics and the public at large are persuaded that the company's performance standards are adequate and that the company's claims of performance are true. The MNC will be expected to create and pay for a system of policing, monitoring, and judging its performance while ensuring that the system is completely independent of the MNC—both in perception and in reality. The MNC must also bear the ultimate responsibility that its code provisions, implementation mechanisms, transparency and objectivity of performance measures, and independent external monitoring and verification are scrupulously observed and rigorously enforced. Otherwise, these measures will not create the necessary public trust. Rather than enhancing corporate reputation, they will diminish it.

The first step in the development of a workable code of conduct is to define its scope of action. This includes:

- *Definition.* What aspects of corporate business activities are to be included in the code of conduct?
- *Measurement and Verification.* How should corporate performance of these activities be measured, and how should accuracy be verified?
- *Accountability and Reporting.* To whom should the corporation be accountable for its performance, and how should this performance be made public?

The following sections will discuss the first two elements: creating a code and implementing it. The third element—independent monitoring and public reporting—will be discussed in the next chapter. The notion of independent external monitoring and public reporting of MNCs' compliance efforts has been the subject of heated debate, with MNCs offering a multitude of arguments against independent external monitoring and reporting. Our analysis suggests that most of these arguments are logically untenable and empirically refutable. Where these arguments have some validity, we will show how MNC concerns can be handled, and their legitimate interests protected, without diminishing the need for transparency in monitoring compliance and making these findings available to public.

PRINCIPAL ASPECTS OF A COMPANY'S ACTIVITIES TO BE COVERED IN THE CODE

The code of conduct must address the relevant concerns of the affected communities—as seen from the perspective of the community—in the manner the corporation prefers to define them. The issues covered must be seen to have some relation to the company's activities, and corporate action and resources must be able to do something about them.

The MNC should resist all efforts—even at the expense of alienating the community—to include issues that are outside the reach of the company or that cannot be improved, even if the company was willing to devote resources in that direction. Thus, it would be quite appropriate for the MNC and its local suppliers to pay their workers more than the minimum wage, improve their working conditions, offer basic educational programs, create skill-enhancement training programs, and improve health care facilities. However, it would be imprudent to expect the MNC to undertake these improvements for the entire community in a given area. Similarly, a commitment to improve the waste treatment or emission standards of a company's plant should be expected of the corporation. It would be unrealistic, however, to commit the company's resources to improve the infrastructure of an entire locality. In such a case, a multiplicity of political and economic constituencies would be involved, all of them with their own agendas, and the issues would be outside the control of the corporation.

Conversely, a company should not "load the code" with activities that are peripheral to the core issues of concern to the community. For instance, a company might start a youth self-help program or open an orphanage as an expression of good corporate citizenship, but if the community is demanding better treatment of workers in the company's plants, these other programs—however praiseworthy in themselves—will be seen as cynical attempts by the company to distract public attention from the issues that the community most cares about.[2]

It is critically important that the MNC specify the scope of its code-related activities in objective and outcome-oriented terms. It is not sufficient to define the MNC's commitments as "continuous improvement," "best effort," or "dollars to be spent" in remedying a particular situation. The standards must be specific about the current state of a given problem and about when that problem will be resolved. If the company promises to improve existing standards to another level, it must clearly specify the time frame within which this improvement will take place.

The MNC must also define zero tolerance issues on which it will not accept any shortfall under any circumstances—issues such as use of children and payment of wages that are below the minimum wage required by the country.

A third aspect of the code standards has to do with the measures the company will take where its performance, or that of its suppliers and strategic partners, falls below its avowed commitments.

A review of current codes of conduct—whether group-based or individually created—suggests that an overwhelming majority of these codes fail to meet any of the three conditions just outlined. The sole exception to this statement is the case of Mattel, Inc., which is discussed in Chapter 13. The author is also aware of a small number of companies that are currently taking tentative steps in this direction.

A number of companies, such as Disney and Mattel, have indicated that they have indeed created areas of zero tolerance where the company's suppliers will immediately lose any contractual relationship with the MNC if they fail to meet the code's requirements. However, these MNCs as yet have declined to publicly identify the companies so terminated, or disclose the precise nature of their standards and the manner in which they plan to enforce compliance. Even where MNCs have publicly stated that they have indeed placed some companies on their watch list or have even refused to do further business with them, the MNCs have been extremely reluctant to identify these companies publicly. The only exception has been where such information was made public as a consequence of exposés by public interest groups.

MEASUREMENT AND VERIFICATION

The code must be translated into a quantifiable and standardized audit instrument that lends itself to objective and consistent measurement by different auditors. The auditing procedure must develop four qualitative and quantitative criteria:

1. Enable the firm to continuously monitor its activities to make sure that programs are developing most efficiently and are yielding the desired output.
2. Create measurements such that two independent, unrelated auditors examining a plant should come to essentially similar conclusions.
3. Generate data to assist management in improving performance and selecting future activities in anticipation of future changes in objectives.

4. Enable management to report accurately and objectively on its activities in order to provide the interested public with a true index of the corporation's performance and a basis for comparing it with the activities of similarly placed corporations.

These issues have been major weaknesses in the area of MNC code compliance. Even when the companies have created viable codes of conduct and have publicly committed themselves to independent external audits, they have lagged in creating more precise standards of measurement. In the case of the FLA, we have noted some of the problems that occur when standards are ambiguous and are not outcome-oriented.

Vague standards allow the auditor wide latitude in accepting or rejecting an audited plant's performance in a given category. This is especially worrisome when:

- An auditing firm is required to complete the audit in a specific time and for a given fee.
- The auditing firm has been retained by the plant itself—the so-called second party audit—when the local plant wants to present itself to the MNC as a "precertified" manufacturing facility.
- The auditing firm has been retained by the MNC to act as the company's internal auditor and, therefore, must meet the MNCs expectations with regard to the adequacy and quality of audits. There is pressure to deliver "acceptable reports" if the auditing firm wishes to continue business with the company. Even where such audits are by NGOs, there is pressure to accommodate the MNC, if only to encourage the company to continue on this path.
- The problem is further compounded when the MNC declines to publicly disclose the full text of the audit and instead asks the public to accept the company's statement that the audited plants are in compliance with the company's code. As noted in Chapter 8 on the FLA, this approach casts serious doubt on the integrity of the audit process and the credibility of the MNC.

It should also be noted that similar concerns have jeopardized the credibility of independent external audits conducted by a group called SA-8000, which is one of the more frequently used independent auditing organizations. A case discussion of SA-8000 is presented in Chapter 12.

Corporate Commitment to the Code of Conduct

No code of conduct is likely to succeed without the endorsement and support of the company's board of directors and top management. The company's top management must be strongly and unequivocally committed to implementing the code. Executive performance at all levels of management, including code compliance, must be closely linked to management performance evaluation and compensation.

The company must also be willing to expose its operations and code compliance to public verification if it expects to garner the "reputation effect" and thereby benefit from increased consumer patronage and public approval. And finally, adequate financial and human resources must support the code process to ensure that code compliance is carried out in a timely fashion. As argued elsewhere in the book, the cost of creating systems and procedures for code compliance is not significant enough to make material financial impact on the company's bottom line.

Creating and implementing a meaningful code of conduct entails certain risks that are associated with any type of innovative and entrepreneurial activity. In the case of codes of conduct, there is also the added risk of combining economic and social criteria where performance measures of success are not easily determined a priori, but can be demonstrated with certainty only after the fact and over the long term. However, it is precisely this long-term aspect of calculated risk taking, and self-confidence in doing the right thing, which separates corporate leaders from the also-ran, and distinguishes corporations for their long-term success in the financial and sociopolitical arena.

History is replete with instances where corporate leaders were willing to break the mold of conventional wisdom to preserve the corporation's reputation in the face of adversity. Alternately, a bold new leader will take over the helm of a corporation facing an adverse external environment and succeed in a sharp turnaround with strategies that respond to a changing sociopolitical environment rather than defend the status quo.[3]

In the current debate on sweatshops and human rights issues, there is only one company, Mattel, Inc., that has broken the mold of industry resistance and opted for a code of conduct with strong performance measures, transparency, and independent external monitoring of compliance verification and public reporting. The circumstances confronted by Mattel in this case are no different from those of a host of other companies embroiled in the issues of sweatshops and human rights abuses. The primary reason for

Mattel's distinct conduct must be found in its top management, corporate board, and corporate culture. The importance of top management's leadership qualities also become apparent when one examines the wide disparity in response patterns to the same set of problems by other companies, such as Disney, Nike, Wal-Mart, and McDonald's, to name a few.

Current Approaches to Creating and Implementing Codes of Conduct

MNCs are currently following two approaches as they develop codes. The first one may be termed "reaction to perceived reality" and is externally based and motivated. The second approach may be termed "maximum capability utilization and best effort" and is internally based. Both approaches are based on certain assumptions and corporate goals that will lead these approaches to different courses of action and results. When used exclusively, each may yield less than the maximum attainable benefits to the corporation as measured in terms of public acceptance of the firm's performance and the most efficient use of its physical and human resources. Each approach, if used alone, may not provide maximum discretion in decision making that is free of outside interference or pressure.

REACTION TO PERCEIVED REALITY

Under this approach, a corporation assumes that there is really no criterion to determine what is socially responsible behavior and what is acceptable to the general public or to various interest groups at a given point in time. Consequently, the code includes whatever the public expectations are in a particular set of circumstances. The MNC would do well to satisfy these expectations to the maximum extent possible. Thus, it is not the real social needs, however defined, that are important; it is the perceived needs as advocated by the most influential, or most vocal and strident, corporate critics.

The MNC can gauge these perceptions through a variety of means, including public opinion surveys, news media, and the agendas and priorities of NGOs that represent affected communities whose opinions are considered important to the company. Another approach, also externally oriented, is to determine how the public ranks a company among different firms of similar size or among industry members that face similar issues worldwide or in specific geographical areas. This approach often forms the basis of creating industry-wide or group-based codes of conduct.

The perceived reality approach has certain advantages. It helps a corporation keep its goal posture more in tune with societal expectations. To some extent, perceived reality is partly a function of what a corporation does and partly a function of what the public believes that an individual MNC and all similarly placed MNCs are doing about the issue; in such cases, the corporation is likely to maximize its short-run gains by meeting societal expectations. The cost of conformity is similar to that of other companies, which reduces competitive pressures. Societal expectations are also moderated by creating the impression that all forward-looking companies are doing the best that can be expected under the circumstances.

This approach allows the MNC to find an easy fix to its problems of public pressure. The corporation may also expend considerable resources in public relations and public education to alter public perceptions without actually improving its performance on the key issue. Evolving shifts in societal expectations are easily accommodated through marginal changes in corporate performance.

This approach, however, suffers all the problems of (1) putting emphasis on public information and education and (2) relying on a group-based approach—issues that were discussed in earlier chapters. Extensive reliance on public relations can seriously endanger the company's credibility when unexpected public exposés of corporate conduct or conduct of its industry partners lead to serious erosion of the public's trust. In addition, group behavior, in the absence of a priori and externally accepted standards, is pressured toward the lowest common denominator because of adverse selection and the free rider problem.

A totally external approach to goal determination does not take into account a firm's own strengths and weaknesses in attacking certain problems and may lead the firm to allocate its resources poorly. Such an external approach narrows the discretion management can exercise to select remedial and preventive actions and to establish the time frame in which to execute them efficiently.

MAXIMUM CAPABILITY UTILIZATION AND BEST EFFORT

This approach allows management maximum discretion to select areas of action—within the multiple areas of concern to the public—that make the best use of the corporation's ability to deliver desired and socially relevant outputs at the least cost. This approach is internally oriented, is deliberately planned for the long term, and does not entirely depend on current issues and approaches advocated by corporate critics.

This approach has the advantage of allowing the really innovative corporation to fashion solutions to the problems envisaged by the community in a way that gives the firm the first mover's advantage. As has been argued elsewhere in this book, this approach, when followed in a deliberate manner and with the intention of ameliorating real problems, will provide the firm the most advantage, in terms of return on efforts, and will deliver the greatest amount of societal good.

Suggested Framework for Developing Programs for Corporate Social Audits

A prerequisite for an effective code is the creation of new procedures and changes in organization to enable a corporation to (1) evaluate the external social environment; (2) generate internal data for program development and evaluation, decision-making points for delegating authority, and guides for pinpointing responsibility; and (3) select alternate courses of action for utilizing the organization's physical and manpower resources most efficiently, while effectively responding to external constraints. This arrangement is similar to the organization of a firm for its primary activities—the production of goods and services for profit—where the organization is geared to respond efficiently to market conditions, profit centers are created to assign responsibility for various activities, and financial data are generated in a form that is useful for both internal control and external reporting of financial health.

Figure 11.1 is a flowchart that shows how to adapt an internal organization. The primary aim is to develop effective long-range goals and medium-range strategies. It is assumed that once a suitable decision structure has been developed, it should be able to respond automatically and effectively to short-run and day-to-day operational problems and tactics within the framework of long-range goals and medium-range strategies. The model recognizes four types of external constraints to which a firm must respond and adopt its behavior: existing legal constraints, anticipated legal constraints, pressure from the general public and special-interest groups, and performance of other companies against which a firm is compared by various groups. Existing legal constraints are considered to be

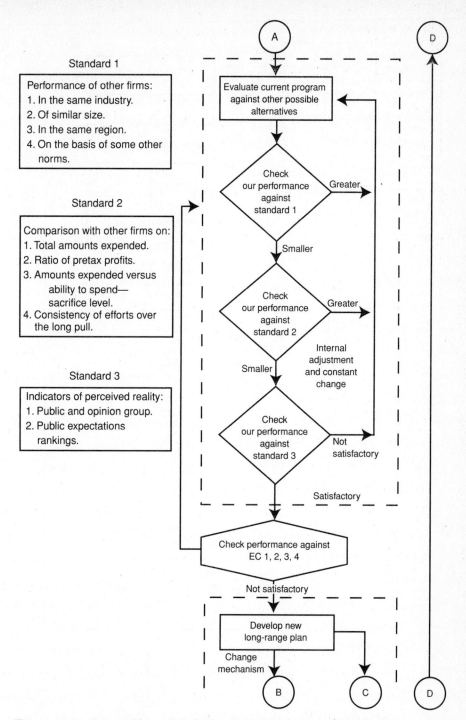

Figure 11.1 Process Flow of Understanding Environment Constraints and Rationale for Creating and Implementing MNC Code of Conduct

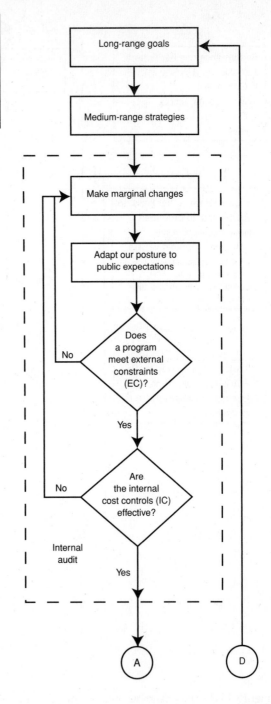

Long-range goals

Medium-range strategies

Make marginal changes

Adapt our posture to public expectations

Does a program meet external constraints (EC)?

No

Yes

Are the internal cost controls (IC) effective?

No

Internal audit

Yes

A

D

Figure 11.1 (*Continued*)

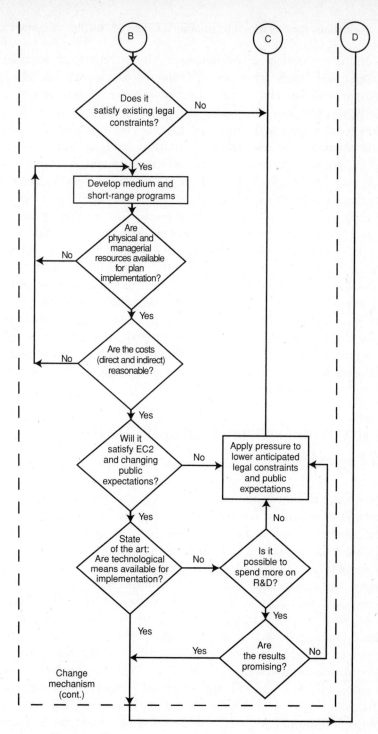

Figure 11.1 (*Continued*)

given and uncontrollable. The remaining three constraints are presumed to interact with each other with positive feedback loops in which the firm's input is likely to have some effect on the level of constraints.

Briefly, the first step is to make an internal audit to evaluate how well the firm is complying with the current code. The next step is to compare existing programs against other alternatives and to make continuous changes to improve internal operational efficiency and adaptability to external constraints. This is followed by a comparison of the effectiveness of a firm's programs with those of other firms. The final step has two aspects: (1) the firm makes changes in the internal mechanism to alter its long-range goals and medium-range strategies, and develops new programs to meet these goals and strategies; (2) the firm tries to exert pressure to relax those external constraints it finds either difficult or impossible to meet.

It should be noted here that this is a generic model to illustrate the desirability of a systematic approach to creating a viable code of conduct. It can also help in designing internal systems and procedures to ensure that code compliance, monitoring, and performance evaluation are integrated into the company's operating systems. And finally, it allows for timely evaluation of external forces that may necessitate changes in the code components and implementation procedures.

Industry-Wide Common Standards Are the Next Logical Step

Chapter 5 argued that in the early stages of business-society conflicts, such as demands to reform sweatshops, MNCs should create their own codes of conduct, and also suggested that this was the best approach, both from the viewpoint of the companies and of society at large, because it minimizes the problems of free riders and adverse selection.

During the preproblem and problem-identification stages, there is no consensus as to the nature and magnitude of the problem or how best to address it. This is true for both the MNCs and the NGOs. At this stage, an individual, company-based code of conduct would give the sponsoring corporation the advantage of being recognized as the innovator, which would enhance its reputation and contribute to its customer franchise. The corporation will thus receive benefits that are commensurate with the risks that the company took in developing and implementing such a code.

Although rewarding in itself, such an effort alone will not be enough in the long run to engender a hospitable operating environment for business in different countries around the world. Therefore, the successful efforts of the innovator company must be expanded to encompass larger segments of the industry. For this to happen, good corporate conduct must become the rule rather than the exception. At this stage, the innovator company can play an important role by helping other companies follow its example and thus establish common standards of conduct that will be congruent with societal expectations. This is especially likely to happen if these expectations have been crystallized during the problem-identification and remedy and relief stages.

By this time, the lead MNC's code of conduct may be widely regarded as the best one and the most acceptable to all of the important stakeholders. In the process, the lead company has created new systems and procedures, management structures, and training protocols. This in-house expertise, developed at significant expense in human and physical resources, is a strategic asset that a company can now deploy for greater competitive advantage in the marketplace. The innovator company can help the next group of companies by sharing this information and thereby reducing the fixed costs of code development and implementation on the part of the larger business community.

The lead company's reputation ensures that the follower companies will escape undue public criticism and scrutiny because of their association with the innovator company. The lead company also gains from this cooperative effort through enhanced reputation effect. It benefits from the infusion of new ideas and approaches developed by other companies. However, for this approach to work, it must meet four conditions:

1. These companies must commit themselves to meeting the lead company's code with uniform standards of measurement, monitoring, and verification before they can share the reputation effect of the lead company.

2. All participating companies must have a commitment to maintain the highest possible code standards, to ensure that there is no erosion in public trust and confidence and to minimize the free rider problem, although there may be a short transition period during which code implementation is phased in.

3. The top management of these companies must have a long-term commitment to code compliance and, where necessary, to enhancing code standards to meet changing societal expectations as new problems emerge and new issues are identified.

4. As a group, these companies should benefit from essentially similar reputation effects and not be burdened with the excessive baggage of a bad reputation from prior actions.

Notes

1. S. Prakash Sethi and Paul Steidlmeier, *Up Against the Corporate Wall: Cases in Business and Society*, 6th ed. (Upper Saddle River, N.J.: Prentice-Hall, 1997).
2. See Chapter 9, which describes Nike's undertaking of a similar approach with poor to negative results.
3. The case of Johnson & Johnson and its CEO James Burke illustrates the first point during the Tylenol tampering issue, while the case of boycott against Nestlé over the infant formula controversy illustrates the second point. See "Johnson & Johnson Seeks Quick End to Tylenol Tragedy," Dow Jones News Service (April 10, 1982); "Johnson & Johnson Begins Bid to Revive Sales of Tylenol," Dow Jones News Service (October 25, 1982); Sam Passow, "Corporate Terrorism: Thinking about the Unthinkable," *Wall Street Journal* (March 26, 1984); S. Prakash Sethi, *Multinational Corporations and the Impact of Public Advocacy on Corporate Strategy: Nestlé and the Infant Formula Controversy* (Boston: Kluwer Academic Publishers, 1994). Similarly, it was the leadership of the CEOs of 12 of the largest U.S.-based multinational corporations that made Rev. Leon Sullivan's vision into the Sullivan Principles in South Africa. The first signatures to the Sullivan Principles were: American Cyanamid, Burroughs, Caltex Petroleum Corporation, Citicorp, Ford Motor Company, General Motors, IBM, International Harvester, 3M, Mobil, Otis Elevator, and Union Carbide. See S. Prakash Sethi and Oliver F. Williams, *Economic Imperatives and Ethical Values in Global Business: The South African Experience and International Codes Today* (Boston: Kluwer Academic Publishers, 2000; pap. ed. Notre Dame, Ind.: University of Notre Dame Press, 2001).

Independent Monitoring Systems: Transparency in Code Implementation, Compliance, and Verification

MNCs and their critics continually argue about the requirement that MNCs subject their claims of code compliance to independent external monitoring and verification. MNCs have offered a variety of arguments against such monitoring.

The following sections examine the arguments advanced by MNCs against independent external monitoring and assess their validity. The analysis concludes that these arguments are, for the most part, untenable. When MNCs do have substantive concerns, it seems they can be satisfactorily handled by creating structural and procedural safeguards in the monitoring and disclosure systems, especially if temporary variance from full-fledged monitoring is permitted during a clearly defined transition period.[1] These measures would protect trade secrets from competitors when such information would harm a company's legitimate interests. The measures should also provide for an orderly implementation of the external monitoring system, keeping it within reasonable time limits and resource constraints.

MNCs' Assertions about External Monitoring of Code Compliance

When a company has to produce factual information in response to specific legal and regulatory provisions, one should expect that most companies would be in substantial compliance. Otherwise, they will be subjected to legal penalties, with adverse consequences for the company and the executives responsible for producing inaccurate information. Corporations expect to be audited by independent outsiders for their financial performance, to ensure their investors of accurate information. The same applies to other filings by the companies when required by law, in the case of air emissions and water quality standards, for instance. Requirements of independently audited statements are considered necessary disincentives (through the threat of civil and criminal penalties) to restrain companies from violating relevant laws and regulations. However, if we look at the recent examples of Enron, Tyco, and Global Crossing, even these strictures have not been sufficient to deter some of the largest companies from violating various securities and other laws.

A similar logic applies to voluntary codes of conduct, in which the case for credible and factual information is even more pertinent. A critical element in the conflict between the MNCs and their critics involves the extent to which corporate critics and the public at large should believe the MNCs' claims that they are complying with their own codes of conduct. Without casting any aspersions on corporate integrity, the fact remains that MNCs have a poor track record when it comes to providing factual information about working and living conditions in their overseas plants and those of their suppliers. And yet the companies continue to insist that people should have faith in their claims of code compliance, which is a somewhat dubious proposition even under the best of circumstances. Why then should companies be so reluctant to open their performance to public scrutiny if they have nothing to hide and everything to gain, especially when their good performance would create public trust and improve corporate reputation?[2]

Corporate Credibility and Public Trust

The issue at hand is trust. Public acceptance of self-regulation is directly related to the extent that people trust the corporation and its executives. In this sense, trust is an economic asset with a market value. Trust also has some of the attributes of a public good. If some companies prove trustworthy, other companies in the industry are likely to be trusted as well. Unfortunately, the reverse is equally true.

When it comes to MNC conduct in the sweatshop issue, important segments of public opinion, advocacy groups, and corporate critics trust the corporations very little. Instead, there is a large element of distrust, which is a negative public good and a corporate liability. The reasons for this lack of trust are to be found in structural conditions of the marketplace and in corporate conduct. It is unfortunate, but nevertheless true, that the highest growth rates in the current wave of offshore production have been recorded in countries that generally have dictatorial and repressive regimes with deplorable records of human rights violations. These countries also offer a hospitable environment for locating offshore plants. Under these conditions, even the most enlightened companies would be tainted in public eyes and would suffer from guilt by association.

Publicly owned corporations are legally required to generate and publicly disclose financial information—even when it is negative. It is hard to argue that they shouldn't be able to generate and disclose other types of information that affect their vital constituencies and that are also of interest to the public at large. It is likely that once enough corporations have provided substantive information about their activities, they will establish the parameters of public expectations, which will be based on the reality as projected by the corporations and not on the reality advocated by their critics.

Public sentiment and perspective play an important role in defining the parameters of discretion that a society will allow the leaders of its various social, political, and economic institutions. In the present instance, as well as in many previous instances involving social issues, the fight for the hearts and minds of the public has invariably been led by the corporate critics who take the initiative. The companies, fearing lack of public trust, have refrained from proactive public debate and have instead limited themselves to disputing their critics' charges. This is a losing battle and will always remain so. By yielding the initiative to their critics, MNCs have allowed them to shape the agenda of public debate in ways that put MNCs in a perpetually defensive mode. They are always answering charges about "what MNCs have done wrong" instead of taking credit for "what MNCs are doing right." History is replete with instances in which otherwise highly successful and economically powerful corporations failed to address public concerns in a timely fashion—when these concerns were in an embryonic state—and were forced to incur enormous financial penalties and loss of markets. In many cases, companies lost their public franchise or even went out of business.

Lack of Transparency Also Undermines Internal Corporate Compliance Efforts

In the absence of transparency, independent evaluation, and accountability, corporate actions—no matter how enlightened and well-meaning in the initial phases—become hostage to organizational inertia and degenerate into window dressing. Without external credibility, corporate codes generate neither economic benefits nor public goodwill. In a self-fulfilling prophecy, they are viewed as a waste of corporate resources by insiders who object to such external intrusion on both philosophical and practical grounds.[3]

Experience has shown that code compliance invariably brings into scrutiny other corporate activities that are impacted by the company's conduct. Thus, excessive overtime during peak demand periods may be a business necessity; it may also reflect lack of strategic planning and poor supply chain management, causing one part of the company to demand urgent deliveries and its attendant evil, forced overtime, while another part of the company is working to minimize excessive and involuntary overtime.

Similarly, we have noticed that a company will often place orders with two suppliers who offer similar price, quality, and delivery assurances; but one supplier is in full compliance with the company's code with regard to labor practices while the other one is charged with excessive violations. The explanation offered is the need for having diverse sources of supply. In reality, the reasons are the buying agents' comfort level with a particular supplier and a lack of pressure from the company to make code compliance an integral part of the internal performance evaluation and compensation system. Experience also indicates that a supplier is highly unlikely to be in a bimodal stage, with excellent performance in one area and unacceptable performance in another. Suppliers that abuse workers are likely to cut corners in other areas when given an opportunity. Doing business with these companies may yield the MNC a short-term gain, but will expose the company to greater harm and potential risk in the long term.

External Monitoring Is Expensive and Unjustified on a Cost-Benefit Basis

The MNCs often make quite fallacious arguments about the alleged high cost of independent external monitoring. A common refrain is that a comprehensive program of independent external monitoring is very expensive and that its cost cannot justify its perceived benefits. MNCs further argue that worker conditions in poorer countries will be improved more efficiently if these moneys were instead devoted to worker training and other forms of assistance to local vendors. This argument has also been used by the Fair Labor Association, which agreed to offer partial subsidies to some of its poorer members to jump-start external monitoring programs.

Consider the following statement by Elliot Schrage, a senior vice president of Gap Inc. In discussing the problems his company encountered in starting a monitoring system, he states: "Then there is practicality. Gap spends $10,000 a year for independent monitors at Charter, which is owned by Taiwanese investors, and thousands more for management time to arbitrate disputes and for its own company monitors to recheck the facts on the ground. For the company to duplicate these intensive efforts at each of the 4,000 independent factories it contracts with would have taken about 4.5 percent of its annual profit of $877 million last year."[4]

In our view, these figures, when presented without context, create an extremely distorted picture. They are misleading and are designed to enlist sympathy for the embattled MNCs. They must be debunked with equal bluntness.

Let's accept for the sake of argument that Gap spends $10,000 for independent monitoring at a plant, although our survey of various monitoring groups certified by both FLA and SA-8000 suggests that the cost of a single factory audit ranges between $3,000 and $8,000, based on the size of the plant and the thoroughness of the audit required by the MNC. We will give credit to Gap for insisting on exceptionally rigorous standards and incurring higher costs for its audits.

Now let's assume that a typical plant employs about 5,000 workers, each of whom earns about $2 per day based on a wage rate of 25 cents per hour for an eight-hour workday. Therefore, the $10,000 cost would be equal to one day's wages per year for the entire plant. Further assuming that employees work only five days per week, this cost represents 0.38 percent of the normal yearly wage cost of the plant.

It should be apparent to the reader that this cost estimate is the most liberal interpretation of the relation between employee wages and the cost of monitoring. In reality, very few plants operate on the schedules of 40 hours and 5 days per week. Instead, most employees work 10- or 11-hour days and 6-day weeks. Since some of these hours are worked on an overtime basis, their combined effect would further depress the cost of audit in relation to work hours and total wages in a given plant. Add to it the fact that a great many plants work two shifts or even three, and one would be hard-pressed to come up with a number higher than 0.2 percent of the actual yearly wage costs of a typical plant.

Why is this cost not justifiable as insurance to ensure that workers are paid their legally mandated, and MNC-recognized, wages and benefits, and that they work in a relatively safe and healthy environment? How much does it cost the company and its vendors to ensure that products manufactured by its overseas suppliers meet the company's standards of quality product, safety, and delivery schedules?

Looking at it another way, we might ask how much these workers are being robbed of their legitimate wages every year, and what, if anything, the MNCs and their local vendors are going to do by way of restitution for years and years of expropriation of the wages of the workers who are at the bottom of the food chain and are least able to defend themselves? And what about the potential injury to their health and well-being from an unhealthy and unsafe work environment? Do MNCs and their local vendors realize that they are looking at huge potential liability 15 to 20 years down the line, similar to the costs confronted by tobacco companies and asbestos users?

Now let's consider Mr. Schrage's estimate of the total bill of monitoring 4,000 factories at a cost of $39.5 million per year representing about 4.5 percent of the company's annual profit in the year 2000. Let's assume that the audits are similar in character to financial audits that all publicly owned companies are required to do on an annual basis. Even under the most stringent audit standards, the audit process requires a careful sampling of a small portion of all transactions that are examined to assess the accuracy of all such transactions in a database. This process is highly scientific and statistically valid, with a high degree of confidence as to its accuracy. And it can be accomplished at a fraction of the cost of an audit involving all transactions. Furthermore, this approach has also been found to be superior and more efficient, even where it is possible to undertake an audit of all transactions in a database.

Why is it not possible to use a similar approach in the case of code of conduct audits? A carefully designed, objectively determined, and randomly selected sample of factories from the total universe of 4,000 factories would not need to be larger than 500 factories under the most difficult circumstances imaginable. Given the randomness of the sample, all factories would stand an equal chance of being audited and thus would have strong incentives to comply with the company's code or risk losing business for noncompliance. Our cost of audits has now been reduced to 20 percent of the previous estimate and now stands at 0.04 percent of a typical plant's annual wage cost. This would also allow the MNC to undertake even more rigorous independent audits. One might even suggest that MNCs should put these savings into a reserve fund, which could be used to reimburse workers for past illegal confiscation of their wages, to pay accurate wages at present, and to improve wages in the future.

Refusal to Disclose the Identity of Local Suppliers

MNCs and their suppliers have vociferously opposed identifying vendors' names in code compliance reports that are made public. This is true even in the case of Mattel, which has otherwise committed itself to complete external monitoring and to public disclosure of the findings of its independent external monitoring group, without any censorship from the company. In a small number of cases where supplier names have become public, they have been revealed by the efforts of activist groups and corporate critics who were investigating sweatshop conditions in these plants. In the process, these groups have exposed the names of both the local manufacturers and the foreign multinationals for whom the intended products were manufactured. This situation is most prevalent in China,[5] although the insistence to remain anonymous is endemic to most manufacturers in developing countries where sweatshop conditions are prevalent and widespread.

Identification Would Make Vendors Targets of NGOs

MNCs and their suppliers claim they are quite willing to comply with the MNC codes and to have their compliance—warts and all—publicly reported as part of the MNC's overall compliance record. They also assert that the NGOs will invariably target them—even when they are identified as the good guys—in order to besmirch their reputations.

We contend that this argument is unsupportable. To date, only two groups of plants have been publicly identified. The first consists of plants that are wholly owned by Mattel or those owned by local entrepreneurs whose total output is dedicated to Mattel's products. Externally monitored reports of these plants were made public in 1999–2001. These reports did not paint a perfect picture. They listed many shortcomings on the part of plant management in code compliance, outlined steps that both Mattel and plant managers agreed to undertake to rectify these deficiencies, and required follow-up audits to ensure that corrective action had indeed been taken.[6]

It should be noted that not one of these plants, whether owned by Mattel or its vendors, was targeted by NGOs for special treatment. Most moderate NGOs recognize that no plant will ever be perfect and that it is more constructive to recognize and praise proactive efforts when they merit such praise. As a matter of fact, a number of prominent and respectable NGOs, such as the Investor Responsibility Research Center (IRRC) and the Interfaith Center on Corporate Responsibility (ICCR), have publicly praised Mattel's efforts in code compliance and independent external monitoring. They have cited Mattel as a role model other companies should emulate.[7]

Given this evidence, it would seem that local manufacturers should be only too happy to be publicly identified and benefit from their forward-looking and enlightened management practices. The reasons for their reluctance and the MNCs' acquiescence are likely to be more complex and less obvious.

Individual local manufacturers are under extreme pressure from other local companies not to publicize their compliance record for fear that it would bring unwanted attention to other companies that are unwilling to take similar steps. This situation is further aided and abetted by trade groups and industry associations in these countries, which have resisted the creation of meaningful codes and credible compliance monitoring systems.

MNCs have an equally strong incentive to resist universal vendor identification to enforce code compliance. To date, only a handful of vendors can claim to be in substantial compliance with any type of code. Identifying these few vendors would put the MNCs in the uncomfortable position of admitting that they have not done enough—after a decade-long effort—to make substantial code compliance by local manufacturers a general rule rather than an isolated exception.

MNCs have argued that it makes no sense to identify vendors that may not be currently in full compliance with their codes, but are making genuine efforts toward improvement. Exposure at this stage would bring added pressure from NGOs and force the MNCs to withdraw their business and thereby deprive thousands of innocent workers of their jobs.

This argument has some legitimacy. It has even been recognized by many NGOs, who have refrained from identifying individual plants in their investigative reports for fear that rather than helping these plants improve, the MNCs will simply abandon them in favor of other plants, which may be just as bad, but have not yet been discovered by antisweatshop activists.[8] This argument, however, fails to meet its stated rationale when examined in light of actual practices in the field.

For example, if MNCs are serious about this assertion, they should provide data about what percentage of their vendors fall in this category, how long they are likely to stay there, and when they are expected to reach the full compliance stage. Furthermore, what happens when these plants fail to meet MNC expectations within a reasonable time frame? Are they dropped from the approved vendor list? And if so, what is the logic of withholding their names when this information would serve a larger public purpose?

The argument that identification of bad vendors would only hurt their workers is only partially true when applied to specific vendors, and completely false when applied to a broader area in which this vendor is only one of many. In the first place, workers fired from one plant may find jobs in other plants that are doing well in terms of code compliance because of added business from the MNCs. Even in the worst-case scenario, jobs lost by these workers would create similar jobs elsewhere that would be filled by other workers, leaving the overall employment in the area unaffected.

Another argument made by MNCs for keeping the identities of their vendors secret is to protect them from being poached by the MNC's competitors. This is a valid argument, but only when it is applied in rare circumstances and to a very small group of vendors.

In the real world, all MNCs develop market intelligence about available sources of supply and the quality of different suppliers—both their own and those of their competitors. Similarly, local manufacturers bid for business from various MNCs, using their current list of customers as references. Manufacturing plants simultaneously produce goods for multiple MNCs, who may be competing with each other in their home markets. Therefore, it is highly unlikely that good vendors could be kept secret for any length of time. In rare cases in which an MNC has devoted substantial resources to improve a vendor's capacity and quality, the MNC should have no problem in making contractual arrangements restricting a vendor from doing business with that MNC's competitors. Therefore, a case for confidentiality can be justified only under restrictive circumstances and for limited periods. One cannot foresee a situation that would justify such secrecy on a permanent basis because the competitive marketplace would not allow it.

Alternative Forms of Independent External Monitoring and Public Disclosure of Code Compliance

A number of MNCs, yielding to public pressure, have adopted alternative forms of publicly reporting their code compliance. These measures provide a degree of public disclosure while allowing the MNCs greater flexibility to withhold most information about code compliance from public scrutiny.

One such approach, as discussed in Chapter 8, is currently being used by the Fair Labor Association. Among the flaws of the system cited there were the unrepresentative sample and its pro-industry bias, vaguely defined measurement standards that allow the auditors/monitors wide latitude in interpreting compliance levels, and economic pressure on the monitors to favor plant owners and MNCs in order to retain their business.

The system was also saddled with two additional fatal flaws, which destroyed the credibility of the monitoring system. The first one was the certification by the FLA that the entire product line or brand of an MNC would be considered to be in full compliance despite the fact that this claim was based on a nonrandom, unrepresentative sample of the universe of plants. The second fatal flaw was that none of the auditors' complete reports would be available for public review. Instead, people were expected to trust the FLA's assertions about the auditors' findings when (1) companies involved had played a major, if not decisive, role in the sample selection and when (2) many of these companies were represented on the FLA's board of directors.

Social Accountability International (SAI) and SA-8000

Another approach to external auditing and certification, similar to FLA, is SA-8000, which has been promoted by Social Accountability International (SAI). The Council on Economic Priorities (CEP), a well-known

NGO based in New York, is the entity behind the creation of SAI and SA-8000.

As the name implies, SA-8000 is modeled after similar UN standards of ISO 9000.[9] It purportedly builds on the merits of ISO auditing techniques: specifying corrective and preventive actions, encouraging continuous improvement, and focusing on management systems and documentation proving these systems' effectiveness. In addition, the SA-8000 system includes three elements essential for social auditing:

1. Specific performance standards set with minimum requirements.
2. Requirements that auditors consult with, and learn from, interested parties, such as NGOs, trade unions, and, of course, workers.
3. A complaints and appeals mechanism, which allows individual workers, organizations, and other interested parties to bring forward issues of noncompliance at certified facilities.

SA-8000 PRINCIPLES AND STANDARDS

These are described in general terms and are quite similar to a large majority of codes currently in vogue with individual companies and industry groups. These include provisions pertaining to child labor, forced labor, occupational health and safety, freedom of association and rights to collective bargaining, discrimination, disciplinary practices, working hours, and compensation.[10] In addition, the standards require that a company's management act in the areas of policy for social accountability, management review, company representatives, planning and implementation, control of suppliers, concerns and corrective actions, outside communication, and access for verification of records.

SA-8000 contends that it advocates a living wage for the workers while none of the corporate or industry-sponsored codes currently do so. However, in practice SA-8000 has failed to meet this goal. According to SA-8000's own records, the living wage provision has not been applied in any of 85 factories that have been audited and certified by SA-8000 accredited auditors as of December 1, 2001.[11]

ORGANIZATIONAL STRUCTURE AND AUDITING PROCEDURES

CEP-SAI also created an organizational structure to manage SA-8000 activities around the world. The system is quite similar to the pyramid form of a selling organization in which each level in the pyramid draws compensation based on the success of the level below it. Examples of such systems in the commercial world include companies like Amway and Avon. At the top of the pyramid is SAI, which receives its fees from the eight organizations that have been granted exclusive franchises to accredit other organizations, which will then accredit organizations and individuals to perform SA-8000 audits.

TRAINING

SAI's training program provides the foundation that supports the expertise of its auditors and the quality of their audits. There are two training courses available: the Auditor Training Course and the Supplier Training Course (for company management and suppliers to understand SA-8000 and help them to obtain certification).

These programs are a major revenue producer for SAI, with individuals paying fees of $1,600 for the auditing course. Training programs are offered almost once a month in different parts of the world and may draw between 20 to 40 candidates per training session. To date, SAI has certified approximately 1,100 candidates under its auditor training program.[12]

A majority of the trainees have been drawn from plant owners and suppliers of consulting services, such as accounting, quality assurance, and so forth. Critics have argued that for these firms SA-8000 is one more, albeit rather small, service in their portfolio of services. There is strong incentive to help the client achieve SA-8000 certification. A critical study of SA-8000 by an NGO group also found that the training instructors did not possess the knowledge or actual field experience to understand the standards and train new candidates.[13]

The training program lasts one week, and the candidate must pass an examination upon completion. Successful completion, however, does not make a candidate a qualified SA-8000 auditor. SA-8000 strongly urges that trainees also take the ISO 9000 lead auditors course and gain field experience before performing independent audits.

SA-8000 SUCCESS FACTORS AND DRAWBACKS

The success of the entire structure depends on the size of the bottom level of the pyramid, which actually conducts field audits. These auditors pay SAI an up-front fee of $15,000, followed by a graduated yearly fee starting with $2,500 in the first year and declining in subsequent years thereafter. It should be noted that in contrast FLA's accreditation is free of charge for individuals and organizations that take FLA's training program and are qualified to conduct audits for plants designated by FLA. Two NGOs that are active in external code compliance programs, when contacted by the author, indicated that, given the high certification fees and few potential clients, NGOs are unlikely to become SA-8000 certified auditors. Instead, commercial firms are currently doing almost all of the SA-8000 work. It was also indicated that no one could survive doing SA-8000 audits alone. Instead, firms certified for SA-8000 also qualify to do other certification work, such as ISO 9002 and ISO 14000.

In the case of SA-8000, there is tremendous pressure for field operators to extend the scope of their activities, which would generate revenues for them and in turn benefit members at the upper level of the pyramid. SA-8000 also encourages its auditors to be flexible and to work with plant owners and managers to enable them to meet SA-8000 standards. Plants are required to make a minimum three-year commitment, during which SA-8000 auditors will work with the plants to improve their operations. The cost of a typical SA-8000 audit ranges between $3,000 and $5,000, inclusive of all expenses, and is borne by the plant being audited. The plant is expected to meet the standard obligation of a three-year commitment. A failure to do so will cancel certification and remove the manufacturer's name from the SA-8000 web site (usually after six months' notice).

The system's strengths are obvious. It encourages plants to improve their performance by introducing proper systems and procedures. It provides a financial incentive to the auditors to work closely with plant management to improve performance in accordance with SA-8000 standards.

The shortcomings of the system are equally glaring. The financial pressure to succeed, when combined with its avowed flexibility, provides auditors with tremendous latitude to interpret plant compliance with SA-8000. This combination creates tremendous pressure on the auditors to cut corners and run the risk of accrediting plants that should not be certified.

PLANT CERTIFICATION

The ultimate and perhaps the fatal flaw is the SAI's plant certification process under SA-8000. Once an auditor has certified a plant and has notified the SAI, the plant name is posted on the SAI web site. This action completes the loop. There are no checks and balances to review the auditor's work, no systemic oversight, and no opportunity for outsiders or the public to review the quality of the auditor's work. The system is even inferior to that of the FLA, in that, at least on paper, the FLA headquarters in Washington, D.C., reviews all the reports submitted by the FLA-approved auditors. In the case of SA-8000, no such process exists.

ACCOMPLISHMENTS TO DATE

SA-8000 started audits with certain built-in advantages, which should have made it highly successful.

- It offers MNCs and their vendors a respected NGO sponsor in SAI and CEP. CEP and SAI count among their supporters and advisers a number of companies with global operations that would be candidates for SA-8000 audits.
- It provides the plants with a flexible and friendly system to seek certification and an auditing system with wide latitude and implicit bias toward approval.
- The plants are spared the danger of having the reports examined by others, which may lead to embarrassing disclosures.

It is therefore surprising that SAI's progress has been quite disappointing. According to SAI, during the four-year period ending December 1, 2001, SA-8000 had certified a total of 85 plants worldwide, of which 55 were located in Asia, 25 in Europe, 3 in South Africa, and one each elsewhere in Africa and in North America.[14] The current number of plants producing goods for MNCs for export to industrially advanced countries runs into many thousands. The number of plants that supply MNCs, which are in some way affiliated with CEP and SAI, would also run into the thousands. One wonders why these MNCs have not taken advantage of SA-8000. Is it possible that most MNCs are unwilling to subject themselves to even the most innocuous form of external auditing, as offered by the SA-8000? Alternatively, it is also possible that while they see the downside of such audits, they do not see the upside.

The situation with regard to the individual auditors is equally discouraging. The SA-8000 provides certification to the plants that wish to use this certification as a tool to gain contracts from MNCs. This is not independent, external monitoring in the sense that the term is commonly used. Instead, it is a form of internal audit commissioned by a company using non-company sources. Although SAI has declined to provide any data, anecdotal evidence from the field suggests that a majority of SA-8000 certifications to date fall in this category. In the end, SA-8000 itself and its clients and affiliates have been poorly served with such a fungible system of monitoring and lack of meaningful oversight.

Essential Elements of a Credible Independent Monitoring System

We now come to the final part of our discourse on the creation of an independent monitoring system. We have seen that systems like those proposed by the FLA or SA-8000 suggest some movement in the direction of independent external monitoring and public disclosure. These systems fail to meet the criteria of independence, representative character, and transparency. Without any one of these, the system will not persuade the public to trust corporate claims.

A successful independent monitoring program would require policies and procedures in three important areas:

1. A comprehensive and meaningful code and its implementation by the MNC.
2. An external auditing program to monitor corporate compliance with the code.
3. An independent institutional mechanism to verify corporate performance on code compliance, through careful oversight of the external auditing system with freedom to report its findings to the public.

Creation of a Comprehensive and Meaningful Code

The critical elements of an economically feasible and socially credible code were discussed in Chapter 11. The important points that need to be emphasized are the following:

- The code of conduct must be translated into a quantifiable audit instrument that lends itself to objective and consistent measurement by different auditors.

- The corporation's top management must be strongly and unequivocally committed to implementing the code. Executive performance at all levels of management, including code compliance, must be closely linked to executive compensation.

- The corporation must establish policies and procedures in which compliance with code provisions becomes an integral part of a manager's activities. Code implementation should not be peripheral to the company's normal operations.

- As part of this program, the corporation must create an internal auditing system that is parallel to its regular financial internal auditing program. The independence of the "code compliance internal auditing system" is absolutely necessary if the company expects to gain meaningful control and accurate information from its field operations. The internal auditing program should be responsible for regular, periodic audits of all of the corporation's operations that are impacted by its code of conduct. It should recommend corrective actions and have the authority to ensure satisfactory compliance. Recent incidences of financial fraud and conflict of interest in the United States suggest the dangers of having internal auditing and compliance functions report to the executive who is in charge of line operations.[15] This process weakens the checks and balances that are necessary to protect the corporation from misconduct on the part of employees and line managers.[16] Therefore, both internal auditing and compliance departments should have a direct line of reporting that separates them from the operating divisions whose activities are being monitored under the code. It is highly desirable that the overall findings of this program should be made available to the company's top management and to the audit committee of the corporation's board of directors.

- The corporation must be willing to expose its operations, and code compliance, to public verification and scrutiny. Otherwise, the corporation will fail to gain the reputation effect and lose the benefit of increased consumer patronage and societal approval.

External Monitoring (Auditing) of the Corporation's Performance with Code Compliance

The integrity of the internal auditing program would be strengthened by having an external auditing organization verify the company's compliance effort. This program should be based on well-established audit procedures that place the emphasis on verifying the accuracy of information generated by the company's internal audit program.

External audit programs should not be required to duplicate the effort of the corporation's internal audit program. Instead, they should be based on a thorough follow-up audit of a carefully selected, and statistically valid, sample of the entire universe of companies in such a manner that findings can be considered representative of the conditions prevailing in the entire universe of plants that manufacture products of the company.

We also strongly recommend that this external audit program should be directed and supervised by the independent external monitoring group set up to monitor and verify the corporation's overall compliance with its code and to ratify its accuracy to the public at large. The activities of this group comprise the third element of the code compliance, monitoring, and verification system, and are described in the next section.

- It would be preferable that the organization doing the external audits had no other business interest with the corporation. When this is not feasible for an auditing firm, the company should make sure, for instance, that there is a fire wall between the people involved in code compliance audit and people within the auditing organization who are engaged in other types of work for the same client.
- The corporation should also experiment with and encourage the use of NGOs in the external auditing function. However, extreme care should be exercised to ensure three conditions:
  1. The NGO group must understand that in the present case its role must be solely to verify corporate performance against existing code standards which the corporation has agreed to adhere to.
  2. When a particular NGO has a difference of opinion about the adequacy of principles and standards in the code of a particular corporation, this NGO should not be involved as an external auditor.
  3. NGOs involved in the external audit program must abide by the terms and conditions of confidentiality, and procedures for resolving disagreements of audit findings must be established.

Independent External Monitoring and Oversight

The corporation must establish an appropriate formal institutional mechanism that will be responsible for creating and managing the external code compliance audit program. This institutional mechanism plays a vital role in a corporation's effort to engender public trust in the corporation's performance. In the absence of such a system, the integrity of the corporation's entire code creation and implementation effort would be in jeopardy.

The primary role of the independent external monitoring body is to ensure the public at large and important stakeholders as to the accuracy of the corporation's claims with regard to code compliance. By putting its own reputation behind the corporation's claims, this institution provides a protective shield against unsubstantial allegations. The organizational structure of this mechanism is not yet fully evolved and is currently in flux. However, there are three operational models that have been tried with varying degrees of success: city manager model, cooperative model, and executive and oversight monitoring model.

CITY MANAGER MODEL

This approach places the primary responsibility for managing the entire process of code compliance, monitoring, and verification on one person, who works with the assistance of an advisory board. This model was used in the case of the Sullivan Principles in South Africa.[17] Single-person responsibility allowed for a focused approach and a speedy resolution of the problems that invariably emerge during various stages of implementation. Unfortunately, the system also suffers from the "capture theory of monitoring." The single person is under enormous pressure to show results. Since there is more contact with the corporation, the single person tends to treat the corporation as a friend and to consider the larger society as an amorphous and diffused entity that is unable to provide a counterbalance to the corporation. This situation is further exacerbated if the advisory board turns out to be largely ceremonial and perfunctory.

This process becomes even more vulnerable to undue corporate influence if the monitor is not required to provide complete details of compliance reports and instead simply certifies that the corporation has complied with the code in a satisfactory manner. As noted elsewhere in the book, this has been the most critical flaw in the monitoring and verification processes established by the Fair Labor Association and the SA-8000.

COOPERATIVE MODEL

This approach provides for a shared and combined responsibility of a group of individuals in performing the oversight and verification functions of the corporation's code compliance program. This approach was used by Nestlé during the infant formula controversy.[18] The cooperative group is generally much larger than in the two other approaches discussed here. The large size is deemed necessary to accommodate diverse interests and constituencies. Moreover, in the case of the infant formula controversy, the group's members also carried out all the investigative work. The FLA governance structure is somewhat similar to the cooperative model with three important distinctions:

1. The governance structure includes representatives of the corporations whose performance is to be monitored and verified. This creates the potential for conflict of interest.
2. The voting power is strictly regulated to ensure that no group would dominate the board's decisions. However, this has the effect of giving almost veto power to the corporate members on decisions they may view as contrary to their interest. Consequently, it undermines the credibility of the governance structure.
3. The representative character of the NGO board membership is inadequate.

The strength of this model lies in the collective knowledge of the group and its ability to represent many constituencies. Its weakness is its difficulty in creating focus and cohesiveness in such a large group. The size of the group also makes it somewhat difficult to organize and manage. Over a period of time, the group's focus tends to shift in favor of the agendas of those members who can devote more time to the group's business than other members can do. The effectiveness and efficiency of the cooperative group approach is particularly vulnerable to situations in which code principles and standards are not precisely stated and leave a wide latitude for interpretation by group members.

EXECUTIVE AND OVERSIGHT MONITORING MODEL

Under this approach the oversight function is located in a small group of people who are nationally and internationally known experts in one or more aspects of the issues involved. They also have impeccable credentials as public citizens, with reputations for independence. The group's primary role is that of compliance verification.

In its executive role, the monitoring board is responsible for organizing and implementing all aspects of external audits that will be undertaken to verify the code compliance of the corporation's own plants and those of its vendors and licensees. The entire process of sample selection (i.e., the plants that will be selected for verification audits), the scope and integrity of these audits, as well as the timing, will all be under the control of the board.

The monitoring board will also be responsible for issuing public reports of its findings, without any prior censoring by the corporation. The contents and frequency of these reports will be at the discretion of the board. There will, however, be appropriate procedures for the MNC management to resolve disagreements and to respond to the findings of the board. When these differences cannot be resolved, the monitoring board will be obliged to include management's response—without any editing—in its reports to the public. The MNC management, however, cannot change the content of the report as prepared by the monitoring board.

The executive board format is currently being applied at Mattel, Inc., under the name of the Mattel Independent Monitoring Council for Global Manufacturing Principles (MIMCO). This model, or something similar, appears to offer the best approach among the three models described here. The detailed workings of this approach in the case of Mattel are discussed in the next chapter.

Notes

1. As discussed in Chapter 5, I believe there may be other, more questionable, reasons that explain MNCs' reluctance to pursue effective code implementation and independent external monitoring and verification. It was suggested that until recently most MNCs have constantly asserted their full compliance with their own codes, which, among other things, claim that MNCs and their local manufacturers substantially meet all local labor and environmental laws. This has opened the MNCs to potentially large financial liability (and a public relations nightmare) should it now appear that this was indeed not the case. Thus MNCs and their local suppliers may be obliged to compensate those workers for wages that were due but not paid.

2. As of this writing Mattel, Inc. is the only company in the world that has committed itself to external independent monitoring and public disclosure of compliance reports. The company's program has been in operation since 1998 and is discussed in Chapter 13.

3. S. Prakash Sethi, *Multinational Corporations and the Impact of Public Advocacy on Corporate Strategy: Nestlé and the Infant Formula Controversy* (Boston: Kluwer Academic Publishers, 1994).

4. Leslie Kaufman and David Gonzalez, "Labor Standards Clash with Global Reality," *New York Times* (April 24, 2001), A1.

5. "Toys of Misery: A Report on the Toy Industry in China," published by the National Labor Committee, December 2001 (www.nlcnet.org). See also "How Hasbro, McDonald's, Mattel and Disney Manufacture Their Toys," report on the labor rights and occupational safety and health conditions of toy workers in foreign investment enterprises in Southern Mainland China, by the Hong Kong Christian Industrial Committee, December 2001.

6. Mattel Independent Monitoring Council (MIMCO), Audit Report 1999 (November 1999); MIMCO, Audit Report (May 25, 2000); MIMCO, Following Audit Report for Guan Yao (Zhangmei) Plant and Chang An (Metei) Plant (April 1, 2001); MIMCO, Audit Report, Mattel Manufacturas de Monterrey, S.A. de C.V. (MX3), Mexico (April 30, 2001).

7. Rodney Ho, "Some Companies Say Being Green Doesn't Mean a Red Bottom Line," *Wall Street Journal* (December 3, 1999), A6; Lisa Bannon, "Mattel's Asian Plants Will Address Problems," *Wall Street Journal* (November 18, 1999), 1–2; Tim Smith, letter to Mr. Alan G. Hassenfield, Chairman and CEO, Hasbro Toy Co., June 18, 2001. Mr. Smith is a vice president of Walden Asset Management, a Boston-based company that specializes in social investment funds. Prior to joining Walden Asset Management, Mr. Smith was the founder and executive director of the Interfaith Center on Corporate Responsibility (ICCR); for IRRC comments, see Investor Responsibility Research Center (IRRC), *Social Issues Service, 1998 Company Report—M, Mattel, Executive Compensation* (Washington, D.C.: IRRC, 1998), 1–9.

8. "Toys of Misery." See also "How Hasbro, McDonald's, Mattel and Disney Manufacture Their Toys."

9. Cited from the web site of the Council on Economic Priorities Accreditation Agency (CEPAA), www.cepaa.org/introduction.htm.

10. For detailed list refer to SAI web site at www.cepaa.org.

11. Ibid.

12. Social Accountability International (SAI) and SA-8000 e-Update, January 2002.

13. Cited in report "No Illusions: Against the Global Cosmetic SA-8000," by Labor Rights in China, Asia Monitor Resource Center, June 1999.

14. For detailed list refer to SAI web site, www.cepaa.org.

15. Charles Gasparino, "Lehman Broker in Alleged Big Swindle also Supervised Compliance Officer," *Wall Street Journal* (February 20, 2002), C. See also Charles Gasparino, "Broker Oversight or Tunnel Vision? Two Case Histories— Letter by Accused Raised Questions for Lehman, Cowen," *Wall Street Journal* (February 13, 2002), C1.

16. Gasparino, "Lehman Broker in Alleged Big Swindle." Also see what Barbara Whitekar wrote about Global Crossing, "An Accountant Who Raised Enronian Issues," *New York Times* (February 17, 2002), sec. 3.

17. S. Prakash Sethi and Oliver F. Williams, *Economic Imperative and Ethical Values in Global Business: The South Africa Experience and International Codes Today* (Boston: Kluwer Academic Publishers, 2000; pap. ed. Notre Dame, Ind.: University of Notre Dame Press, 2001); S. Prakash Sethi, "Creating and Implementing Global Codes of Conduct: An Assessment of the Sullivan Principles as a Role Model for Developing International Codes of Conduct—Lessons Learned and Unlearned," *Business and Society Review* (Summer 2000), 169–200.

18. S. Prakash Sethi, *Multinational Corporations*.

Mattel, Inc.: Global Manufacturing Principles—A Model Approach to Code Implementation and Independent Monitoring

O n November 20, 1997, Mattel, Inc. announced the joint establishment of a code of conduct for production facilities and contract manufacturers, as well as the development of a worldwide independent audit and monitoring system for the code. Mattel asked Dr. S. Prakash Sethi, University Distinguished Professor at the Zicklin School of Business, Baruch College, City University of New York, and an international expert on corporate governance, corporate strategy, codes of conduct, and business ethics, to assist in the development of measurement standards for effective code compliance. The announcement went on to state that Dr. Sethi would work with Mattel to design an ongoing "independent monitoring program headed by an independent panel of commissioners that will select a percentage of the company's manufacturing facilities for annual audits, and monitor compliance with the new code. The company plans to have the panel in place early in 1998. It will have full autonomy in its operations."[1]

Called the Global Manufacturing Principles (GMP), the code covered such issues as wages and hours, child labor, forced labor, discrimination, freedom of association, legal and ethical business practices, product safety and product quality, protection of the environment, and respect for local culture, values, and traditions (Exhibit 13.1).

Mattel also asked Dr. Sethi to make recommendations that would enhance existing systems that had been designed to support worker education, training, and skills, and that could significantly improve workers' income and standard of living. The news release emphasized that the code was intended to "create and encourage responsible manufacturing business practices around the world—not serve as a guideline for punishment. . . . However, manufacturers that do not meet standards, or refuse to take swift, corrective action to do so, will no longer work for Mattel."[2]

The new group of external monitors was named the Mattel Independent Monitoring Council for Global Manufacturing Principles (MIMCO). It included three people: Dr. Murray L. Weidenbaum and Dr. Paul F. McCleary,[3] with Dr. Sethi as chairperson.

With this announcement, Mattel, Inc., the world's largest toy maker, took the unprecedented step of committing the company to have its code compliance monitored by an independent outside group with complete authority to select plants for monitoring and to make full reports of findings to the public without prior censorship by the company. Mattel also indicated that it expected the monitoring process to be in place by early 1998.

At the time of this announcement, Mattel was the only company in the world to make such a commitment. Responding to increasing public pressure, a great many multinational corporations had created codes of conduct promising their compliance with local labor and environmental laws, and ensuring that their overseas operations and those of their suppliers would be free of child labor and involuntary overtime, and would respect freedom of speech and association, among other things. However, none of these codes gave the public any reason to believe the corporations' assertions about their performance.

It has been more than four years since Mattel launched its initiative in independent external monitoring. To date, Mattel stands alone as the only company in the world that has made such a commitment, has carried it out over the past four years, and plans to continue doing so for the foreseeable future.

Exhibit 13.1   Global Manufacturing Principles, Mattel, Inc., 1997

These Manufacturing Principles set standards for every facility manufacturing our products in every location in which they are produced. Compromise is not an option.

Wages and Hours: All Mattel factories and vendors must set working hours, wages and overtime pay that are in compliance with governing laws. Workers must be paid at least the minimum legal wage or a wage that meets local industry standards, whichever is greater.

While overtime is often necessary in consumer product production, Mattel factories and vendors must operate in a manner that limits overtime to a level that ensures humane, safe and productive working conditions. Overtime, if necessary, must be paid in accordance with local laws.

Child Labor: No one under the age of 16 or the local legal age limit (whichever is higher) may be allowed to work in a facility that produces products for Mattel. Simply stated, Mattel creates products for children around the world—not jobs.

We encourage the creation of apprenticeship programs tied to formal education for young people as long as students will in no way be exploited or placed in situations that endanger their health or safety.

Forced Labor: Under no circumstances will Mattel, Inc. use forced or prison labor of any kind nor will we work with any manufacturer or supplier who does.

Discrimination: Discrimination of any kind is not tolerated by Mattel, Inc. It is our belief that individuals should be employed on the basis of their ability to do a job—not on the basis of individual characteristics or beliefs.

We refuse to conduct business with any manufacturer or supplier who discriminates either in hiring or in employment practices.

Freedom of Association: Mattel is committed to abiding by all the laws and regulations of every country in which we operate. We recognize all employees' rights to choose (or not) to affiliate with legally sanctioned organizations or associations without unlawful interference.

Working Conditions: All Mattel, Inc. facilities and those of its business partners must provide a safe working environment for their employees. Facilities must engage in efforts including:

- Complying with or exceeding all applicable local laws regarding sanitation and risk protection and meeting or exceeding Mattel's own stringent standards.
- Maintaining proper lighting and ventilation.

(Continued)

Exhibit 13.1   *(Continued)*

- Keeping aisles and exits accessible at all times.
- Properly maintaining and servicing all machinery.
- Sensibly storing and responsibly disposing of hazardous materials.
- Having an appropriate emergency medical and evacuation response plan for its employees.
- Never using corporal punishment or any other form of physical or psychological coercion on any employee.

Facilities that provide housing to their employees as a benefit of employment must ensure that such housing be kept clean and safe.

Legal and Ethical Business Practices: Mattel will favor business partners who are committed to ethical standards that are compatible with our own. At a minimum, all Mattel business partners must comply with the local and national laws of the countries in which they operate.

In addition, all of our business partners must respect the significance of all patents, trademarks and copyrights of our and others' products and support us in the protection of these valuable assets.

Product Safety and Product Quality: All Mattel, Inc. business partners must share our commitment to product safety and quality and must adhere to those operational and workplace practices that are necessary to meet our stringent safety and quality standards.

Environment: Mattel, Inc. will only work with those manufacturers or suppliers who comply with all applicable laws and regulations and share our commitment to the environment.

Customs: Because of the global nature of our business and our history of leadership in this area, Mattel, Inc. insists that all of our business partners maintain a strict adherence to all local and international customs laws. Our business partners must comply with all import and export regulations.

Evaluation and Monitoring: Mattel, Inc. is committed to ensuring that all facilities manufacturing our products meet or exceed our Global Manufacturing Principles and we will audit all facilities to ensure compliance. Consequently, we insist that all manufacturing facilities provide us with:

- Full access for on-site inspections by Mattel or parties designated by Mattel.
- Full access to those records that will enable us to determine compliance with our principles.
- An annual statement of compliance to our Global Manufacturing Principles signed by an officer of the manufacturer or manufacturing facility.

Exhibit 13.1   *(Continued)*

Acceptance of and compliance to the Mattel Global Manufacturing Principles is part of every contract agreement signed with all of our manufacturing business partners.

Compliance: These principles are intended to create and encourage responsible manufacturing business practices around the world—not serve as a guideline for punishment.

We expect all of our manufacturing business partners to meet these principles on an ongoing basis. At the same time, our current business partners can expect us to work with them to effect change if certain aspects of the principles are not being met. Future business partners will not be engaged unless they meet all of our manufacturing principles.

If Mattel determines that any one of its manufacturing facilities or any vendor has violated these principles, we may either terminate our business relationship or require the facility to implement a corrective action plan. If corrective action is advised but not taken, Mattel will immediately terminate current production and suspend placement of future orders.

Mattel, Inc., 1997

Public Pressure for Improved Corporate Conduct in Foreign Sourcing

Like many other MNCs with major foreign sourcing operations, Mattel was not spared NGO criticism for the prevalence of sweatshop-like conditions in plants that it owned or controlled, or where its suppliers made products for Mattel.[4] The watershed event in this case was a documentary entitled "Toy Story," which was aired by NBC's *Dateline* on December 17, 1996.

The creation of the Global Manufacturing Principles was not an unusual event. It was partially a response to external pressures faced by many other corporations about working conditions and environmentally harmful operating practices in many manufacturing plants in developing countries. It made little difference whether these plants were owned by foreign multinationals or were enterprises based in the home country. Some plants were in private hands, while others were government-owned. Similar responses have also been forthcoming from other multinational corporations and industry groups. However, as stated earlier, Mattel took a number of steps that made the GMP distinctly different in terms of its commitment to create objective, outcome-oriented standards of performance. In addition, Mattel assumed a number of obligations external to the GMP, notably by establishing independent external monitoring and verification of its performance. Most important, Mattel did not censor the findings or control their public dissemination.

Why is it that companies in a given industry, when confronted with an external crisis, respond differently to similar situations? Our analysis in this instance, and in a number of others examined by this author,[5] indicates that a large part of the differences can be traced, first, to the character and vision of the company's CEO and its top management. Equally important factors are the corporate culture—its values and traditions—and how people in the company view themselves and their company, and are in turn viewed by the outside community. Without a supportive corporate culture (internal) and corporate reputation (external), the CEO and its top management team are likely to meet strong resistance from within and without when trying to impose discrete and substantive changes in corporate strategy and conduct. Similarly, a CEO who is not in sync with corporate culture and prevailing societal expectations is unlikely to maximize the value of these resources. He or she will find it difficult to create a viable strategy that the company's managers and employees will enthusiastically implement and the company's stakeholders will accept.[6]

A company's physical resources, market position, and relative level of profits, although important, are unlikely to be determining factors—except in extreme cases—in influencing corporate conduct. Innovative changes in strategic direction, when undertaken with due regard for risk and uncertainty, seldom expose the corporation to potentially serious adverse consequences. By contrast, they can provide significant upside potential for improved corporate reputation, shareholder satisfaction, and prospects for higher market presence and profitability.

In the case of Mattel, there were two distinguishing elements that influenced its conduct. The company's products were aimed at children, and the company emphasized children and family values. It could not be seen to be undermining these values by employing children and young adults to make toys under sweatshop conditions. The company also had a strong CEO who favored entrepreneurial approaches to business strategy and operations. Mattel's board included a number of directors who were imbued with the ethics of corporate social responsibility and were fully supportive of the GMP. And finally, Mattel's employees generally took pride in being part of the company.

There was a dramatic change in the top leadership of Mattel in May 2000, when a new chief executive officer, Robert A. Eckert, was brought in to lead the company following serious strategic missteps by the departing CEO, mistakes that caused significant financial losses for the shareholders. The new CEO faced major challenges in restoring the company's financial health and could easily have relegated the GMP to lower priority. Eckert, however, chose a different course. He did not see a conflict between restoring the corporation's financial health and reinforcing the corporate culture and values. He insisted that the two were inseparable. In his first meeting with MIMCO and his senior managers, he declared, "I am a libertarian by conviction. I also believe that the corporation's freedom to manage its operations cannot be sustained without our assuming our social responsibility to the community." He indicated that Mattel would behave in all its actions with "unwavering integrity" and that the company's commitment to the GMP remained unequivocal and undiminished.[7]

Through the GMP, Mattel committed itself, its strategic partners, and its primary suppliers to comply with all provisions of the GMP. As part of its commitment to operate as a responsible company and a good corporate citizen, Mattel undertook three hitherto unprecedented initiatives in implementing the code.

1. GMP audits would not be a one-time proposition. They would be undertaken on a regular basis as an integral part of the company's operational philosophy.
2. The GMP-related compliance efforts by Mattel, its strategic partners, and primary suppliers would be audited by an independent outside group of respected and knowledgeable experts. This group would have complete access to all facilities, workers, and supervisors, as well as to payroll and financial records, pertaining to the plants owned and operated by Mattel, its strategic partners, and primary suppliers.
3. The external monitoring group would have complete discretion in making its findings public, as to both their content and their frequency.

Antecedent Events to GMP Implementation

As part of its overall strategy of code compliance, Mattel's top management also undertook to:

- Make compliance with the principles an integral part of management evaluation and compensation.

- Develop training procedures and information systems by which all levels of the company's managers and employees would be familiarized with these instructions and implementation procedures.

- Constantly revise and improve these instructions and operational procedures in light of experience gained from Mattel's own operations and those of other companies facing similar operational challenges in countries where Mattel has its operations.

- Verify that all of the company's operations, and those of its major suppliers and strategic partners, remain in full compliance at all times with the principles and the company's implementation procedures and instructions.

PRE-AUDIT FIELD VISITS BY MIMCO

During the first six months of 1998, MIMCO undertook to visit all of Mattel's owned or controlled facilities in Asia and Mexico to gain firsthand knowledge and familiarity with the plants and management and to establish baseline data as to the operating conditions in those plants.

DEVELOPMENT OF QUANTIFIABLE OBJECTIVE STANDARDS FOR PERFORMANCE MEASUREMENT

Both MIMCO and Mattel realized that any set of principles is at best an expression of policy goals and operating philosophies, which can be subjected to widely divergent interpretations. To accomplish its goals, Mattel created two task forces, one based in the company's headquarters in El Segundo, California, and the other in its major field office in Hong Kong. These task forces were comprised of more than 50 managers and technical experts. This group, along with MIMCO and its own team of academic experts, worked extensively over a 12-month period to create detailed operational standards and performance measures, and to secure agreement with Mattel's top management and field managers as to those standards.

This was one of the most critical phases of the audit process. Any operational definitions that are subject to alternative interpretations would make the audit process less credible and therefore unacceptable to MIMCO and the public at large. Conversely, local managers would not take operational standards seriously if they expected an unrealistic level of performance. Such standards could not have any real impact on improvement in the plants' operations or the workers' quality of life.

These standards had to meet four criteria:

1. ***The standards must be quantifiable and objective in measuring and evaluating performance.*** In other words, two different people observing compliance with a given criterion must draw similar conclusions.
2. ***They must be outcome-oriented.*** It is not enough to indicate that moneys are being spent or that policies and procedures exist. Rather, the plant management is required to show that there are so many bathrooms per 100 workers and so many square feet of living space per worker in a dormitory, that the injury rate per 1,000 worker hours meets acceptable levels, and so forth.
3. ***They must meet the country's legal criteria.*** At a minimum, these standards must meet the legal criteria mandated by the labor and environmental laws of the country where a plant is located. Where country-specific standards do not exist or are lower than Mattel standards, local plants must meet Mattel's own standards. As a long-term proposition, Mattel must endeavor to have its plants meet or exceed the best industry practices prevailing in their specific regions or localities.
4. ***The standard-setting process is dynamic and interactive.*** Standards of performance must continue to evolve in light of experience gained from existing operations, competitor conduct, and the company's desire to continue building on its leadership position. In addition, standards must evolve to meet changing societal expectations because of new data and conduct of major players in the industry, the NGO community, public opinion, and behavior of host country governments.

This process led to the creation of more than 200 specific standards. They define the compliance parameters for each principle and cover all aspects of manufacturing operations; environment health and safety standards; worker hiring and training; working conditions; working hours, performance bonuses, wages, and overtime; conditions in dormitories and recreational facilities; and non-job-related skill-enhancement programs. An illustration of this approach appears in Exhibit 13.2, which presents a small segment of performance standards from the GMP compliance document for China. The China document alone is 60 pages long. Similar compliance documents

Exhibit 13.2   Excerpts from GMP Standards Check List—China

		Yes	No	Remarks
Hiring, Wages, and Working Hours				
1. Does the facility have the most current copy of the local minimum wage requirement? Is that information communicated to all employees? **(National Labor Law, Article #19)**	C	❑	❑	

a. The facility must have the most current copy of the minimum wage requirement and have implemented it within the specified time period.

b. Information on how pay is calculated must be communicated to employees.

c. During new employee orientation, employees must be briefed on the minimum wage and how pay is calculated. They must be informed of any changes.

d. The facility must have access to copies of the current Labor and Social Security Laws and Regulations.

Suggested Assessments:

1.1   Review new employee orientation to see if it is covered. Ask questions during employee interview.

The facility should show the auditor a copy of the laws and regulations.

		Yes	No	Remarks
2. Are all employees paid correctly and at least at the minimum wage for the country or region? **(National Labor Law, Article #48)**	H	❑	❑	

a. **Calculation must be: (365 – 104 – 10 = 251 annual work days) (251/12=20.92 workdays per month) (minimum wage/20.92 = daily wage) (daily wage/8 = hourly wage)**

b. **Minimum wage standards (See Attachment 1)**

Suggested Assessments:

2.1   Verify compliance by reviewing the facility's payroll records on a sample basis. Determine the minimum wage for the area.

Exhibit 13.2   *(Continued)*

		Yes	No	Remarks
	2.2 The pay stub should reflect calculation of the minimum wage and all additions and deductions from gross pay.			
	2.3 If a piece rate is used as the pay structure, it can be reflected on the pay stub, but the primary calculation is the equivalent hourly wage.			
	If there are deductions from the pay, they must be listed along with a precise explanation.			
3.	Are employees properly paid for overtime worked? **[National Labor Law, Article #44]:** a. **1.5 times regular wage for O/T on working days after 8 hours and/or after 40 hours.** b. **2.0 times regular wage for O/T on rest day(s).** c. **3.0 times regular wage for O/T on statutory holidays.**	H ❏	❏	
	Suggested Assessments: 3.1 Verify compliance by reviewing the facility's payroll records during desk audit. 3.2 If piece rate system is used at the facility, verify compliance by recalculating the gross wages based on equivalent working hours for the sample selected. 3.3 Pay stubs or the method of reporting pay to employees must indicate hours and overtime rates of pay. 3.4 Time cards should be reviewed to verify hours worked. 3.5 Employees should be questioned about pay rates for overtime.			
	. . .	. . .	. . .	. . .
				(Continued)

Exhibit 13.2   *(Continued)*

	Yes	No	Remarks
Age Requirements			
1. Are all employees hired in the facility above the age of 16? **[National Labor Law, Article #15]**	Z ❏	❏	
a. **The law in China requires employees working in factories to be at least 16.**			
b. **There is a provision for underage employees, between 16 and 18, to work but they must meet the criteria listed in number 2 below.**			
c. **If employees below 16 are found working in the factory, the facility relationship must be terminated. This is a zero tolerance item.**			
Suggested Assessments:			
1.1 Verify the age of a sample number of employees hired at the facility by reviewing appropriate personnel records maintained by the vendor. Pay attention to the age of employees during employment.			
1.2 The employee ID cards should be reviewed to determine if there is any evidence of tampering with the card. Also, the photo should be compared to the employee.			
1.3 Interview employees with questions about age, birthdate, and family.			
Forced Labor			
1. Is each employee at the facility employed at his or her own free will? **[National Labor Law, Article #96]**	Z ❏	❏	
a. There must be a written policy or procedure that recognizes employee's rights.			
b. The facility must understand how employees are recruited and must not tolerate forced situations.			

Exhibit 13.2 *(Continued)*

	Yes	No	Remarks
c. **The facility must not withhold custody of an employee's residency permit, work permit, national identification card, or other document verifying an individual's personal status. [Minister of Labor Document 118 (1994)]**			
Suggested Assessments: 1.1 Review facility documentation to determine if there is a written policy which states that employment is voluntary. 1.2 During employee interviews, stress the nature of employment at this facility. 1.3 Review employee files for official documents retained by the facility and ask employees if they keep their own official identification cards/permits.			
Freedom of Association **1.** Does the facility's management recognize all employees' rights to choose to affiliate, or not to affiliate, with legally sanctioned organizations or associations without unlawful interference? **[National Labor Law, Article #7]**	C ❏	❏	
Suggested Assessments: 1.1 Inquire whether the facility is unionized or nonunionized. 1.2 Inquire whether the facility has been found guilty of any unfair labor practice charges. 1.3 Inquire if the freedom of association rights have been communicated to the employee.			

C: Critical; H: Highly critical; Z: Zero tolerance.

have been prepared for 20 other countries where Mattel has operations. These documents are continuously revised in light of changes in local labor and environmental laws, Mattel's field experience through internal audits, and the upgrading of GMP standards. The process was completed in October 1998, when Mattel's top management agreed to these standards. The next step was to institute an audit timetable for external independent monitoring and compliance verifications.

Creation of a Viable External Monitoring Program

A basic premise of the entire code compliance and verification program was that Mattel would create an intensive internal audit organization. This organization would be responsible for conducting regular GMP compliance audits of all of Mattel's own and Mattel-controlled plants, and the plants of its vendors and licensees. Thus, MIMCO will not be responsible for conducting initial GMP audits of Mattel-related plants. Instead, MIMCO will focus almost entirely on the verification audits of plants that have already been audited by Mattel's internal audit teams.

This is a critical distinction, and its importance cannot be overemphasized. MIMCO was not designed to undertake the GMP audit of Mattel's plants and those of its vendors. It was designed to *verify* that all of Mattel's facilities and those of its vendors are in substantial compliance with GMP standards. For this purpose, it is not necessary or even desirable that MIMCO should independently monitor each and every Mattel-related facility. Such a process would be tremendously wasteful, because it would duplicate Mattel's internal audit efforts. Instead, MIMCO would use sampling procedures to identify and examine various Mattel-related facilities in order to provide a statistically rigorous and scientifically valid measure of all of its facilities.

When Mattel's internal audit program has certified that vendor plants are in compliance with the GMP, MIMCO can choose a small random sample of plants for its verification audits. Given their representative character, it would follow that the findings for this sample would be applicable to all plants in the larger group.

This approach has three important advantages over auditing the entire group and has been effectively utilized in other areas of field research.

1. Every plant in a group has an equal chance of being selected for verification audit, and no plant has prior knowledge of which one will be

selected. This puts enormous pressure on every plant in the group to maintain its compliance efforts to avoid being found in violation of GMP standards.

2. A similar situation applies to Mattel's internal audit program. Mattel's GMP auditors must monitor every plant with equal diligence to avoid missing a plant that might be the subject of a MIMCO verification audit. The random sample selection approach encourages Mattel's internal audit teams to hold to high standards in their audits since MIMCO's audit findings are a reflection on their work as well.

3. The small size of the group creates opportunities of undertaking really intensive audits within reasonable cost and time constraints.

MIMCO Audit Schedule

MIMCO established a systematic three-year cycle to meet its obligations for external audits. The first year of the cycle would concentrate on Mattel facilities. These include all of the company-owned plants and other plants in which Mattel controlled 100 percent of the output. The second year would focus on a statistically selected sample of the plants that are owned and operated by Mattel's strategic partners and primary suppliers, and from which Mattel buys 70 percent or more of the plant's output. The third year of the audit cycle would focus on a statistically selected sample of second-tier plants from which Mattel buys between 40 percent and 70 percent of the plant's output. This audit cycle would be repeated on a three-year basis. Thus plants in each group would be subjected to MIMCO audits once every three years. In addition to this general rule, MIMCO also had complete discretion to include additional plants in its audit sample in order to arrive at a more accurate picture of how well Mattel's strategic partners and primary suppliers were complying with GMP requirements.

MIMCO decided to exclude plants from the purview of the audits if less than 40 percent of their total output was devoted to Mattel. It was not an unreasonable decision. These plants represent a small part of the company's annual purchases. The cost of auditing these plants was not justifiable in terms of potential benefits, and funds could be spent more effectively elsewhere.

Unfortunately, this ambitious schedule could not be maintained when actual field conditions turned out to be far more complex and time-consuming than the planners had estimated. Analyzing voluminous data from field audits took more time than originally anticipated. Discussions between MIMCO and plant managers, and MIMCO and Mattel headquarters, also took more time than scheduled because the parties lacked the experience to implement the process efficiently. And lastly, vendor audits had to be delayed because Mattel's internal audit group could not hire and train enough auditing personnel to complete initial vendor audits, which was a necessary precondition for MIMCO's verification audits.

Notwithstanding, the progress made to date has been impressive. As will be noted in a later section of this chapter, the extended time period in the first round of audits was used to iron out areas of future disagreements and to make audit schedules more realistic.

MIMCO Audit Protocols

MIMCO also had to create its own audit protocols and audit instruments. The objective was to ensure that MIMCO's audit reports were comprehensive and provided the public at large a fair, objective, and unbiased picture of conditions in the audited plants. These reports would also provide a representative sample of conditions that were likely to be found among all the plants belonging to the particular group from which the sample was selected.

The audit instruments were designed to elicit information about all aspects of plant operations as covered in the GMP. In particular, they would focus on employee wages and working hours; living and working conditions; freedom of speech, religion, and association; protection from discrimination based on age, sex, religion, or ethnicity; and access to all levels of management with regard to issues concerning employees' living and working conditions, and procedures for handling grievances and resolving conflicts.

MIMCO field audits were comprised of four elements: management compliance reports (MCRs), payroll and personnel files desk audits, systematic walk-through examinations of the plants and dormitories, and one-on-one worker interviews.

MANAGEMENT COMPLIANCE
REPORT (MCR)

This document is prepared by the plant management and provides data on the plant's compliance in considerable detail with regard to all the standards pertaining to GMP. The MCR obligates the plant management to provide in writing its detailed compliance to all items on the GMP performance standards (checklist). Plant managers are encouraged to acknowledge the extent to which their compliance has fallen short of GMP standards and to explain their reasons for shortfall. The plant's owner or general manager signs the MCR certifying the accuracy of the data. Should the data turn out to be at variance with the findings during MIMCO's plant visit, the plant management should be seriously concerned because discrepancies erode MIMCO's trust, and all other information provided by the plant becomes suspect.

SYSTEMATIC WALK-THROUGH
OF THE PLANTS

MIMCO team leaders and other experts accompanying the team undertake an extensive walk-through of the plant, storage facilities, work areas, dormitories, and recreation facilities. Walk-throughs take between four and six hours on the part of two to three MIMCO team members, either working together or individually. MIMCO experts also examine the plant's maintenance records including workers' injury data, environmental standards, air quality, and waste disposal. The records are compared with physical conditions observed by them, verified with the MCR, and evaluated from the perspective of their experience with other plant audits conducted by MIMCO. The team members also meet individually and in private with different managers who are responsible for various plant functions, such as worker training, work scheduling, human resource management, environment, or health and safety, as the team seeks clarification of various issues and assesses the quality of information that was provided by the plant management as compared with observations by the MIMCO team. In follow-up meetings with MIMCO, the plant's top management seeks clarification and explanation of observations made by the MIMCO team. When plant data appears to be too good to be true, the MIMCO team becomes especially vigilant and places special emphasis on worker interviews.

Sample Selection

MIMCO has complete access to Mattel's internal audit reports of various plants, recommendations for corrective action, and findings of any follow-up audits. These provide valuable information to MIMCO audit teams in their preparation of field audits.

Before the actual audit can start, plant management is asked to provide the MIMCO team with a complete list of all the workers—assembly-line and administrative staff. Organized in sequence based on worker ID numbers, this data is used to select a random sample of all workers, which will provide the basis of the actual audit. The size of the sample is determined by the complexity of the workforce. For example, the sample is larger if different groups of workers are engaged in distinct job categories, such as sewing, injection and blow molding, storage and packing, or if they are divided between night and day shifts. Notwithstanding, the size and composition of the final sample must meet the statistical test of representing the entire workforce of the plant.

This process ensures that plant management cannot influence which workers will be selected for inclusion in the sample. Nor is it likely the management could coach the entire workforce, under the threat of reprisals, to give only innocuous answers to the MIMCO interviewers.

The plant management might also try to mislead the MIMCO audit by excluding all workers whose employment might in some way be in violation of the GMP. Again, this is possible but not plausible. Any break in the ID number sequence or aberration in the worker list would raise red flags with MIMCO and call for explanation on the part of the plant management. In addition, MIMCO's worker interview questionnaire has built-in questions that seek information about other issues. The information sought is scattered in different parts of the questionnaire, making it extremely difficult to distort data and conceal worker-related information from MIMCO.

The worker sample selected by MIMCO is used in two different types of audits. The first one is the payroll and personnel files desk audit. The second one pertains to workers who are selected for one-to-one confidential interviews.

PAYROLL AND PERSONNEL FILES DESK AUDIT

This document is designed to examine the system of recording regular and overtime working hours, wages paid for regular and overtime work, performance and other types of bonuses paid to workers, and any deductions from the workers' pay. The intent is to ensure that all workers receive wages and benefits and work regular and overtime hours in accordance with local laws and GMP standards. The pay stubs are analyzed to ensure that workers understand how their wages and deductions are calculated and that they have received all they are entitled to. Examination of personnel files is designed to ensure that workers are treated fairly, that any disciplinary action is recorded properly and is processed in accordance with company policies and local labor laws, and that there are accurate records of worker training, incidents of injury, and other pertinent data.

The payroll and personnel files desk audit is conducted by a three- or four-member group of professional accountants/auditors under the oversight and supervision of a senior MIMCO team member to ensure complete cooperation on the part of the plant management. At present, MIMCO uses auditors from the firm Global Social Compliance (GSC, formerly a part of PricewaterhouseCoopers). These professionals are citizens of the country in which the plant is located. They are drawn from the local office of GSC and are very knowledgeable about local labor laws and record-keeping practices. They are thus able to ferret out any inconsistencies in the data.

It should be noted that GSC auditors are bound by a legal agreement with MIMCO that prohibits them from working in any capacity with the plants being audited. Nor are they allowed to share any information generated through MIMCO audits with either the plant management, members of Mattel, or other GSC auditors. They themselves do not analyze the data they collect. This is done by MIMCO in New York to minimize the possibility of contaminating this data.

WORKER INTERVIEWS

These are conducted through a questionnaire that elicits information from the workers on all aspects of their working and living conditions at the plant. Workers selected for one-on-one interviews are the same ones whose personnel files and payroll data are examined in that phase of the audit. This approach seeks to find out from the workers whether the plant's financial records contain accurate data about their wages and working hours, and personnel-related activities. Data sought are factual and experiential-perceptual, and both quantitative and qualitative. The questionnaire contains more than 115 questions, many with multiple choices, and provides opportunities for both structured and unstructured open-ended responses.

The questionnaire was designed by MIMCO experts and rigorously tested for objectivity, clarity, and coherence. There is also built-in redundancy to minimize the possibility of workers giving answers that they might consider to be appropriate, but which might not accurately reflect the conditions prevailing in the factory. The questionnaire was initially prepared in English, translated into various local languages, and then translated back into English by another set of translators to minimize ambiguity in the language and questions.

The one-on-one worker interviews are conducted by a three- or four-person team of professionally trained and experienced interviewers provided by Verite, Inc., a nongovernmental organization with considerable experience in this type of work. The interviewers are based in the country or region where the plant is located. They speak the local language and are sensitive to nuances of local culture and traditions of the workers. The interviewers also tend to reflect the demographic profile of the workers to be interviewed at each facility. These interviewers follow strict interviewing protocols using only the questionnaire instrument designed by MIMCO. All interviews are conducted with individual workers in complete privacy and in the language of the workers.

Considerable time is spent with the interviewers prior to the start of the interview process. The training of the interviewers is an important dimension of the process to ensure that questions are fully and clearly understood by the interviewers. The interviewers are also instructed to develop a level of trust with the workers who are being interviewed. They are also instructed to report responses as given by the workers and without any bias or interpretation on the part of interviewers.

Upon completion of the audit, the MIMCO team leader takes personal charge of the data collected through questionnaires, payroll audits, and examination of personnel files and other documents. These are brought to New York for further analysis by MIMCO personnel in preparation of the final report.

Prepublication Review Process of Audit Findings

To ensure complete accuracy of the audit findings, MIMCO and Mattel established a three-step review process before the audit findings could be made public. Once the draft report is prepared, it is sent to the plant manager for review and comments. The plant manager is offered three choices:

1. When plant managers can demonstrate to MIMCO's satisfaction that MIMCO's audit findings are in error because of overlooked information or misinterpretation of data, MIMCO removes those findings from the draft report without even showing it to Mattel. This is an important safeguard and is designed to ensure that a plant manager's reputation and, possibly, career are not unjustifiably compromised. It should be noted that to date this has not happened in any of the audits conducted by MIMCO.

2. A more common scenario is for the plant management to accept MIMCO's findings and work out a schedule for taking corrective action in agreement with Mattel and MIMCO.

3. In the event of differences of opinion between MIMCO and the plant management as to MIMCO's findings and recommended action, the matter is referred to Mattel's head office. The review process at Mattel's headquarters level follows similar procedures and is expected to be completed within 30 days.

It is important to note that in all such cases, MIMCO's public report will clearly state both the shortcomings discovered by the audit and the corrective action agreed to by the plant management and Mattel. In the unlikely event that Mattel and MIMCO cannot agree on certain findings and corrective action, Mattel cannot prevent MIMCO from making its findings public, without any prior censorship from Mattel. MIMCO, however, is obligated to include Mattel's response to its findings and the company's explanation of its disagreement as given by Mattel and without any editing on the part of MIMCO.

In all the audits conducted by MIMCO to date, such disagreements have not occurred. Both plant managers and Mattel have agreed with MIMCO's findings and have completed corrective action as previously agreed. One should also keep in mind the fact that all the plants audited by MIMCO to date have been either owned or controlled by Mattel and have not included any of the vendor plants.

Notwithstanding the review process just described, MIMCO has complete discretion in undertaking one or more follow-up audits—including unannounced audits—to ensure that all corrective action has been taken by the plant management and that changes in policies and procedures have been implemented and are being adhered to.

Public Dissemination of MIMCO Reports

MIMCO has complete control over the content and frequency of its reports to the public. So far, MIMCO has published reports on individual plants including separate reports on follow-up audits it has undertaken. These reports are immediately posted on Mattel's web site (www.Mattel.com) and can be freely downloaded. They can also be requested directly from MIMCO's office in New York. Both MIMCO and Mattel independently issue press releases highlighting findings of the reports and bringing them to the attention of the news media, NGOs, and the general public.

Brief Summary of MIMCO's Audits

Toward the end of 2001, MIMCO completed the first round of audits, including follow-up audits, of all Mattel-owned and -controlled plants (Table 13.1). Our overall conclusion, based on these audits, is that Mattel's overseas plants have, in general, met all of the important standards promulgated in the GMP. A number of plants have since invested considerable sums of money to repair and improve work environments and living facilities so as to eliminate most of the adverse conditions noted by MIMCO during the pre-audit field visits in early 1998. The result has been that these plants have suffered from none of the complaints commonly associated with Asian plants, such as insufficient and inadequate toilet facilities, unsafe drinking water, and lack of hot and cold running water in dormitories. In contrast, we noted many instances of improved cooling and heating measures in plants and dormitories, improved cleanliness, more balanced and varied food services, improved safety, and so on.

All evidence indicated that workers, with few exceptions, were 18 years of age or older. Younger, albeit legal workers, had been employed prior to the company's commitment to the GMP standards. Since then, no worker below 18 years of age had been hired in any of these plants. Interviews with workers indicated that Mattel was considered a preferred employer, and

Table 13.1 MIMCO's Field Visits to Mattel's Vendors, February 1999 to January 2002

Date	Country	Plant	Nature of Visit
February 7–10, 1999	Malaysia	MMSB	Formal plant audit
		MTSB	Formal plant audit
		MKL	Formal plant audit
		Sitiawan	Formal plant audit
March 8–10, 1999	China	Chang An	Formal plant audit
		Guan Yao	Formal plant audit
		PML	Formal plant audit
April 4–10, 1999	Indonesia	MJS	Formal plant audit
		MJD	Formal plant audit
	Thailand	MBK	Formal plant audit
August 2–6, 1999	Mexico	Mabamex	Formal plant audit
		Montoi	Formal plant audit
June 19–20, 2000	China	Chang An	Follow-up audit
		Guan Yao	Follow-up audit
August 11–25, 2000	China	Field visits to eight vendors' plants to understand the complexity of their operations.	
August 21, 2000	China	MDC	Formal plant audit
November 7–9, 2000	Mexico	Monterrey (MX3)	Formal plant audit
		Montoi	Formal plant audit
December 12–15, 2000	China	Field visits to five vendors' plants to understand the complexity of their operations.	
February 5, 2001	Mexico	Monterrey (MX3)	Follow-up audit
November 26, 2001	Mexico	Monterrey (MX3)	Follow-up audit
January 5–16, 2002	China	Field visits to seven vendors' plants to understand the complexity of their operations.	

new hires had been recommended to work there by other Mattel employees. Quite often, there were waiting lists of workers who wanted to work in a Mattel plant. Interviews with workers also indicated a high level of satisfaction on the part of the employees with regard to their wages and their working and living conditions.

Desk audits of employee payroll data and personnel files generally confirmed that employees were paid according to company policies and met legal requirements as to wages, overtime, and so on. Similarly, there was no evidence of systematic ill treatment or harassment of workers based on sex, race, or other considerations.

At the suggestion of MIMCO during the pre-audit field visits in early 1998, Mattel instituted a program whereby all workers received a regular pay stub indicating total amounts earned and distribution of wages among regular, overtime, and holiday work, deductions for dormitory and food services, taxes, and all other charges. It was also required that the pay stubs should be prepared in a format that the employees could understand.

Plant facilities appeared safe and comfortable, with employees working under conditions and with protective gear that were appropriate to particular tasks and with equipment that was properly maintained. A majority of the plants were air-conditioned or climate controlled. Of the approximately 30,000 workers covered under this audit, 47 percent worked in air-conditioned facilities. Where air-conditioning was not available, adequate heating and cooling systems, including ventilation, were provided.

Workers in large numbers expressed their satisfaction with non-job-related training programs, such as courses in English, computer literacy, and so forth, when these programs were offered by the plant management. However, the demand for these courses constantly exceeded their availability, and workers expressed a strong desire for additional training opportunities.

In one sense, this outcome should not come as a surprise. After all, it was Mattel's own code of conduct and Mattel's own choice to establish an independent external monitoring commission. Clearly, it would not have done Mattel any good if it had failed to meet its commitments under the GMP. Nevertheless, the audits show that companies can maintain safe working conditions, pay fair wages, and still maintain a viable outsourcing program in developing countries.

If Mattel is able to satisfy a group of independent experts with regard to its compliance, there is no reason why other MNCs cannot do so, especially when the plants in question are totally or largely dedicated to producing for the MNC. Unfortunately, as noted earlier, this has not been the situation in the case of Nike, which has 68 plants worldwide that are fully dedicated to producing Nike's footwear products.

Vendor Audits

As of March 1, 2002, MIMCO had not completed any vendor audits and thus was approximately 18 months behind schedule for reasons explained earlier in this chapter. Both MIMCO and Mattel used this period to improve their planning process for vendor audits. Mattel used its intensive vendor audit process to help vendors improve their compliance by building additional facilities and changing their operating procedures to enhance their compliance with GMP standards. According to Tom Debrowski, Mattel's Executive Vice President for Worldwide Operations, "Our aim has always been to work with our established vendors and to assist them in GMP compliance. We have also used this process, and the opportunity it presented, to curtail our vendor list by discontinuing our business with those vendors who are unwilling or unable to meet our expectations. Consequently, in the last few years we have reduced our vendor base significantly."

In preparing for vendor audits, MIMCO undertook field visits to a cross section of Mattel's vendors to understand the scope and complexity of their operations and to better prepare for formal vendor audits, which are scheduled for the second half of 2002 (Table 13.1).

An analysis of the recent database on Mattel vendors also suggested that the old two-phase audit cycle for vendors needed to be revised. The original plan called for first-phase audits to include all plants in which Mattel accounted for over 70 percent of output. Field visits by MIMCO indicated that this process would include a large number of relatively small plants. Conversely, it would exclude some very large plants in which Mattel accounted for a small percentage of total output, which was, nevertheless, significant in volume of products and dollar value of output. Consequently, a new definition of first-phase plants was created. It would now include all those plants that currently do more than $8 million worth of business with Mattel per year. This group of plants accounts for more than 85 percent of all vendor-related business by Mattel. The second-phase vendor audit would include vendors that do less than $8 million per year of business with Mattel. The exact parameters of this group will be determined once the first-phase vendor audits have been completed and both MIMCO and Mattel have better information about the remaining group of vendors.

Mattel's Revision of GMP

From the very start of the GMP process, Mattel and MIMCO had agreed that GMP would be a dynamic process and that its standards would be revised and upgraded with changing conditions and with experience gained in implementing the GMP. Mattel's new management has continued its commitment. In a recent meeting with MIMCO, Bryan Stockton, Mattel's Executive Vice President, commented, "[CEO] Bob Eckert wants a systematic progress report on a regular basis that reflects our commitment to be an industry leader not only in product quality and variety, but also in meeting our obligations to our workers all over the world, and also be responsive to all of our stakeholders."

An illustration of this approach can be seen in the fact that Mattel undertook to enhance significantly the GMP standards for all new plants. The company was equally willing to raise its compliance standards above the current GMP standards in those plants that were undergoing significant expansion or renovation. Furthermore, in January 2001 Mattel revised and enlarged its Global Manufacturing Principles (Exhibit 13.3). This was in response to the NGO interest in seeking more information on Mattel's detailed criteria for measuring compliance with various standards.

Furthermore, at Eckert's initiative, on January 1, 2001, Mattel issued four policy initiatives to further enhance internal GMP compliance. These dealt with (1) the roles and responsibilities of Mattel's corporate organization worldwide; (2) Disney sourcing policies and procedures, which apply to all Mattel facilities and contractors that source Disney products worldwide; (3) policies and procedures that apply to all contractor, subcontractor, supplier, and licensee manufacturing facilities seeking certification for Mattel Global Manufacturing Principles (GMP) compliance; and (4) policies and procedures that apply to all Mattel facilities and operations that license Mattel-branded products.

Exhibit 13.3   Global Manufacturing Principles, Mattel, Inc., 2001

Scope:
Mattel's Global Manufacturing Principles (GMP) policy applies to all parties that manufacture, assemble or distribute any products or package bearing the Mattel logo.

Purpose:
GMP is the cornerstone of Mattel's ongoing commitment to responsible worldwide manufacturing practices. The establishment and implementation of GMP provides a framework within which all of Mattel's manufacturing must be conducted. GMP provides guidance and minimum standards for all manufacturing plants, assembly operations and distribution centers that manufacture, assemble or distribute Mattel products. GMP requires safe and fair treatment of employees and that all locations protect the environment while respecting the cultural, ethnic and philosophical differences of the countries where Mattel operates.

Introduction:
As "The World's Premier Toy Brands—Today and Tomorrow," Mattel takes pride in the quality of its products, its customer relationships, its employees, its communities and its global reputation, as well as the value built for its shareholders. Mattel is committed to executing GMP in all areas of its business and will only engage business partners who share its commitment to GMP. Mattel expects all its business partners to enforce GMP, and will assist them in meeting GMP requirements. However, Mattel is prepared to end partnerships with those who do not comply. Compromise is not an option.

Our Values:
The foundation for the successful implementation of GMP lies within the Mattel core values. It is essential that the company's business partners share these values.

We Value:
1. *Our Customers*
The well-being of children is an inherent part of the reason that Mattel exists and this is reflected in all aspects of our business. A child's well-being is our primary concern in considering the quality and type of toys produced, and in the way Mattel toys are manufactured. At Mattel, we want to inspire children's imaginations and enrich their lives with our products. Accordingly, Mattel is committed to creating safe and quality products for children around the world. Mattel products will be manufactured in a manner which will meet its GMP stringent standards.

(Continued)

Exhibit 13.3   *(Continued)*

2. *Our Work*

We strive for excellence and creativity in every aspect of our business. Mattel understands that the implementation of GMP is an ongoing process, and is committed to making continuous improvements to its GMP performance as the company strives for full compliance.

We are dedicated to a creative approach in addressing areas of particular concern and resolving compliance issues. We will protect the environment and continue to reduce our use of resources and materials. In every aspect of our business, we will conduct ourselves with unwavering integrity.

3. *Our Partners*

We will share success with our customers, our suppliers, our shareholders and the communities where we operate. Our shareholders and customers demand that Mattel products are manufactured and assembled under ethical working and living conditions. Enforcement of the company's GMP policy illustrates to customers and shareholders that Mattel shares their concern and is committed to ensuring that Mattel products are manufactured under conditions that meet GMP standards. We are also committed to supporting and working closely with our individual vendors in complying with GMP.

4. *Ourselves*

We operate with unwavering integrity and take ownership of all issues that pass in front of us. We are accountable for the results of our business and the development of our fellow employees. We are dedicated and committed to implementing GMP with honesty and have incorporated measures to ensure continual improvement in our performance. While the development of GMP is essential to success, enforcement of the code is equally as important. Mattel has initiated an extensive three-stage auditing process that is overseen by an independent monitoring council to thoroughly inspect both the company's owned-and-operated facilities around the world, as well as those of our contractors.

We will continue to refine GMP to ensure that all employees are treated fairly, with respect, and work under safe and healthy conditions that encourage dignity and pride for themselves and their workplace.

Our Commitments: Mattel will operate its facilities in compliance with applicable laws and regulations of every country where the company operates. In countries where the laws are not well defined, Mattel has developed country-specific standards that govern our operations and those of the companies that manufacture, assemble or distribute our products. Mattel has defined the following basic standards of conduct to guide Mattel and each of its business partners' operations in implementing GMP. These standards are dynamic and evolving to ensure ongoing protection of employees and the environment.

Exhibit 13.3 *(Continued)*

1. *Hiring, Wages and Working Hours*
   a. Work Hours: Mattel will comply with country laws. Overtime work must be voluntary.
   b. Work Week: We will comply with country laws but require at least one rest day per week.
   c. Wages: Wages must meet or exceed legally mandated minimum wage. Wage rates for overtime work must also meet legally mandated rates.
   d. Benefits: All benefits provided to employees must comply with country laws.
   e. Payment of Wages: Employees must be paid at least monthly. Accurate records for each employee's regular and overtime hours must be maintained either through time cards punched by each employee or through other similar systems. Pay records must include employee work hours; and every employee must be provided a pay stub with pay calculations and deductions clearly listed.
   f. Deductions: Deductions must comply with local laws. Deductions for company-provided food and living must be reasonable, affordable and if employees choose to live and eat outside of the company facilities they will not be charged.
   g. Hiring: Every employee must be provided a written document which outlines their work hours, wages and wage calculations, benefits, costs for food and living and length of employment contract. Mattel and its partners will not charge employment fees and we will monitor our hiring agencies to ensure that fees are reasonable.

2. *Age Requirements*
   a. No one under the age of 16 will be employed. If the local law requires a higher minimum age, we will comply with the local law.
   b. In cases, where employees are hired between 16 and 18, special considerations must include annual physical and will exclude hazardous duties.
   c. A system must be in place to detect forged and false identity documents.

3. *Forced Labor*
   a. Under no circumstances will forced or prison labor be used to manufacture, assemble or distribute Mattel products. Each employee must be provided with a document stating that employment and overtime is voluntary.
   b. Mattel will not allow or condone physical or verbal abuse, or any form of physical or psychological coercion of employees.

(Continued)

Exhibit 13.3   (*Continued*)

c. There must be a written grievance procedure in place.
d. Every employee must be provided with general orientation on GMP as well as local company code that includes: wages, working hours, dormitory rules, canteen procedures, grievance procedures, disciplinary procedures, safety training, evacuation, fire prevention, self-improvement opportunities and a plant tour.

4. *Discrimination*
   a. The location must have a procedure on hiring, promotion and disciplinary practices that addresses discrimination. Discrimination or harassment on the basis of age, religion, sex, or ethnicity will not be tolerated.
   b. Mattel will make every attempt to further employee job skills through training. The company will give strong preference to promotion from within the ranks of the current employees. No employee will be denied promotion opportunities for reasons of age, sex, ethnicity, or religion.

5. *Freedom of Expression and Association*
   a. Each employee has the right to associate, or not to associate, with any legally sanctioned organization.
   b. Management must create formal channels to encourage communications among all levels of supervisors and employees—without fear of reprisal—on issues that impact their working and living conditions.
   c. Senior managers must hold quarterly meetings with all levels of employees to share information and discuss plant-wide issues.

6. *Living Conditions*
   a. Dormitories (if provided)
      • Every employee must be provided with adequate living space.
      • Ventilation must be provided.
      • Showers and bathrooms must be convenient, centrally located or in the room.
      • Lockable storage space for each employee must be provided.
      • Hot water must be provided.
      • Dormitories must be maintained, clean and safe.
      • Safety hazards must be eliminated.
   b. Canteens (if provided)
      • Canteen staff must have annual physical examinations.
      • Canteen staff must wear clean clothing with proper protective equipment when serving food.
      • Canteens must be clean, well lit and free of food scraps.
      • Refrigeration must be available if perishable food is stored.
      • Tables and chairs must be provided.
      • Meals provided must meet nutritional requirements.

Exhibit 13.3 *(Continued)*

7. *Workplace Safety*
   a. There must be trained or certified safety professionals and a written safety program must be developed.
   b. Combustible materials must be properly handled with special precautions taken in spraying and mixing areas.
   c. Machines with revolving or moving parts must be guarded and employees will receive special training on the use of this machinery.
   d. Hazards must be eliminated where possible. Employees must be provided and trained on the use of Personal Protection Equipment where hazards cannot be fully eliminated.
   e. Mattel will identify all hazardous materials and properly train employees on the appropriate procedures for handling these materials.
   f. Safety training must be conducted for special work categories (industrial trucks, electricians, maintenance, painters, molding operators, etc.).
   g. Employee exposure to chemicals and vapors must be below legal requirements or Mattel standards, whichever is the most stringent. In special cases where ventilation cannot eliminate the exposure, respiratory protection will be used and employees trained.
   h. All accidents must be investigated and corrective actions documented.
   i. All locations must continuously reduce accident rates and have specific targets on reductions.

8. *Health*
   a. In locations where there are more than 1000 employees, there must be on-site medical facility for routine medical treatment and work-related injuries. In locations where there are less than 1000 employees, treatment must be available within 15 minutes if there is not a clinic on site.
   b. The facility must have lighting which meets Mattel's standards or local requirements, whichever is higher.
   c. Temperatures must be measured during hot and cold seasons and if they exceed local or Mattel standards, corrective actions must be taken.
   d. Noise must not exceed 85dBA. Hearing protection must be used in any areas that exceed this limit. If the local limit is lower, the lower limit will be used.

9. *Emergency Planning*
   a. Emergency plans for evacuation, spills and natural disasters must be current and identify key responsibilities.
   b. Emergency evacuation signals must be understood and audible in all locations of the facilities.
   c. Emergency exits must meet local or Mattel standards.
   d. Emergency lighting must provide immediate (within 5 seconds) and sufficient lighting to allow evacuation.

(Continued)

Exhibit 13.3 *(Continued)*

e. Fire extinguishers must be provided and employees designated to use fire extinguishers must be trained.

f. Employees must be trained on reporting emergencies and evacuation procedures.

g. Emergency equipment and respective documentation must be maintained.

h. Special protective and prevention system like "hot work" must be used when open flames are present.

10. *Environmental Protection*

   a. Trained environment personnel must be assigned to manage the areas of air and water emissions and waste management.

   b. Hazardous wastes must be properly contained, stored and only disposed of at approved facilities.

   c. Water discharges must meet local requirements or Mattel's standards.

   d. Mattel will quantify its wastes and continually reduce them.

   e. Air emissions must meet local requirements or Mattel's standards.

   f. Any and all spills or releases must be immediately cleaned.

   g. Odors and noise that cause undue disruption to the community must be eliminated.

   h. Plans to handle environmental emergencies must be current and identify key responsibilities.

11. *Evaluation, Corrective Action and Monitoring*

   a. Mattel and its business partners will undergo an audit process to assess compliance with GMP. This process must include a corrective action plan to ensure that audit findings are corrected and GMP compliance achieved. Mattel will work closely with all business partners to ensure that corrective actions are completed in a timely manner.

   b. In cases where corrective actions are not taken in a timely manner, Mattel will identify alternative suppliers. However, Mattel is prepared to terminate any operation or partnership where compliance is not achieved within the time frame agreed upon. Mattel will not engage potential business partners unless they meet the company's stringent requirements or are committed to achieving full compliance.

   c. Mattel's commitment to the public includes verification audits by an independent monitoring organization to assess the GMP performance of Mattel and its business partners. An independent monitor will conduct periodic evaluations of a select number of locations of its choosing to verify compliance with GMP standards. They will be provided with complete access to all information and facilities in order to make an evaluation of Mattel's performance in ensuring that Mattel locations and those of its partners meet GMP standards. The independent monitor has the discretion to periodically issue reports to the public on our progress.

Notes

1. Mattel, Inc., "Mattel, Inc., Launches Global Code of Conduct," press release, Mattel, Inc., El Segundo, California, November 20, 1997.

2. Ibid., 2.

3. Dr. Murray Weidenbaum is professor and director, Center for the Study of American Business, Washington University, St. Louis. Dr. Weidenbaum was the first chairperson of the Council of Economic Advisors under President Reagan. Dr. Paul McCleary was until recently president of For Children, Inc. Dr. McCleary is a prominent church leader (former associate general secretary of the General Council of Ministries, United Methodist Church, and associate secretary for the Division on Overseas Ministries, National Council of Churches of Christ in the USA (NCCC)). He served as president of the Non-Governmental Organizational Committee on UNICEF.

4. Citations given here are illustrative of the type of media criticism directed at Mattel. They are neither representative nor comprehensive. We are also making no claims as to the extent of their accuracy. In most such media coverage, MNCs have alleged media bias and factual errors in reporting, and Mattel is not an exception to this line of argument. See, for example: Dinah Lee and Rose Brady, "International Business Long, Hard Days—At Pennies an Hour—Chinese Teenagers Are Toiling in the Foreign-Owned Sweatshops of the Special Economic Zones," *Business Week* (October 31, 1988), 46; Haider Rizvi, "Toying with Workers (Consumer Campaign against Toy Transnational Companies That Hire Asian Subcontractors Violating Labor Rights)," *Multinational Monitor* (April 1, 1996), 6; Elizabeth Razzi, "Did Child Labor Make That Toy? Here's How You Can Tell—and What, If Anything, You Can Do About It," *Kiplinger's Personal Finance* (December 1, 1996), 46; Anton Foek, "Sweatshop Barbie: Exploitation of Third World Labor," *The Humanist* (January 11, 1997), 9; Sean M. Fitzgerald, "Barbie Talks Back," *The Humanist* (July 17, 1997), 29; Anton Foek, "A Reply to Mattel," *The Humanist* (July 17, 1997), 30; "Mattel Launches Global Code of Conduct for Plants, Contractors," *Dow Jones Online News* (November 20, 1997); Michael White, "Shareholders Reject Plan to Link Executive Pay to Labor Practices," Associated Press Newswire (May 6, 1998); "Where the Furbies Come From," *The Economist* (December 19, 1998), 95.

5. S. Prakash Sethi and Oliver Williams, *Economic Imperatives and Ethical Values in Global Business: The South African Experience and International Codes Today* (Boston: Kluwer Academic Publishers, 2000; pap. ed. Notre Dame, Ind.: University of Notre Dame Press, 2001); S. Prakash Sethi and Paul Steidlmeier, *Up Against the Corporate Wall: Cases in Business and Society*, 6th ed. (Englewood Cliffs, N.J.: Prentice-Hall, 1997); S. Prakash Sethi, *Multinational Corporations and the Impact of Public Advocacy on Corporate Strategy: Nestlé and the Infant Formula Controversy* (Boston: Kluwer Academic Publishers, 1994); S. Prakash

Sethi and Dow Votaw, *The Corporate Dilemma: Traditional Values and Contemporary Problems* (Englewood Cliffs, N.J.: Prentice-Hall, 1973).

6.   This situation was dramatically stated in the case of Nestlé and the infant formula boycott controversy. During the early stages of the controversy, the decentralized organization proved ineffective in responding to public pressure because the source of the problem was in one region while the source of public pressure was in another part of the world. Thus the problems of turf, budgetary constraints, and the differing management style and operational tactics in the two regions contributed to an exacerbation of the problem. Consequently, the top management of Nestlé in Switzerland took control of the problems, and installed a separate management team in Washington, D.C., which would report directly to Nestlé's top management and bypass the authority of area managers in the United States as well as the managers responsible for the worldwide marketing of infant formula products. This turned out to be a most innovative and effective approach. Within four years, the new organization not only resolved the issues but caused a 180-degree turnaround in Nestlé's reputation from a highly negative to a substantively positive level.

The ad hoc organization, however, could not be integrated into Nestlé's existing global organization and decision-maker structures. Soon after the issue was resolved, the new organization was dissolved and all authority to manage infant formula marketing reverted to the regular managers. Once in power, these managers undertook to erase all credit for resolving the issue from the new ad hoc organization. Instead, Nestlé commissioned a journalist to write a book for general public distribution at Nestlé's expense. This book rewrote the history of the infant formula controversy as Nestlé's executives wanted the world to see it. It placed all the blame of the controversy on Nestlé's critics and projected Nestlé as the hapless victim of NGOs' less-than-ethical conduct and spreading of inaccurate and misleading information. It also largely credited Nestlé's seasoned managers with successfully handling the issue with only a minor role assigned to the ad hoc organization. See Sethi, *Multinational Corporations*; S. Prakash Sethi and Bharat B. Bhalla, "A New Perspective on International Social Regulation of Business: An Evaluation of the Compliance Status of the International Code of Marketing of Breast-Milk Substitutes," *Journal of Socio-Economics* 22:2 (1993), 141–158.

7.   Comments made by Robert A. Eckert, chairman and CEO, Mattel, Inc., to MIMCO members at a meeting at Mattel headquarters in El Segundo, California, on October 4, 2000.

PART SIX

Lessons Learned and Unlearned— Guidelines for the Future

Corporate Social Accountability and International Codes of Conduct: An Assessment

This book began with a description of globalization and its impact as its supporters describe it and as it has been experienced by large segments of the population in poorer countries of the world. As stated in the first chapter, trends in globalization and the move toward open markets over the past 20 years have created an increase in the aggregate wealth and in movement of capital from industrially advanced countries to developing ones. There is, however, considerable debate about the real and alleged benefits of globalization, because many assessments ignore most, if not all, of the negative second-order consequences of globalization, especially its effects on environment, workers, and sociopolitical institutions in developing countries. The book also examined how MNCs have exploited opportunities that arose in the new wave of globalization, and demonstrated that the increased wealth and economic benefits have flowed disproportionately to the multinational corporations at the expense of other factors of production, notably labor.

The focus in this chapter is not on the past, but on the future. Emphasizing the need for charting a new direction on the part of MNCs, the aim is to create more proactive cooperation between the MNCs and other players with whom they interact in the global economic arena. Given the critical role of MNCs in increasingly integrated global markets, we believe that enlightened leadership on the part of MNCs will elicit a similarly positive response from other important constituencies and institutions of civil society. In particular we address four issues:

1. The new wave of globalization has brought about tremendous increase in economic power and political influence of the MNCs. They have become custodians of enormous concentrations of economic assets, while the countervailing power of national political institutions and regulatory bodies has not kept pace in the developing countries. The MNCs must demonstrate that they are using their power with a measure of self-restraint. In particular, they must consider the legitimate interests of other stakeholders who are affected by MNC decisions in the marketplace, but who are poorly equipped to protect their interests.

2. Increased globalization of economic activity has also weakened social and cultural bonds between MNCs, local communities, and related constituencies. Consequently, traditional notions of corporate social responsibility and people's expectations thereof have become somewhat outmoded. A new dimension of corporate social responsibility is necessary, one that takes into account not only the needs of the MNCs' home countries, but also those of communities around the world where MNC operations are located.

3. The twin factors of increased MNC economic power and political influence, and a weakening of the traditional notions of corporate responsibility, call for a reexamination of the relative responsibilities and obligations of the MNCs to their various stakeholders and other impacted constituencies—in particular, certain corporate activities whose impact on corporate constituencies should not be left solely to the discretion of corporate management (i.e., actions voluntarily taken by the MNCs under the rubric of corporate social responsibility and corporate citizenship). Instead, they should be considered as necessary imperatives in which MNCs should be held accountable for an externally determined level of performance.

4. And finally, we assess the role of international corporate codes of conduct as important instruments through which the MNCs can bridge the credibility gap between corporate promises and their delivery. We shall also consider the legitimacy gap between corporate performance

and societal expectations. The past 15 years have provided considerable experience in international corporate codes of conduct, first in South Africa and more recently in Asia and Latin America. The MNC sponsors of these codes represent a wide spectrum of large, well-known multinational corporations from a cross section of industrial sectors and from a variety of industrially advanced countries. These codes are seen as voluntary corporate efforts that bridge the gap between legally mandated standards and evolving social needs. These codes, with few exceptions, have been disappointing. They have not delivered on corporate promises, nor have they met sorely needed societal expectations. Consequently, large segments of the population, especially opinion makers and corporate critics, view business codes of conduct as no more than public relations hype.

Need for Altered Expectations of Multinational Corporations

Multinational corporations are at a crossroads. The path they choose will impact the scope and direction of globalization. Even more important, it will define the terms of engagement between business institutions, notably large multinational corporations, and other sociopolitical institutions.

Commenting on the recent World Economic Forum in New York, Alan Murray of *The Wall Street Journal* wrote: "In the big picture view that is encouraged at these conferences, seemingly unconnected events begin to look like a trend. The rise of the anti-globalization protesters, the collapse of the Nasdaq, the terrorist attacks on September 11, and the Enron scandal, all are cited as challenges to the reigning social order. . . . Such sentiments could prove ephemeral—the temporary by-products of recession, an outbreak of terrorism, and a passing corporate scandal. But there are at least some here who sense more. 'I think we are at a turning point,' says David Rothkopf, chief executive of Intellibridge Corp., which advises companies on global trends. 'In every meeting I've been in there is an undercurrent of resentment to the U.S. corporate establishment. There's a sense that the system doesn't work for everybody.' What comes next, he says, is unclear; but the order is changing."[1]

Murray went on to describe how at the same forum Richard Edelman of Edelman Public Relations reported his findings from a survey of how American public attitudes have changed in just the past year. "The number of people who held favorable attitudes toward business declined only modestly, he said, to 40 percent from 43 percent; but those with favorable attitudes toward government shot up to 46 percent from 23 percent. Attitudes toward nongovernmental organizations such as Amnesty International and the World Wildlife Fund, who often find themselves pitted against corporate interests, have improved sharply as well."[2]

Murray felt that a preponderance of sentiment at the forum suggested that this might be a decisive decade in the history of capitalism. "Twenty-five years of increased reliance on markets and reduced interference by governments produced an unprecedented era of prosperity, particularly for the world's fortunate few. But like all social trends, this one nurtured the seeds of reaction. Something new is afoot, and America's corporate leaders may not find it entirely to their liking."[3]

Under the new globalization, market conditions are highly imperfect and give great advantages to the multinational corporation. MNCs cannot argue that wages paid to workers in developing countries are the outcome of demand-supply conditions in the marketplace when it is apparent that both the industrially advanced countries and MNCs have skewed these conditions in their favor. The lack of competition is further exacerbated by structural rigidities in the labor markets and production processes introduced by the MNCs. At the lowest level of labor-intensive production— where most of the sweatshop conditions and human rights abuses predominate—production systems (implemented by the MNCs) discourage skill- and knowledge-based differences in the local labor market and reduce labor to the level of commodity. MNCs prefer this approach because it diminishes the need for capital. It creates conditions in which most production economies must emanate from low-wage labor. This commoditization of labor then forces developing countries to compete with each other to attract business from the MNCs.[4]

The power of the MNCs and the resultant distributive gains have three sources.

1. *Information imbalance.* MNCs have greater access to information regarding labor supply and market conditions that impacts demand for labor. MNCs use this information leverage to induce greater competition among local workers and entrepreneurs. This puts the local workers and entrepreneurs at a competitive disadvantage. Companies use this leverage to demand ever-lower prices for the products they buy from manufacturers in developing countries.

2. ***Bargaining power imbalance.*** MNCs exercise substantial control over the markets where these products are sold. This results from brand-name recognition and control of technology, supply chains, and retail outlets. Foreign entrepreneurs must depend on the MNCs as the primary, if not the only, outlet for their products, which are invariably made in response to specific contracts from the MNCs. The branded products have only one buyer, the MNC. This situation gives the MNCs enormous power to learn the minutest details of the cost structure of local entrepreneurs. MNCs can dictate prices at which they will purchase goods. MNCs can force the lowest possible operating margins on the local entrepreneurs and appropriate for themselves the maximum profit that can be squeezed from such an exchange.[5]

3. ***Remedy and relief, and adjudication imbalance.*** In dealing with local manufacturers, the MNCs hold all the cards. They dictate the prices at which they will buy local products, especially in industries that are labor intensive and employ low-skilled and unskilled workers. MNCs can also dictate the conditions under which these products are made. Given their substantial control over the prices to be paid to local manufacturers, MNCs can, and quite often do, exercise considerable influence on how local manufacturers deal with workers, wage rates, and working and living conditions.

This situation is quite evident when we realize how MNCs induce their local partners to comply with codes of conduct. Quite often, local manufacturers strongly resist these impositions because the same MNCs that insist on code compliance are generally unwilling to share increased costs. Local manufacturers then have to cut corners, which results in shortchanging local workers. It is apparent that MNCs are quite aware of this situation since they are such a significant contributory factor. Instead, the MNCs put the entire blame of sweatshop conditions and human rights abuses at the door of local manufacturers. When confronted with public pressure to curb these conditions, these MNCs are apt to plead helplessness because they "have no control over the local entrepreneurs."[6]

Moving from "Cost" Culture to "Value" Culture

The traditional approach to efficiency in competitive markets is through cost reduction at the micro level. At the macro level, market competition is supposed to allocate resources among different factors of production. This condition does not hold true when a single buyer or a handful of buyers controls total demand and access to markets. Under these conditions, a seller is reduced to opting out of the market unless the seller accepts what the buyer is willing to pay.[7]

A more equitable manner for sharing gains from production is to consider not the minimum cost that the MNC can extract from the supplier, but the total value that the MNC generates from the use of local sources. This point can be best illustrated by using labor costs in developing countries. For ease of explanation, assumptions and relative labor costs have been somewhat simplified.

Most experts agree that average hourly wages range between 20 and 30 cents in most developing countries that make labor-intensive products using low-skilled and unskilled workers. The cost to the MNC, if these products were to be made in its home country (e.g., the United States), would be at least $5.50 per hour, if not higher. Thus the added value of this $0.30/hour worker to the MNC is about $5.00 per hour. If markets were more efficient (i.e., competitive), the workers in poorer countries would certainly earn more than 30 cents an hour.[8] This would hold true even after accounting for extra costs associated with overseas production, such as transportation, long lead times, customs duties and tariffs, and additional requirements for quality control. As it stands now, almost all of the value gains are appropriated by the MNC and are shared by other elements of the supply chain.[9] Now assume that effective demand for these products would decline if the MNC tried to pass on the additional costs to the consumer. Therefore, the increased costs of labor cannot be passed on to the consumer. In that case, all other elements of the supply chain would have to adjust their prices, which would now be closer to the real value of their contributions to the making and selling of these products.

And why should this readjustment be considered unreasonable or irrational? It does not depress ultimate consumer demand. It forces other elements in the supply chain to become more efficient and makes the entire process more productive. The reason why this is not currently happening should also be apparent. The other elements of the supply chain have no incentive to become more efficient—to work harder or smarter—when it is easier to squeeze costs from those who are least able to resist such pressure. My extensive experience with companies that depend on outsourcing in developing countries has repeatedly demonstrated the flaws in supply chain management. Often, inefficient management leads to imbalances between demand and supply for products, poor planning of production schedules, and frequent changes in product design. These problems lead to additional manufacturing costs, transportation delays, and filling distribution centers with products for which there is little demand, causing inventory write-downs and millions of dollars in losses. These are only a few of the problems.

Therefore, in the new world of globalization: The socially responsible MNC would be judged by the extent to which it does not maximally exploit its market power against those stakeholders, especially labor, who are unfairly situated because they suffer from asymmetric information and unequal bargaining power. This could take many forms, including information sharing, technological assistance to achieve increased productivity, a more enlightened policy of pricing aimed at a more equitable sharing of "surplus value" created by the outsourcing process, and investment in building human capital through education and training of the workers in poorer countries.

Thus an MNC might voluntarily consider (1) paying wages approaching the level of a living wage appropriate for that country and (2) investing money in training programs for workers to enhance their non-job-related skills, which would equip them for better paying jobs once they leave their current employment. It should be noted that U.S. companies in South Africa under the aegis of the Sullivan Principles previously tried this approach.[10] The apartheid laws of South Africa had forced lower wages on the black workers. The U.S. companies voluntarily paid anywhere from 25 to 75 percent premium on the legally mandated minimum wages. This was often done against the wishes of the South African government so as to provide black workers with pay equity—equal pay for similar work—and compensation that was at least equal to something approaching a living wage.[11]

In the current circumstances, a similar approach can be justified on ethical and economic grounds. The ethical rationale is that of equity and fairness. The economic rationale is that of imperfect markets in which wages are based on unequal bargaining power and MNCs are the beneficiaries. Reforms would not be an unbearable burden for the MNCs. As noted elsewhere in the book, the ex-factory cost of goods produced in these countries is generally less than 15 percent of the retail price. And the labor component of the ex-factory cost is even smaller.[12] Thus even a significant percentage increase over the current low base in the labor cost component would not materially affect the overall cost of these products. Furthermore, the MNC should be able to recover these costs through extracting efficiencies in other components of the supply chain.

The socially responsible MNC would also be held accountable for restitution of lost wages that have been misappropriated by local manufacturers, especially when the MNC's own code of conduct specifically prohibits such practices.

Our investigation with codes of conduct all over the world has shown that one of the major violations of host country labor laws and MNC codes occurs when local manufacturers cheat workers by not paying even the legally mandated minimum wages.[13] However, to the best of my knowledge, upon discovery of such violations, no MNC has required its vendors to pay back the wages that were literally stolen from the workers.[14] At best, the vendor is asked to refrain from this practice in the future, but is allowed to keep the ill-gotten gains. This approach rewards the plant owners while penalizing the workers. If the MNCs are willing to work with these vendors then they should also be held responsible *and* accountable for such conduct on the part of their vendors. They should force the vendors to make good on those wages. But since that is not always possible, at the very least the MNCs should insist that local manufacturers should pay all back wages for the entire period to those workers who are currently on the factory payroll or those who had been on the factory payroll during the previous 12 months. Otherwise, the MNCs must compensate these workers from their own resources. There can no ethical, economic, or legal rationale that gives MNCs the right to act otherwise.[15]

RECOMMENDATIONS

It would best serve the long-term interests of the MNCs and all groups who are impacted by their actions, either directly or indirectly, to incorporate the following elements in their codes of conduct:

- Provide expeditious enforcement of corrective actions to *compensate individuals and groups* that have suffered monetary losses or a diminution in their employment conditions through illegal or inappropriate actions on the part of the MNC and its vendors.
- The MNC will hold itself *accountable and liable* for ensuring that effective remedial actions are taken in a timely manner.
- The implementation process will be made known to all the parties involved. It will be made *transparent* and subject to independent external monitoring and verification.

- With regard to wages paid to workers, the legally mandated wages will be treated as a *benchmark of corporate accountability*, which must be adhered to without exception.

- As a measure of *corporate social responsibility and enlightened self-interest*, the MNCs will create a plan of action to share their gains from the value-added surplus with workers and other factors of production. MNCs will be able to provide some improvement in the workers' current income and also invest in human capital for future growth.

Acts of Good Corporate Citizenship

The conventional notion of a socially responsible corporation is that of a financially successful and economically efficient company that marries profit making with social responsibility, provides stable and well-paid jobs with generous benefits, supports culture and the arts, encourages employees to become involved in their communities, and is a good corporate citizen. In a word, we seek a corporation that is paternalistic and benevolent. The reason that a good corporation is also socially responsible should be all too apparent. It is based on the notion of voluntariness.

Corporate managers do not have to be "good" or "socially responsible" in the sense that social responsibility is a necessary prerequisite for the company to gain its social franchise. Instead, the notion of good conduct is embedded in the ethical values of the individual managers and those of the corporation as an institution. Another ancillary reason for corporate social responsibility is ethnocentric, since most corporations have a local-national orientation, if not in terms of products and services, then in terms of the people who control and manage assets and resources.

Unfortunately, the current trends in globalization have drastically changed these historical assumptions. The new forces of globalization have unlinked, to a large extent, the connection between market imperfections, the ethnocentric notion of community, and corporate citizenship and social responsibility.[16] How might one otherwise justify the conduct of large corporations over the past two years, when they have laid off hundreds of thousands of workers, unilaterally reduced pensions and health care benefits, and seen drastic dilution in the shareholders' equity? At the same time, corporate leaders have managed to increase their own salaries and stock options to unprecedented levels.[17] These disparities should be even more apparent in the international arena when we consider the coexistence of sweatshop conditions with the enormous power and profitability of multinational corporations. The increasing globalization and resulting competition in the market-place have made it highly improbable that we will ever find modern business institutions playing the older role of the benevolent corporation. What is more, we should not even seek that role for these corporations. A more appropriate approach would be to move from corporate social responsibility to corporate social accountability. Corporate social responsibility may supplement, but it should not supplant, corporate social accountability.

RECOMMENDATIONS

In the area of corporate citizenship, we recommend that the MNCs consider incorporating the following elements in their codes of conduct as a measure of *corporate citizenship and corporate responsibility*:

- The MNC will provide a minimum level of support to improve social and cultural conditions and undertake quality of life measures at a level that is commensurate with practices of other MNCs of similar size and profitability.
- The MNC will distribute its corporate citizenship dollars in a manner that is not ethnocentric and does not favor the city or country where its home office is located. Instead, it will allocate resources fairly and equitably to all locations, worldwide, where its operations are located.
- The MNC will consult with its local partners and workers with regard to activities that will be suitable for the MNC to support.
- For the socially responsible MNC, it is not the magnitude of effort on the part of the "good corporation" that would be the determining factor, but rather its capacity to undertake such actions and the extent to which the corporation acts voluntarily.

Improvements in the Scope and Implementation Practices of Current International Codes of Conduct

A major part of this book has analyzed the strengths and shortcomings of current codes of conduct. Also discussed have been the essential elements of creating codes that will meet certain standards of sufficiency, acceptability, transparency, and verifiability.

Notwithstanding the current level of public distrust, corporate codes of conduct offer perhaps the best and last opportunity to create a new framework in which conflicts between business and society can be voluntarily resolved through a consensus-building process that takes into consideration:

- The ethical and moral dimensions of business-society conflicts.
- The issues of fairness in distributing productivity gains among various players when competitive markets have largely failed to provide acceptable levels of distributive justice.
- Strengthening of the forces of democratic capitalism, including open economies, competitive markets, consumer choice, and voluntary compliance.

We should learn from the lessons of the past 15 years to find ways to improve the scope, effectiveness, and public credibility of these codes. A failure in this area will lead to dire consequences by imposing greater regulation and oversight on corporate conduct.

It is imperative that leaders of large multinational corporations take steps to restore public confidence in their ethics and professionalism. People must believe in the integrity of their corporate leaders. Transparency of corporate actions and public trust in corporate leaders go hand in hand. Therefore, given the current low level of trust, a high level of transparency is called for if MNCs are to gain public confidence. Another important part of this effort has to do with the corporation's commitment to what the institution stands for, both legally and as a measure of good corporate citizenship. Creating and implementing meaningful codes of conduct will be the first step the MNCs must take to achieve this goal. This is not going to be easy, because the MNCs need to undo a large measure of the rhetoric and many of the practices that they have advocated to date. MNC leaders face a number of challenges.

Voluntary Codes of Conduct to Implement Legally Mandated Actions

It is ironic that a majority of the MNC codes of conduct currently in vogue have, for the most part, confined themselves to complying with the legally mandated conditions of wages, working hours, and safe and healthy work environment. To this minimum standard other measures are added, such as refusing to exploit child labor; but these are no more than minimum decencies in civilized societies.

At the expense of being absurd, one might ask: Why is it necessary to have a code of conduct in which the company commits itself to do only what it must do as a law-abiding corporate citizen? And to add insult to injury, these corporations insist that they will not publicly disclose any information as to how well they are complying with these minimal, and legally mandated, standards. Instead, they expect the public to accept corporate assurances at face value.[18]

Compliance with legally mandated and otherwise minimal standards should be considered a *measure of corporate social obligation*. These standards are benchmarks of corporate social accountability. MNCs should not be allowed to withhold information from the public as to their compliance.

NECESSARY AND IMPORTANT ELEMENTS OF INTERNATIONAL CODES OF CONDUCT

The earlier part of this book provided a detailed framework for creating a viable code of conduct that meets societal expectations while challenging corporate ingenuity to become economically efficient and socially responsible. In particular:

- From the corporate viewpoint, such a code must be economically viable and competitively feasible. While it should meet the industry benchmarks, it is not necessary or even desirable that a company's code should merely mimic other corporate codes in the industry. If product differentiation is desirable for a company to gain competitive advantage, it is even more important to have a code of conduct that differentiates the MNC from other companies in terms of corporate vision, ethical values, and performance standards in the social arena.[19] Such an individual code will enhance corporate reputation and build public trust.

- MNC codes should not attempt to indulge in PR hype by promising more than they can deliver. Nothing damages a corporation's reputation more than a sense of betrayal when it fails to live up to its promises.

- MNC codes of conduct must be substantive and address issues that are of concern to society while at the same time they highlight corporate contributions to building an economically and socially viable community.[20]

- No code of conduct will be successful unless it has the total commitment of corporate leadership. It must also be integrated in the corporate value system and be part of corporate strategy and operations. In the final analysis, a corporation can do more good, and more harm, through its normal business operations and their second-order effects on the community. Therefore, the notion of corporate citizenship and social responsibility cannot be a peripheral activity but must be part of the corporation's raison d'être.

- Codes must provide for highly objective measurement standards that are transparent and outcome oriented.[21]

- Finally, codes must be subject to independent, external monitoring to verify compliance.[22]

FILLING THE ETHICAL VOID

Most often, these voluntary codes of conduct do no more than agree to comply with the legal norms of society. But MNC rhetoric has increasingly equated them with the ultimate achievement of high moral rectitude. In the process, MNCs have debased these codes from "promises voluntarily made" as an expression of the MNC's higher ethical and professional standards of responsible corporate citizenship. Thus reduced to mechanistic measures of evaluating corporate performance, they have become yet another aspect of corporate governance that is mindlessly repetitive, boringly bureaucratic, and eventually devoid of any sense of social responsibility. Nothing differentiates one corporation from another for its level of corporate citizenship by going beyond these benchmarks and becoming good corporate citizens in how they conduct their business in the economic and sociopolitical arena.

The MNC codes of conduct must stand for something above and beyond legally required standards of conduct, or minimal standards that are considered as the absolute musts for individual and institutional members of a society. Whether we like it or not, the notion of "above and beyond" must be rooted in our concepts of human values. And yet corporations have consistently resisted ceding any moral justification for business actions. This tendency is even more pronounced in the case of multinational corporations when their leaders avoid any reference to ethical norms or human values, allegedly for fear of alienating their local hosts. And yet it goes without saying that in the real world a corporate action of any significance simply cannot take place in a moral vacuum. Instead of taking the high moral ground, even the most enlightened corporate leaders fabricate tortuous arguments to justify their actions in economic terms only, while these actions clearly contain elements of human values of compassion, fairness, and respect for the environment.[23]

Whither Goes the Future?

The emerging global economic order of the 1980s and 1990s saw capitalism and its principal actor, the large corporation, reach the apex of social institutions. This was in sharp contrast to the 1960s, when the multinational corporation was seen as a threat to national sovereignty and political freedom. This new world viewed the multinational corporation as an agent of positive change. However, in less than two years—less than a wink of an eye in terms of history—all our senses have been assaulted by the excesses of capitalism. It has once again raised all the hidden fears of the public that underneath the veneer of hope and expectation lies the ever-present danger of the unaccountable corporate behemoth, and its potential for doing harm through abuse of power. The paradox of economic globalism has inevitably created two societies that are quite disparate in their needs and resources, as well as in their aspirations and potentials for fulfillment.[24]

The economic and sociopolitical problems of the twenty-first century will be largely connected with the interdependent nature of the world and its people, a world in which individual goodwill is not possible without thought for the common good. It makes no sense to separate moral principles from institutional behavior, political power from economic influence, and environmental values from material rewards. To do so is to divorce the social system from its basic element, the human being, who does not behave in a fragmented manner.

The large corporation, and especially the multinational corporation, must become an active agent for social change if it is to make the world safe for democracy and, indeed, for capitalism. For the latter can survive only in an environment of individual choice, voluntarily exercised, in both the political and economic arenas. As a dominant institution in society, the corporation must assume its rightful place and contribute to shaping the public agenda instead of simply reacting to policy choices advocated by others. The right of advocacy, however, cannot be taken for granted. It must be earned through public trust in corporate intent and faith in corporate promises made in the name of the public interest.

Notes

1. Alan Murray, "Aura of Social Change Cloaks Economic Forum," *Wall Street Journal* (February 4, 2002), 1.
2. Ibid.

3. Ibid.
4. For a further discussion of these arguments, see Chapter 1.
5. See Chapters 1 and 3. See also S. Prakash Sethi, "Globalization and the Good Corporation," text of keynote speech, *International Conference on Business Ethics in the Knowledge Economy*, Hong Kong Baptist University, Hong Kong, April 2–4, 2002 (to be published in a forthcoming issue of *Journal of Business Ethics*, approximate publication date, 2003).
6. See Chapter 9.
7. See Chapters 1 and 3.
8. See Chapter 3.
9. See Chapter 9.
10. S. Prakash Sethi and Oliver F. Williams, *Economic Imperatives and Ethical Values in Global Business: The South African Experience and International Codes of Conduct Today* (Boston: Kluwer Academic Publishers, 2000).
11. Ibid.
12. See Chapter 3.
13. See Chapters 2, 5, 7, 8, 9, and 10.
14. See Chapters 9 and 10.
15. See Chapters 3, 9, and 10.
16. S. Prakash Sethi, "Corporate Codes of Conduct and the Success of Globalization," *Ethics and International Affairs* 16:1 (New York: Carnegie Council on Ethics and International Affairs, 2002), 89–106.
17. Ibid. See also Sethi, "Globalization and the Good Corporation"; S. Prakash Sethi, "Standards for Corporate Conduct in the International Arena: Challenges and Opportunities for Multinational Corporations," *Business and Society Review* 107:1 (2002), 20–40.
18. Chapters 7, 8, 9, and 10.
19. Chapters 11, 12, and 13.
20. Chapter 11.
21. Chapter 11.
22. Chapters 12 and 13.
23. Ronald Dworkin, *Sovereign Virtue: The Theory and Practice of Equality* (Cambridge: Harvard University Press, 2000); Richard DeGeorge, *Competing with Integrity in International Business* (New York: Oxford University Press, 1993); Thomas Donaldson, *The Ethics of International Business* (New York: Oxford University Press, 1989).
24. S. Prakash Sethi, Joel A. Kurtzman, and Bharat B. Bhalla, "The Paradox of Globalism: The Myth of the 'Global Village'—The Changing Role of Multinational Corporations," *Business and the Contemporary World* 6:4 (1994), 131–142.

Bibliography

Abelson, Reed. 1999. "Crisis in the Balkans: Aid; In a Wave of Balkan Charity Comes Drug Aid of Little Use." *New York Times* (June 29).

———. 1999. "Report Outlines Problems with Donated Drugs Sent Overseas." *New York Times* (August 16).

"About the FLA" on the web site of Fair Labor Organization (www.fairlabor.org). The participating companies in the Apparel Industry Partnership (AIP) were: Nike, Reebok, Liz Claiborne, Phillips–Van Heusen, and L. L. Bean, among the more prominent corporate members.

Akerlof, George A. 1970. "The Market for 'Lemons': Quality Uncertainty and the Market Mechanism." *Quarterly Journal of Economics* 84 (MIT Press), 488–500.

"Anti-Capitalist Protest—Angry and Effective." 2000. *The Economist* (September 23), 85–87.

Asia-Pacific Human Rights Network. 2001. "Associating with the Wrong Company." www.aphrn.org (July 13).

Bannon, Lisa. 1999. "Mattel's Asian Plants Will Address Problems." *Wall Street Journal* (November 18), 1–2.

Baterson, Robert, and Murray Weidenbaum. 2001. *The Pros and Cons of Globalization*. St. Louis: Center for the Study of American Business, Washington University, 22.

Baumol, William. 1991. *Perfect Markets and Easy Virtue*. Cambridge, Mass.: Blackwell.

Baysinger, Barry D. 1984. "Domain Maintenance as an Objective of Business Political Activity: An Extended Typology." *Academy of Management Review* 9:2, 248–254.

Bearak, Barry. "Lives Held Cheap in Bangladesh Sweatshop." *New York Times* (April 15), sec. 1, 1.

Benjamin, Media. 1999. "What's Fair about the Fair Labor Organization." *Global Exchange* (February).

Berry, John M. "This Time, Boom Benefits the Poor." *Washington Post* (February 14), C5 (cited in Weidenbaum, *Common Ground*, 6).

Bhagwati, Jagdish. 1998. *A Stream of Windows—Unsettling Reflections on Trade, Immigration, and Democracy*. Cambridge: MIT Press.

Branigin, William. 1996. "Honduran Girl Asks Gifford to Help End Maltreatment." *Washington Post* (May 30), A29.

Bruno, Kenny, and Joshua Karliner. 2000. *Tangled Up in Blue: Corporate Partnerships at the United Nations*. CorpWatch, www.corpwatch.org (September 1).

Burns, Jennifer L. 2000. "Hitting the Wall: Nike and International Labor Practices." HBS Case 9-700-047l, Boston: Harvard Business School, 3.

"The Case for Globalization." 2000. *The Economist* (September 23), 19–20.

Cattaui, Maria Livanos. 2000. "Yes to Annan's 'Global Compact' If It Isn't a License to Meddle." *International Herald Tribune* (July 26).

"Celebrities Sweatshops." 1996. *Denver Rocky Mountain News* (June 30), Editorial, 67A.

Charter Document of FLA. 2001. Section III, "Participation Criteria for Companies," and Section VII, "Monitoring Process." Fair Labor Association, Washington, D.C. 20005 (January 24).

Cohen, Daniel. 1998. *The Wealth of the World and the Poverty of Nations*. Cambridge: MIT Press, 7.

Connor, Tim. 2000. "Still Waiting for Nike to Respect the Right to Organize." *Global Exchange* (June 28).

Corporate Europe Observatory. 2001. "High Time for UN to Break Partnership with ICC" (July 25).

"Corporation, Officers Cleared in Public Relations Misrepresentation Case." 2000. *Corporate Officers and Directors Liability Litigation Reporter* 15:11 (Andrews Publications Inc., April 3), 12.

CorpWatch. 2001. "The Global Compact Corporate Partners." Alliance for a Corporate-Free UN, September 1, 2000. Available at www.corpwatch.org, this includes articles like: Elizabeth Neuffer, "UN: Aventis Accused of Breaking Global Compact" *Boston Globe*, (June 15, 2001).

———. 2001. "UN and Corporations Fact Sheet," under Campaigns: Corporate-Free UN (March 22).

"Costs of Inspection by External Monitors." 2001. *Charter Document of FLA*, Section D of Monitoring Plan. Fair Labor Association, Washington D.C. 20005 (January 24).

Davidow, J. 1980. "Multinationals, Host Governments and Restrictive Business Practices." *Columbia Journal of World Business* 15:2 (Summer), 14–19.

DeGeorge, Richard. 1993. *Competing with Integrity in International Business*. New York: Oxford University Press.

Dell, S. 1990. *The United Nations and International Business*. Durham, N.C.: Duke University Press.

Deutsch, Claudia H. "Unlikely Allies with the United Nations." *New York Times* (December 10), C1.

Donaldson, Thomas. 1989. *The Ethics of International Business*. New York: Oxford University Press.

Dowling, J., and J. Pfeffer. 1975. "Organizational Legitimacy: Social Values and Organizational Behavior." *Pacific Sociological Review* 18:1, 22–136.

Dworkin, Ronald. 2000. *Sovereign Virtue: The Theory and Practice of Equality*. Cambridge: Harvard University Press.

Feld, W. J. 1980. *Multinational Corporations and UN Politics*. New York: Pergamon.

Fikentscher, W. 1982. "United Nations Codes of Conduct: New Paths to International Law." *American Journal of Comparative Law* 30:3, 577–604.

Fitzgerald, Sean M. 1997. "Barbie Talks Back." *The Humanist* (July 17), 29.

Foek, Anton. 1997. "A Reply to Mattel." *The Humanist* (July 17), 30.

———. 1997. "Sweatshop Barbie: Exploitation of Third World Labor." *The Humanist* (January 11), 9.

Gasparino, Charles. 2002. "Broker Oversight or Tunnel Vision? Two Case Histories—Letter by Accused Raised Questions for Lehman, Cowen." *Wall Street Journal* (February 13), C1.

———. 2002. "Lehman Broker in Alleged Big Swindle also Supervised Compliance Officer." *Wall Street Journal* (February 20), C.

"Global Capitalism: Can It Be Made to Work Better?" 2000. *Business Week* Special Report. (November 6), 72–90.

"Globalization and Its Critics: A Survey of Globalization." 2001. *The Economist* (September 29), 30.

Global Policy Forum, which can be found at www.globalpolicy.org, NGO Panel on Corporate Accountability held at the United Nations, February 15, 2001, under the headline "Global Compact with Corporations: 'Civil Society' Responds."

Gwartney, James, and Robert Lawson. 2000. *Economic Freedom of the World: 2000 Annual Report.* Vancouver: Fraser Institute, 15 (cited in Weidenbaum, *Common Ground*, 6).

"Hired Consultant Gives Nike's Labor Practices Good Review." 1997. Associated Press Newswires (June 24).

Hirsch, Fred. 1976. *Social Limits to Growth.* Cambridge, Mass.: Harvard University Press. See in particular Section II, "The Commercialization Bias," 72–114, and Section III, "The Depleting Moral Legacy," 117–158.

Ho, Rodney. 1999. "Some Companies Say Being Green Doesn't Mean a Red Bottom Line." *Wall Street Journal* (December 3), A6.

"How Hasbro, McDonald's, Mattel and Disney Manufacture Their Toys." 2001. Report on the labor rights and occupational safety and health conditions of toy workers in foreign investment enterprises in southern mainland China, by Hong Kong Christian Industrial Committee, December.

"Increased University Representation." 2001. *FLA Update* 1:11 (October 25).

"Indonesia: Update—Nike, Adidas Factories Still Sweatshops—Report." 2002. Reuters English News Service (March 7).

"Indonesians 'Just Do It' Sweating for Nike." 1992. *San Francisco Examiner* (August 30).

Investor Responsibility Research Center (IRRC). 1998. *Social Issues Service, Company Report—M, Mattel, Executive Compensation.* Washington D.C.: IRRC, 1–9.

Jayram, Nityanand. 2001. "Inconsistencies Galore: A Timeline on Unilever's Mercury Dumping in India." www.corpwatch.org (October 4).

———. 2001. "Norsk Hydro: Global Compact Violator." www.corpwatch.org (October 18).

"Johnson & Johnson Begins Bid to Revive Sales of Tylenol." 1982. Dow Jones News Service (October 25).

"Johnson & Johnson Seeks Quick End to Tylenol Tragedy." 1982. Dow Jones News Service (April 10).

Kapstein, Ethan B. 2001. "The Corporate Ethics Crusade." *Foreign Affairs* 80:5 (September–October), 105–119.

Kaufman, Leslie, and David Gonzalez. 2001. "Labor Standards Clash with Global Reality." *New York Times* (April 24), A1.

Kell, Georg, and John Gerard Ruggie. 1999. "Global Markets and Social Legitimacy: The Case of 'Global Compact.'" Paper presented at an international conference *Governing the Public Domain beyond the Era of the Washington Consensus? Redrawing the Line between the State and the Market,* York University, Toronto, Canada (November 4–6), 10–11.

Kline, J. M. 1985. *International Codes and Multinational Business: Setting Guidelines for International Business Operations* (Westport, Conn.: Quorum Books).

Kristof, Nicholas D., and Shery WuDunn. 2000. "Two Cheers for Sweatshops." *New York Times Magazine* (September 24), sec. 6.

Kristol, Irving. 1970. "When Virtue Loses All Her Loveliness: Some Reflections on Capitalism and the Free Society." *Public Interest* (Fall), 3–16.

Lawless, James. 1993. "Child Labor Protested, Wal-Mart Denies Charges." *Plain Dealer* (May 6), Metro, 1B.

Lee, Dinah, and Rose Brady. 1988. "International Business Long, Hard Days—at Pennies an Hour—Chinese Teenagers Are Toiling in the Foreign-Owned Sweatshops of the Special Economic Zones." *Business Week* (October 31), 46.

Maharaj, Raynier. 1996. "Gifts of Love, Made in Hell." *Toronto Sun*, Editorial (January 8), 12.

Mark Kasky on behalf of the General Public of the State of California vs. Nike, Inc. San Francisco County Superior Court, September 25, 1998.

Mark Kasky vs. Nike, Inc. et al. In the Supreme Court of California, Ct. App. 1/1/A 086142, S 087859, May 2, 2002.

Mark Kasky vs. Nike, Inc., Complaint for Statutory, Equitable and Injunctive Relief. In the Superior Court of the State of California in and for the City and County of San Francisco, April 20, 1998.

"Mattel, Inc., Launches Global Code of Conduct." 1997. Press Release, El Segundo, Calif.: Mattel, Inc. (November 20).

Mattel Independent Monitoring Council (MIMCO) Audit Report 1999 (November); MIMCO, Audit Report (May 25, 2000); MIMCO, Following Audit Report for Guan Yao (Zhangmei) Plant and Chang An (Metei) Plant (April 1, 2001); MIMCO, Audit Report, Mattel manufacturas de Monterrey, S.A. de C.V. (MX3), Mexico (April 30, 2001).

"Mattel Launches Global Code of Conduct for Plants, Contractors." 1997. Dow Jones Online News (November 20).

Miles, Robert H. 1982. *Coffin Nails and Corporate Straties.* Englewood Cliffs, N.J.: Prentice-Hall.

Minta, I. K. 1988. "The Code of Conduct on TNCs: In the Twilight Zone of International Law." *CTC Reporter* 25 (Spring), 29–33, 37.

"Monitoring Guidance and Compliance Benchmarks." Manual of FLA. Fair Labor Association, Washington, D.C. 20005, Version 1.1, also available on web site of FLA (www.fairlabor.org).

Murray, Alan. 2002. "Aura of Social Change Cloaks Economic Forum." *Wall Street Journal* (February 4), 1.

NBC Dateline Report. 1996. "Toy Story." New York: NBC, December 17.

"Nike in Asia: This Is Prosperity?" 1997. *Wall Street Journal Europe* (June 17).

Nike, Inc. "Corporate Social Responsibility Report—FY 2001." Beaverton, Ore.: Nike, Inc.

"Nike's Enemies: The Usual Suspects." 1997. *Asian Wall Street Journal* (May 7).

Nike's Form 10-K filed with Securities and Exchange Commission, 2001, pp. 2–4.

"Nike's Image under Attack, Sweatshop Charges Begin to Take Toll on Brand's Cachet." 1998. *Buffalo News* (October 23).

"Nike's Next Move: The Company Has a Long Way to Go in Improving Workers Compensation." 1998. *Pittsburgh Post-Gazette* (May 25).

"No Illusions: Against the Global Cosmetic SA-8000." 1999. Labor Rights in China, Asia Monitor Resource Center (June).

Passow, Sam. 1984. "Corporate Terrorism: Thinking about the Unthinkable." *Wall Street Journal* (March 26).

Perrow, C. 1979. *Complex Organizations: A Critical Essay*, 2nd ed. Glenview, Ill.: Scott, Foresman.

Pilling, David. 1999. "Up to Two-Fifths of Drug Donations Not Requested: Groups Dumping Old Medicines on Developing Countries, Say Critics." *Financial Times* London Edition (August 16), 1.

Pruitt, Dean G. 1983. "Achieving Integrative Agreements." In Max H. Bazerman and Roy J. Lewicki, eds., *Negotiating in Organizations* (Beverly Hills, Calif.: Sage Publications).

———. 1981. *Negotiating Behavior* (New York: Academic Press), 137–162.

Razzi, Elizabeth. 1996. "Did Child Labor Make That Toy? Here's How You Can Tell—and What, If Anything, You Can Do about It." *Kiplinger's Personal Finance* (December 1), 46.

"Report: No Widespread Abuse of Workers in Nike's Factories." 1997. Associated Press Newswires (June 24).

"Report Rips Nike Labor Conditions, Alleges Widespread Abuse at Viet Plants." 1997. Associated Press (March 28).

"Report Says Nike Plant Workers Abused by Bosses in Indonesia." 2001. *New York Times* (February 22), C2.

"Rights Group Says Nike Isn't Fulfilling Promises to Reform Sweatshops." 2001. *Wall Street Journal* (May 16).

Rizvi, Haider. 1996. "Toying with Workers (Consumer Campaign against Toy Transnational Companies That Hire Asian Subcontractors Violating Labor Rights)." *Multinational Monitor* (April 1), 6.

Robinson, P. 1986. *The Question of a Reference to International Law in the United Nations Code of Conduct on Transnational Corporations.* UNCTC Current Studies A, no. 1. New York: UNCTC.

Rodrik, Dani. 1997. *Has Globalization Gone Too Far?* Washington D.C.: Institute for International Economics, 7.

Rondinelli, Dennis, and Jack Behrman. 2001. "The Promise and Pains of Globalization." *Global Focus* 12:1 (2000), 6 (cited in Weidenbaum, *Common Ground*, 6).

Rosenzweig, Philip M., and Pam Woo. 1994. "International Sourcing in Footwear: Nike and Reebok." HBS Case 394–189 (Boston: HBS Press), 2–5 (cited in Burns, *Hitting the Wall*).

Sachs, Jeffrey, and Andrew Warner. 1995. "Economic Reform and Process of Global Integration." *Brookings Papers on Economic Activity* 1 (1995), 1–118.

Salem, D'jamila. 1996. "Human Rights Group Targets Disney, Kathie Lee Apparel Lines; Labor Tells Congress That Imported Clothing Were Made by Abused, Underage Workers." *Los Angeles Times* Business Section (April 30), 1.

"Saving the Brand Name." 1995. *Maclean's* 108:50 (December 11), 30.

Schelling, Thomas. 1978. *Micromotives and Macrobehavior.* New York: W. W. Norton & Co.

Schilling, David M. 1998. Letter to editor, *New York Times* (November 18), A30.

Scott, Robert H. 1972. "Avarice, Altruism, and Second Party Preferences." *Quarterly Journal of Economics* (February) (cited in Hirsch, *Social Limits*, 78).

Sen, Amartya. 1973. "Behavior and the Concept of Preference." *Economica* (August) (cited in Hirsch, *Social Limits*, 139).

Sethi, S. Prakash. 2002. "Corporate Codes of Conduct and the Success of Globalization." *Ethics and International Affairs* 16:1 (New York: Carnegie Council on Ethics and International Affairs), 89–106.

———. 2002. "Globalization and the Good Corporation." Text of keynote speech, *International Conference on Business Ethics in the Knowledge Economy*, Hong Kong Baptist University, Hong Kong, April 2–4 (to be published in a forthcoming issue of *Journal of Business Ethics* (approximate publication date, 2003)).

———. 2002. "Standards for Corporate Conduct in the International Arena: Challenges and Opportunities for Multinational Corporations." *Business and Society Review* 107:1 (Spring), 20–40.

———. 2000. "Creating and Implementing Global Codes of Conduct: An Assessment of the Sullivan Principles as a Role Model for Developing International Codes of Conduct—Lessons Learned and Unlearned." *Business and Society Review* 105:2 (Summer), 169–200.

———. 2000. "Human Rights and Corporate Sense." *Far Eastern Economic Review* (October 19), 37.

———. 1994. *Multinational Corporations and the Impact of Public Advocacy on Corporate Strategy: Nestlé and the Infant Formula Controversy.* Boston: Kluwer Academic Publishers, 18–24.

———. 1987. *Handbook of Advocacy Advertising: Concepts, Strategies, and Applications.* Cambridge, Mass.: Ballinger Publishing Co.

———. 1979. "A Conceptual Framework for Environment Analysis of Social Issues and Evaluation of Corporate Response Patterns." *Academy of Management Review* 4:1, 63–74.

———. 1977. *Advocacy Advertising and Large Corporations.* Lexington, Mass.: D. C. Heath & Co.

———. 1971–1981. *Up Against the Corporate Wall, 1st through 4th eds.* Englewood Cliffs, N.J.: Prentice-Hall; with Paul Steidlmeier, 5th and 6th editions (1991–1997).

Sethi, S. Prakash, and B. B. Bhalla. 1993. "A New Perspective on International Social Regulation of Business: An Evaluation of the Compliance Status of the International Code of Marketing of Breast-Milk Substitutes." *Journal of Socio-Economics* 22:2, 141–158.

———. 1991. "Free Market Orientation and Economic Growth: Some Lessons for Developing Countries." *Business and the Contemporary World* 3:2 (Winter), 86–101.

———. 1991. "The Peril to the Global Environment: The Role of Globalism." *Business and the Contemporary World* (Autumn), 114–125.

Sethi, S. Prakash, and Cecilia Falbe. 1985. "Determinants of Corporate Social Performance." Paper presented at the Stanford Business Ethics Workshop, Graduate School of Business, Stanford University, Stanford, California, August 14–17.

Sethi, S. Prakash, Joel Kurtzman, and B. B. Bhalla. 1994. "The Paradox of Economic Globalism: The Myth and Reality of the 'Global Village'—The Changing Role of Multinational Corporations." *Business and the Contemporary World* 6:4, 131–142.

Sethi, S. Prakash, Nobuaki Namiki, and Carl L. Swanson. 1984. *The False Promise of the Japanese Miracle.* Marshfield, Mass.: Pitman Publishing Inc., 149–166.

Sethi, S. Prakash, and Oliver F. Williams. 2000. *Economic Imperatives and Ethical Values in Global Business: The South African Experience and International Codes Today.* Boston: Kluwer Academic Publishers; pap. ed. Notre Dame, Ind.: University of Notre Dame Press, 2001.

Sethi, S. Prakash, and Dow Votaw. 1973. *The Corporate Dilemma: Traditional Values and Contemporary Problems*. Englewood Cliffs, N.J.: Prentice Hall.

———. 1969. "Do We Need a New Corporate Response to a Changing Social Environment? Part II." *California Management Review* (Fall), reprinted in Votaw and Sethi, *The Corporate Dilemma* (Englewood Cliffs, N.J.: Prentice-Hall, 1973), 191–213.

Smith, Tim. 2001. Letter to Alan G. Hassenfield, Chairman and CEO, Hasbro Toy Co. (June 18).

Social Accountability International (SAI) and SA-8000 e-Update, January 2002.

"Special Report: Globalization." 2000. *Business Week* International Edition (November 6), 52.

Sprote, W. 1990. "Negotiations on a United Nations Code of Conduct on Transnational Corporations." *German Yearbook of International Law* 33, 331–348.

"State Charges Eight McDonald's Restaurants with Violating Pennsylvania Child Labor Laws." 1989. *PR Newswire* (Feb 8), 0208012.

Storm, Stephanie. 1996. "A Sweetheart Becomes Suspect: Looking behind Those Kathie Lee Labels." *New York Times* Editorial (June 27), 1.

Swoboda, Frank. 1990. "Burger King Accused of Child Labor-Law Abuse." *Washington Post* (March 9), A11.

Sylvester, Rachel, and Joe Saumarez Smith. 1996. "Exposed: Shame of Gap's Child Labor Sweatshops." *Sunday Telegraph* (January 21), 1.

"Take a Break, Trade Bullies." 2000. *Business Week* (November 6), 100–101.

Tesner, Sandrine. 1997. *How to Do Business with the United Nations: The 1997 Update*. United Nations Association of the USA, UNA–USA, 226.

Tesner, Sandrine, with the collaboration of Georg Kell. 2000. *The United Nations and Business*. New York: St. Martin's Press.

"Toys of Misery: A Report on the Toy Industry in China." 2001. National Labor Committee (December), www.nlcnet.org.

"Two More Unions Reject Agreement for Curtailing Sweatshops." 1998. *New York Times* (November 6), A15.

Ugarteche, Oscar. 1997. *The False Dilemma: Globalization, Opportunity or Threat*. New York: Zed Books, xiii—xiv.

UN Centre on Transnational Corporations (UNCTC). 1990. *The New Code Environment* Series A, no. 16. New York: UNCTC.

"UNICEF Accused of Forming Alliance with Baby Food Industry." 2000. *British Medical Journal* (July 15).

United Nations. 2000. *The Global Compact*. New York: United Nations.

———. 1999. *The United Nations and Business: The Global Compact*. New York: United Nations.

United States Congress. 1989. "Status of U.N. Code on Transnational Corporations." Hearing before the Subcommittee on Human Rights and International Organizations of the Committee on Foreign Affairs, 101st Congress, 1st Session, November 15.

The Walt Disney Company Annual Reports, 2000 and 2001.

Weidenbaum, M. L. 1985. "The UN as a Regulator of Private Enterprise." *Notre Dame Journal of Law, Ethics and Public Policy* 1, 3.

Weidenbaum, Murray. 2001. *Looking for Common Ground on U.S. Trade Policy*. Washington, D.C.: CSIS Report.

"Where the Furbies Come From." 1998. *The Economist* (December 19), 95.

White, Michael. 1998. "Shareholders Reject Plan to Link Executive Pay to Labor Practices." Associated Press Newswire (May 6).

Whitekar, Barbara. 2002. "An Accountant Who Raised Enronian Issues." *New York Times* (February 17), sec. 3.

Wire Reports. 1999. "Annan, 18 Nations Retooling Civil Rule in Kosovo; Secretary-General Elicits Pledges of Interim Police to Back U.N. Force There." *Baltimore Sun* (July 1).

World Development Indicators 2000. 2000. Washington, D.C.: World Bank, Tables 4.10 and 4.11 (cited in Weidenbaum, *Common Ground*, 6).

"A World of Sweatshops." 2000. *Business Week* (November 6).

Zakaria, Fareed. 2000. "Globalization Grows Up and Gets Political." *New York Times* (December 31), 24.

Index